# THE ADVENT OF SUN MYUNG

*Also by George D. Chryssides*
THE PATHS OF BUDDHISM

# The Advent of Sun Myung Moon

## The Origins, Beliefs and Practices of the Unification Church

George D. Chryssides

*Senior Lecturer in Philosophy*
*Polytechnic South West, Plymouth*

MACMILLAN

First published 1991

Published by
MACMILLAN PROFESSIONAL AND ACADEMIC LTD
Houndmills, Basingstoke, Hampshire RG21 2XS
and London
Companies and representatives
throughout the world

Printed in Hong Kong

British Library Cataloguing in Publication Data
Chryssides, George D.
The advent of Sun Myung Moon.
1.   Unification Church
I.   Title
289.96
ISBN 0–333–49698–1
ISBN 0–333–53836–6 pbk

To Harold W. Turner

# Contents

# List of Illustrations

# Preface

In writing any account of someone else's religious beliefs and practices, any author must find himself between two poles: what members of the religion wish to tell, and what the public wishes to know. Nowhere are these polarities more distant than in the field of new religions. The public wishes to know about 'recruitment', 'brainwashing' and fundraising within the Unification Church, while my discussions with UC members elicited far more material on their own inner spiritual life. After much mental agonising, I have had to conclude that a common meeting ground is simply not possible, and that any book, including this one, has to be a compromise. Just as any mainstream Christian would be irritated by an inquirer's relentless pursuit of questions relating to the precise ingredients of the eucharistic wine, it is understandable that UC members should feel that I have given too much attention to the more obviously external manifestations of their faith in some of their ceremonies. However, while recognising the importance of the insider's definition, I still believe that it is important to answer many of the commonly asked outsider's questions too, and it is simply not possible to speak of sets of internal religious experiences which I do not share. If those Unificationists who were willing to discuss their beliefs with me hoped that they might be able to endorse this book's contents, then I fear they may be disappointed: the account which they wanted can, I believe, only be written by themselves.

In normal circumstances a phenomenological account of a religion is relatively problem free. The author reads, listens, observes, and writes as far as possible without imposing his or her own value judgments. In the area of new religious movements, however, it seems that no neutral ground is possible. Even using the phrase 'new religious movement' is a conscious choice which involves rejecting terms like 'cult', 'sect' or 'fringe group', terms which some commentators would claim to be more suitable substitutes for what they regard as a euphemism. In this book, however, I decided as far as possible to present the Unification Church (although not uncritically) in terms which would at least be recognisable by its members, in accordance with the normal canons of scholarship – unless, of course, what I saw clearly differed from what they explained to me.

I know that in such a controversial area it is impossible to please everyone, and I fear that I will have pleased no-one by what follows.

The UC's critics would no doubt prefer an attack on 'the Moonies' and feel that this study is 'too objective' and academic. UC members may well feel that I have been unfair to them and that they deserved more sympathetic treatment. I also know that some colleagues insist that a phenomenological approach is inappropriate and that the Unification Church (together with most if not all new religions) is only worth taking seriously as a sociological phenomenon. My aim throughout has been that of inter-religious understanding, although in an area of this kind I know that it would be foolish to over-estimate my chances of success!

I have been enormously helped and encouraged by many friends and colleagues who have agreed that this project was worth undertaking. It is obvious, I think, that this book would not have been possible without the help of UC members who have been willing to spend large amounts of time clarifying points of difficulty. In some cases this involved traveling long distances to meet me and interrupting their own schedules within the UC. Although some of the UC's critics may deplore my indebtedness to them, I have to thank them in all sincerity for their help.

There are many people outside the UC who have helped to shape some of the ideas expressed in this book. The fact that I mention them here, of course, in no way implies that they endorse the views expressed between these covers or that they are responsible for any errors. I myself must take full responsibility for everything which I have written.

Amongst particular friends and colleagues who have offered suggestions, thanks are due to Margaret Buck, Janet Franklin, Cathy Michell, Eric Pyle and Dr Paul Williams. Professor W. E. Skillend offered valuable assistance in enabling me to ensure some kind of consistency in transliterating Korean vocabulary, and I am greatly indebted to David and Hyesoon Wood for furnishing me with a translation of part of Kyong Bae Min's *History of the Church in Korea*, which would otherwise have remained inaccessible to me. I am grateful to Peter Clark of the Centre for New Religious Movements, King's College, London, for permitting me to use a paper which I read at a conference there on 'Jesus in the New Religions' in December 1986: a revised version of this paper forms the first half of Chapter 6. There are several people who have offered valuable assistance and who do not wish to named here, for various good reasons; and there are others who by some chance remark have unwittingly enabled me to catch some of these rare glimpses of enlightenment which have made some of the more puzzling aspects of Unification teaching suddenly fall into place.

Two special words of thanks are appropriate. On matters relating to the early history of the Unification Church, I have benefited greatly from discussions and correspondence with Dr Rainer Flasche of Marburg

University. Dr Harold Turner deserves special recognition for the role
which he played in shaping many of my thoughts, and for his constant
encouragement throughout the years in which I carried out the research.
It is fitting that this book should be dedicated to him in the wake of his
retirement as Director of the Centre for New Religious Movements at Selly
Oak Colleges, Birmingham.

GEORGE D. CHRYSSIDES

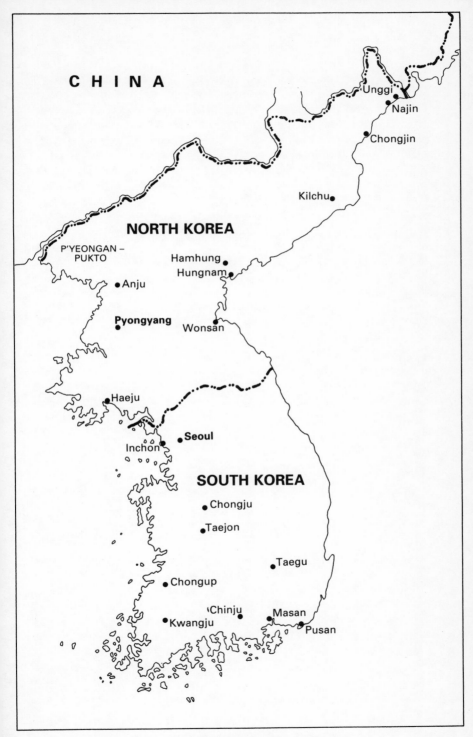

Map of Korea (cartographer Margaret Cree)

# 1 Examining the Evidence

Most accounts of religion have been written 'from the top'. They have been written by those who are academically more gifted than average, and they have focused on the leaders rather than the laity. The history of Christianity is about apostles, saints, bishops and kings, and the teachings attributed to it are about its highest ideals. It is easy to assume that Christianity is equivalent to the Sermon on the Mount and the traditional creeds, the two supreme standards of morality and orthodoxy.

We hear little of those at the bottom. We do not know how well the average lay follower really understood the complexities of the debates about the person of Christ, or the competing doctrines of the eucharist which precipitated such important divisions within the Church. We hear little of those who do not live up to the ideal: although Ananias and Sapphira are identified as a couple of early Christians who failed to live up to the standards of the early Church,[1] they apparently received their just deserts, and their tale is designed to demonstrate how totally committed the rest of the early Christian community was.

When we read of new religions, however, we are led to believe that the opposite is the case. They are typically written about 'from the bottom', and we are led to believe that there are few, if any, laudable Scientologists, Unificationists or Hare Krishna devotees. 'Ex-Moonie turns killer' is a much more probable newspaper headline than 'Rev Moon honoured in Korea'. We are encouraged to think that 'cult members' consist of villains who brainwash the unsuspecting youth or who collect moneys illegally for the uncontrolled disposal of a messianic leader. New religions have formed an area in which, until recently, competent academics have feared to tread, thus leaving the field open to writers who have been inspired by Christian evangelical zeal or anti-cult hostility rather than an ability to provide accurate and balanced exposition. Evangelical writers are swift to criticise new religions for their supposed heresies, but seldom properly set out what they really teach or the ideals to which their members aspire, for it seems only too obvious to these commentators that new religious groups have no coherent sets of teachings and no high ideals to live up to.

In what follows I have attempted to explain the beliefs and practices of the Unification Church. I have endeavoured to discover what it actually teaches, how its teachings arose, and how its members try to put its

1

teachings into practice in ritual and in lifestyle. I have therefore aimed to be objective and not polemical. In the course of writing this book I was frequently asked if I was 'doing an exposé of the Moonies'. Such a question implies that it is a normal expectation that anyone writing about the UC should unmask its alleged malpractices – in other words that I should write about Unificationism 'from the bottom'. I believe this is inappropriate for two reasons. First, all the 'atrocity tales' have been told before: although these are matters of concern, they are not suitable subject matter for a piece of original research such as this. Second, if my work had been on a mainstream denomination, no such question would have been asked, even though traditional Christianity has its 'top' and 'bottom' too. The vicar who is guilty of sexual misconduct, or the church treasurer who embezzles funds is part of the Christian Church too (although maybe not for long), but one never finds such characters in any Christian denominations series!

This account of the Unification Church is an attempt to redress the balance by showing that Unificationism has a 'top' as well as a 'bottom'. Most people have heard the worst: they have heard that the UC (popularly best known as 'the Moonies') was founded by the Korean leader Sun Myung Moon who arranges members' marriages and solemnises them at 'mass weddings' attended by hundreds or even thousands of couples. (For reasons which have never been clear to me, the large scale of these weddings seems to give rise to popular disapproval.) They have no doubt heard that the UC's teachings are viewed unfavourably by most mainstream Christian churches, and that those who join are supposedly subjected to 'heavenly deception' or various 'brainwashing' techniques.[2] What is not so well known is the 'top': it has a carefully developed body of teachings and practices, and sets an ambitious ideal not only for its members but for the whole of humanity. It is not my task here to determine what proportion of members live up to the ideal, or whether they exceed or fall below those ideals which more conventional citizens have a right to expect. These are important questions, but they demand a very different book, and an author must set a realistic limit to a piece of research. Whatever else needs to be written about the UC, its beliefs and practices form a legitimate area of study, and an unduly neglected one.

The attention which has been given to methods of evangelism, fund raising and life-style has caused public interest in the UC to focus on the sociological, psychological and legal aspects. Such a focus, however, denies a new religious movement (NRM) the right to be treated as what it sets out to be – namely, a religion. Those who claim that certain NRMs are basically 'fronts' for political organisations or business companies are thereby depriving the new religion of the right to a specifically religious identity.[3]

Because of the controversial nature of the book's subject-matter, I feel obliged to devote the first chapter to the methods of the researcher, and to defend my approach against a number of common lines of criticism. One would not normally expect such apologetic in a book devoted to one of the world's major religious traditions, where it is taken for granted that they are genuine religions with a recognisable tradition and body of teaching, that one can rely on their members to explain their beliefs and practices, and that the sacred texts truly reflect the tradition.

In the case of the Unification Church, however, there is a radical questioning of whether the normal canons of religious scholarship can be applied. The aspersions cast upon its religious credentials have created doubt as to whether it has a theology to investigate at all. One colleague wrote to me recently, stating that, while it was legitimate to investigate the UC as a social phenomenon, it was unacceptable to treat it academically as a religion. It is further assumed that its self-descriptions are unreliable: the Unification Church has been accused of practising 'heavenly deception' – that is to say, deliberately propagating falsehoods in aid of a supposedly 'higher' purpose. If the 'heavenly deception' thesis were true, then it would cast serious doubts on whether the UC can be trusted to explain its own theology. One particular source of concern for the researcher is the allegation that the UC preaches one set of doctrines to the public, and a different set once one joins the movement. The more publicly available written texts of the UC are said to conceal an esoteric teaching which either adds to, or else supplants, these exoteric portions.

Modern scholars of the world's major religious traditions would normally refrain from offering personal appraisals of Hinduism, Buddhism or Islam. Scholars adopt a 'phenomenological' stance: that is to say, they put into abeyance their own assumptions and value judgements and allow the religious phenomena to emerge uncoloured by any prejudices and predilections of the investigator. In the field of NRMs, there are many pressures on writers to abandon a strictly phenomenological approach. Writers who are committed Christians cannot overlook the fact that Unificationism claims to be Christian, arguing that, if *Divine Principle* is heretical, then it is the task of practising Christians to say so, and not to sit on the fence by offering mere description. Further, it has been suggested that the consequences of becoming involved with NRMs (and perhaps especially the Unification Church, which is often regarded as the epitome of evil) are so serious that anyone who is at all knowledgeable about the movement should sound appropriate 'warning bells' in order to stem the tide of conversion. Finally, the researcher is sometimes accused of using unfortunate 'cult victims' as fodder for research, thus enhancing his or her own reputation at their expense. It is therefore necessary to answer these criticisms of the role of the researcher.

## 'WARNING BELLS'?

Should researchers sound more warning bells? It might be argued that in such an area there is no room for neutrality, since people's minds, lives, health, careers and family relationships are supposedly all at serious risk. A criminologist who witnessed a murder would be failing in duty if he or she merely recorded the data as scholarly research and did not report the crime to the appropriate authorities.

This argument begs many questions. It assumes that minds, lives, careers and relationships are indeed at risk: but this assumption is not warranted simply because a number of atrocity tales exist. One could tell atrocity tales about how, for example, education ruined a person's health or precipitated a marital breakdown, but it is only through serious research that one establishes whether such occurrences are the norm or the exception, or whether the perceived cause (education or religion) is the real one, or whether there might actually be a majority of people who have derived benefit rather than harm.

The suggestion that researchers should sound warning bells against what they see seems singularly inconsistent with another anti-cult criticism, namely that those in academic posts are never *allowed* to see the dark side of the new religions! The 'deprogrammer' Ted Patrick,[4] for example, in his autobiographical account of his anti-cult activities, protests that the 'cults' invite academics on to their premises and then do a whitewash job so that they are reassured that all is well. The truth of the matter is that serious researchers have seen the best and the worst of the new religions they study, and, contrary to much anti-cult belief, the position of the researcher is not non-involvement. Most researchers in this field, like myself, have frequently been asked for counselling and advice and have been called upon to mediate in cases of difficulty. If I ever saw crimes being perpetrated in the name of religion, then I would most certainly take appropriate action and not merely log up more research data.

However, academic writing must seek to be as objective as possible, even in areas where approval and disapproval might be justifiable. No-one would expect a botanist to invite us to admire the beautiful flowers and exhort us to uproot the weeds: the botanist's task rather is to analyse and explain. This is not to say that one should never differentiate between weeds and flowers: anyone who keeps a garden must constantly make such decisions, but making these decisions is not botany, nor does it invalidate the botanist's work. Instead, the respective tasks of the gardener and the botanist are interrelated: the gardener may help to propagate plants for botanical study, and the botanist can provide important information to the gardener, for example about the conditions in which particular species grow or the effects of fertilisers and insecticides. The gardener may even become more aware of a flower's beauty through botanical study or more alert to the dangers of particular varieties of weed.

Just as botany and gardening are both legitimate areas of activity, so are academic studies of religion and the decision making of ecclesiastical bodies and professional counsellors. Just as the serious gardener will use the findings of the botanist, church officials and cult monitoring organisations cannot perform their tasks fairly and effectively unless their decisions are informed by objective and balanced research. Indeed it is a common complaint amongst UC leaders that Christian denominations which have pronounced them heretical have not taken the trouble to inform themselves sufficiently before doing so. Whether fuller information would have resulted in different verdicts is, I think, debatable: all I would contend is that objective examination is a necessary prerequisite for moralising or making pronouncements on Christian orthodoxy. Criticism (which has its place elsewhere) can only be valid if it is based on adequate knowledge, and here the researcher's contribution is invaluable, as well as a legitimate activity in its own right.

## IS UNIFICATIONISM ABSURD?

The criticism that Unificationist beliefs are too absurd to be worth studying must now be addressed.[5] If one assumes that the teachings of the UC are absurd, then it follows that no-one could ever be induced to join by means of rational persuasion, since the beliefs are irrational to start with. One is further enabled to infer that, since evangelising methods cannot be ones which appeal to reason, methods of 'persuasion' must be employed which bypass enquirers' rational thought-processes. Once one starts along this line of anti-cult logic, one has no option but to embrace some form of 'brainwashing' or 'indoctrination' thesis.

However one appraises the evangelisation tactics of the Unification Church, this piece of anti-cult logic is faulty. First, it is doubtful whether anyone converts to any religion, old or new, by means of a completely rational process; conversion is a change of heart rather than of mind. Second, it is extremely problematic, if not impossible, to decide what is rational and what is non-rational in religion. Depending on one's point of view, it can be an absurdity to claim that God is three persons in one, that no-one enters *nirvana* but yet *nirvana* exists, that Allah pre-ordains every human action but yet men and women are responsible, or that the Lord of the Second Advent has been born in the present age in Korea. If one were to imagine a visitor from outer space encountering our planet's plethora of religions for the first time, I suspect our space voyager might find difficulties in traditional world faiths and new religions alike.

There is certainly some truth in reports that the Unification Church teaches by means of constant repetition of its doctrines. When one advances from the 2-day seminar, through the 7-day one, to the 21-day seminar, on each seminar programme one receives lectures on the *Principle*,[6] covering the same main themes of Creation, Fall and Restoration. Nevertheless, I do not think this need be construed as a process of 'brainwashing' or browbeating its enquirers into acceptance. In response to the 'mindless repetition' criticism, it must be said, first, that all religions claim to have a universal message which is proclaimed repeatedly. Most sermons in a mainstream fundamentalist-evangelical tradition follow very much the same theme, yet no-one ever suggests that brainwashing tactics are being employed. Second, it should be noted that subsequent seminars undertake to explain the *Principle* in increasing amounts of detail: thus the enquirer is constantly receiving new teachings, although clearly, in the interests of coherence, a lecturer cannot omit crucial points of doctrine simply because they have already been stated in a previous seminar. Third, the teachings of *Divine Principle* are not at all easy to assimilate, and I can report from first hand experience that, in repeated discussions of the *Principle* with Unificationists (both in formal teaching situations and also informally) the repetition of points which I had heard before often enabled understanding to take place where previously there was bewilderment, or else they corrected earlier misunderstandings into which I had fallen.

If the teachings of *Divine Principle*, the main religious text of the UC,[7] appear to be gobbledegook, requiring psychological coercion to secure acceptance, this may be because the ideas seem difficult and unfamiliar. Where unresolved theological problems become apparent, this can be attributed to the fact that the movement is little more than thirty years old. If its theology is at times exploratory, this is understandable: Christianity certainly did not have everything finalised at the time of St Paul. To those who claim that the convert must be stupid or insane to believe the teachings, I would respond that, on the contrary, one has to be fairly intelligent in order to understand them in the first place! The remarkably high proportion of graduates who convert to Unificationism indicates that it has more appeal to the intelligent than its critics often allow.

## NEW RELIGIONS AND CHRISTIAN INDIGENISATION

The purpose of the present study is to examine the nature of the Unification Church as a religion, and to demonstrate how its distinctive religious beliefs and practices have developed as a result of its Korean origins. The Unification Church has in fact a complicated history surrounding the teachings and practices which it has developed.

Many of the new religions of the world are the by-products of Christian missionary enterprises. This is ironic, since those Christians who are endowed with missionary zeal are often the first to condemn the NRMs. However, as Christianity has spread, it has undergone transformations, and adapted to the cultures in which it has found itself. Sometimes these cultural adaptations have proved acceptable: the Hellenisation of Christianity in the first century is now a *fait accompli*; at other times, the missionary message has combined with indigenous culture to produce either a form of religion whose claims to be Christian have been seriously challenged within the mainstream churches, or else an independent Christian-derived religion. The Rastafarians[8] exemplify the latter, while the Mormons[9] and the Unification Church are examples of the former.

It is not my task to pronounce on the UC's claim to be a Christian denomination: this is a task for official church councils and commissions, and a number of these have already pronounced their verdicts, which have been generally unsupportive of Unificationism.[10] The UC, however, claims that, although it is not mainstream, its teachings represent a legitimate indigenisation of Christianity when it reached Korea. Legitimate or otherwise, undoubtedly the UC was influenced by the indigenous religious climate of Korea, and if we want to understand Unificationism fully it is necessary to examine its roots which lie in the traditional religions of Korea, the arrival of the Christian missionaries, and a number of 'New Christian' groups[11] which emerged as a result of the missionary enterprise. It is naïve to treat Unificationism simply as a 'Christian deviation' by comparing its beliefs and practices with those of mainstream (usually fundamentalist-evangelical) Christianity. Unificationists are aware of such differences, and often consciously acknowledge these, a case in point being their rejection of the literal belief that Jesus Christ will return on the clouds of heaven. The UC must be seen not only against the background of Christianity, but against the backcloth of Korean religion and culture.

Of course, not all UC members are aware of the extent of the influence of indigenous Korean religion, and some have pointed out that my thesis implies that many members do not understand their own religion fully. I believe that such a conclusion is quite tenable. It is supported, for example, by research carried out by James Beckford,[12] and, further, it is a phenomenon also to be found in most mainstream religious traditions. How many Christians, for example, understand what it means when St John refers to Jesus Christ as the '*logos*', when the description can only be understood aright when one knows what the Greek and Hebrew concepts of 'the Word' truly mean? Not everything which this book reveals will necessarily be known by every rank-and-file UC member; but my exposition is based on the UC's own theological writings and oral traditions, much (although not all) of which is explained to enquirers who attend the seminars. Where I have attempted to trace historical origins and philosophico-theological pedigrees, I fully acknowledge that many of my claims are matters for debate: whether I am right depends on the persuasiveness of my material, and UC members may not necessarily agree with all my conclusions. However, insofar as the UC claims to be an indigenised Koreanisation of Christianity, one ought to be able to trace a Korean ancestry, and this, I believe, can be done.

## ESOTERIC AND EXOTERIC TEACHINGS

My investigations are largely dependent on sources supplied to me by the Unification Church. This creates two problems: first, it is often difficult to verify information in the absence of external source material; second, since it is alleged that there are esoteric doctrines which are only disclosed to members at appropriate stages of their spiritual development,[13] it may be asked whether I can be certain to have plumbed the real depths of Unification teachings.

If the more publicly available statements of the UC were factually untrue, this would hardly be a barrier to academic research. Any scholar will evaluate sources, and will adjudicate on whether the stories of the Rev Moon[14] are factual, whether they are hagiographical tales, or whether the matter is undecidable. The UC is not a special case here: the gospel records of Jesus have almost no corroborative external support, but this has not prevented New Testament scholars from forming opinions about the life and teaching of Jesus. If some of the UC's claims have no external confirmation, it is equally true that external sources are at times uncorroborated also. The researcher must subject internal and external sources alike to critical scrutiny: it certainly cannot be assumed *a priori*, as many do, that opponents' statements are true and that those of the UC are false. As I shall show, there is good reason to doubt a significant amount of external testimony.

What constraints are placed on the researcher by the existence of esoteric teachings? The concept of esoteric teachings is a complex one. Yamamoto[15] has defined these as: *Master Speaks, The Divine Principle and Its Application, The 120-day Training Manual* and other works such as *Unification Thought* and *Unification Theology and Christian Thought*.[16] The claim that these last two works are esoteric is absurd: although they are published by a UC subsidiary, which may not necessarily distribute them to general book stores, they are offered for sale to members and non-members alike. Although it is sometimes alleged that *Master Speaks* (transcribed sermons of the Rev Moon) contains strictly classified doctrinal information, I have personally had no problem about gaining access to these sermons, although I have been denied access to an in-house publication which contains obituaries of Heung Jin, the Rev Moon's son who died recently. What members are willing to divulge varies, and no doubt this depends on how they believe such disclosures might be used. If the UC is reticent about making certain texts publicly available it is because many anti-cultists have taken certain statements and wrenched them hopelessly out of context. What might be said in jest, for example, can convey quite erroneous impressions if it is related as if it was in dead earnest. I sometimes wonder what the anti-cult movement would have made of Jesus' statement that one should remove offending eyes and hands,[17] or his apparent rejection of his family when they sought him out on one of his preaching engagements, if they had been around at the time![18] When I have asked Unification Church members about the Rev Moon's notorious statement, 'I am a thinker; I am your brain,'[19] my enquiry has been met with (I believe genuine) bewilderment. No-one to whom I have spoken can recall Sun Myung Moon having said this, and they can only suggest that it was intended as a joke. (Even those who wish to introduce 'codes of practice' for new religious movements[20] have not recommended that humour should be clearly indicated!)

What is to be regarded as an esoteric teaching requires careful definition. Any denomination has its own in-house publications which are not publicly on sale, such as a parish magazine or the occasional transcript of a vicar's Christmas or Easter message – but this does not of course make the material into esoteric doctrine. It must be pointed out that much Unificationist literature falls into this category – since it is primarily designed for its own members there is no real point in making it available more widely.

Further, any religious group has the right to prioritise what is suitable material for those who have newly joined and what should preferably be read at a more advanced stage. When Erica Heftmann,[21] (an ex-member), complains that she was told to put away a UC religious text and rely on spoken lectures instead, a plausible explanation is that the *Principle* is simply too difficult for a new enquirer, who might fare better by studying under a more experienced teacher who can ensure that simpler teachings precede the more difficult ones. Any reasonable clergyman would recommend his congregation to study St Mark's gospel before reading St Thomas Aquinas or the book of Zephaniah.

It is true that there is a body of teaching which is for members only and a further layer of teaching for blessed members. However, the Unification Church is not the first religious group to have 'graded teachings'; the Gnostics, the Graeco-Roman mystery religions and forms of Tibetan Buddhism have had their hidden secrets as well. It is considered necessary to have a basic understanding of the *Principle*, for example, before being told about Unificationist ceremonies, and guidance for married couples is only given as they approach the Blessing or after they have been blessed. In addition, there are a few teachings which appear only to circulate orally, possibly because they lack clear definition at present. Unificationists hold that the Rev Moon has not publicly disclosed all the revelations which he has received, but will do so when the time is appropriate.

If Unification leaders do not appear to explain all their teachings immediately on acquaintance, this is due to two principal factors. First, the sheer complexity of *Divine Principle* makes it unreasonable to expect them to stand and deliver without further delay – and *Divine Principle* is only a part of UC teaching. Second, there can be no doubt that UC members are reticent about defining some of their teachings because of the reaction they expect from the anti-cult lobby. Mainstream Christians have tended to adopt a confrontational stance towards the UC, seeking refutation rather than comprehension, and one counselling organisation regards 'cult membership' (including Unificationism) as a sign that one's rational processes are impaired.[22] Faced with such opposition, it is understandable that the UC would wish to avoid incurring further ridicule or causing offence to the religious sentiments of mainstream Christians. The UC has been subjected to such a volume of attack that it is not surprising if it is now over-sensitive to the possibility of external hostility.

It was inevitable, I suppose, that on certain matters Unification members, although willing to give me direct and full answers, were concerned that I should not publish certain pieces of information, particularly those regarding some of the ceremonies connected with the Blessing. They argued that the principle of religious freedom should afford any religion the right to determine at what stage in a follower's spiritual development a teaching or a practice should be disclosed. A piece of information, revealed at the wrong time or in the wrong sequence, is open to serious misconstruction, and a single book cannot provide the necessary background for a proper understanding of some of practices of the Unification Church. While acknowledging the force of this argument, I believe that the demands of an academically credible book require disclosure rather than suppression. In any case, all the sensitive areas of Unificationist practice have already been disclosed by ex-members and anti-cultists, and not always accurately.

Having considered their concerns, it had to be recognised that many religions grade their teachings and reveal them only at the point at which the acolyte is spiritually and intellectually ready.[23] Members of a religious community are also entitled to reasonable privacy, and have the right to expect that a researcher will not make public things which are told in confidence. Second, the aim of my research is to create understanding of Unificationism, not to sensationalise or provide opportunities for further misunderstanding. Anti-cultists appear only too willing to invent, twist and misconstrue information on new religious movements in order to reinforce their consistently negative stance towards them. Given my intention to generate understanding rather than potential misunderstanding, there proved to be an overwhelming case for insisting that material which had high explanatory powers should be incorporated. Clearly, any information which provides the key to understanding a cluster of problematic theological ideas is essential material, and has been duly incorporated, whereas peripheral material which might only amuse or reinforce existing prejudices has been dispensed with.

Where potentially embarrassing material has already been made public, there have been no ethical dilemmas about taking it aboard – for example Ken Sudo's apparent disclosure of the ingredients of the wine used at the Holy Wine Ceremony.[24] Since any member of the public can gain access to J. H. Grace's book where Sudo's speech is quoted,[25] one cannot conceal what has already been revealed, even if it were desirable to do so.

Throughout my research I bore in mind the possibility that there might be material which would be in the public interest to bring to light, irrespective of the wishes of the Unification Church. From the early stages of my research I made it clear that I would have no hesitation in publishing any material which fell into this category. Now that my research is complete, I am pleased to state that I found no such material. Obviously, since any book's length is finite, I cannot claim to have told *everything* I have learned about the UC: selection has had to be made, but at every point my choices have been determined on the grounds of relevance and my own assessment of the material's importance.

## THE IDENTITY OF THE TEACHINGS

Part of my learning of Unificationist teaching has been from written sources, and part from verbal ones. Not all of these have been in total agreement, and, even when something is written by a prominent leader, it does not necessarily secure general acceptance. This experience runs counter to the commonly held anti-cult view that UC members are brain-washed zombies who are indoctrinated to think alike. In any case, it would certainly be foolish of a researcher to assume *a priori* that there is a single body of belief and practice which we can call 'Unificationism'. The diversity of belief amongst members presents at times the problem of identifying which are the 'official' teachings of the church, and which are the personal opinions of individuals. While some members hold that *Divine Principle* is true in its entirety, other members have expressed the view that it embodies mistakes, and some go as far as to demythologise the teachings which it contains.

Being a young religion, the UC has not yet separated completely its 'official' versions from 'unofficial' ones. Certain texts are authorised explicitly by the Rev Moon, such as *Divine Principle* (1973) and *Outline Of The Principle, Level 4.*[26] Since the UC has had no official councils or courts to define its doctrines (a phenomenon which has only occurred to any large degree in mainstream Christianity), it is difficult to be definitive about what is compulsory and what is optional. At a recent Introductory Seminar which I attended, it was stated that certain parts of *Divine Principle* were negotiable, but others were not. It was never stated which were which, although in any developing religion it would be unreasonable to insist that one must separate the peripheral from the substantial.

In this book I have regarded as peripheral those areas on which there is no official teaching and on which members only speculate privately. Thus, although on occasion I have listened to opinions about whether there are life-forms on other planets, and whether their natures are 'fallen' like humankind, I have felt it unproductive to include such material in the present volume. It is worth emphasising in this context that I have not noticed UC members discuss such matters any more than mainstream Christians, whom I have also heard speculate from time to time on such themes. On the whole, therefore, I have omitted mention of opinions which do not form part of the *Principle* which is attributed to Sun Myung Moon's revelations.

It is evident also that, although most members are much more theologically literate than many of their mainstream Christian counterparts, not all of them are able to give a full account of all the teachings to which I shall refer. In my exposition of Unificationism, then, I am outlining what would be generally agreed by those Unificationists who have seriously studied such ideas. I would be surprised if, say, a seminar lecturer were unfamiliar with the majority of the beliefs I have discussed. Where there are important divergencies of opinion, however, I have endeavoured to indicate this.

## THE CREDENTIALS OF REVELATION

Academic writers are generally conscious of the demands of the anti-cult movement. Yet the fact that NRMs themselves have sensitivities is often neglected, and members of new religions can sometimes feel that the canons of scholarly criticism may destroy their faith. Just as evangelical Christians can feel that modern biblical criticism is cutting the ground from under their feet, so Unificationists may feel that any attempt to explain the origins of the UC means 'explaining away' the teachings of Sun Myung Moon. If the Rev Moon's doctrines are a synthesis of folk shamanism, neo-Confucianism, Buddhism and Christianity, then does not this mean that Sun Myung Moon's teachings cannot be based on direct revelation from God, as the UC firmly holds?

This is not the place to become involved in an extensive discussion of the nature of revelation. A few brief points will suffice. Firstly, any revelation must take place within a context which the recipient recognises. Someone who has a vision of the Virgin Mary must already be familiar with the religious background which enables the vision to be appropriately identified. By analogy, if the Rev Moon has had visions of Jesus Christ, Confucius, Lao Tzu, Satan, and other spirits, their recognition would only be possible if he had the appropriate intellectual and religious framework in which to recognise their identity.

The nature of revelation is itself the subject of much philosophical debate, particularly the question of whether revelation is 'propositional' or 'non-propositional'[27] – that is to say, whether the Rev Moon and Unification members receive direct spoken statements in a final verbalised form from God and the spirit world, or whether revelations are experiences or visions which require further interpretation and systematisation. I have not heard much discussion of this question by Unificationists, although the following exchange in a recent court hearing gives some indication of how the Rev Moon regards his revelations:

> *Q*: '. . . Reverend Moon, did Jesus Christ, Buddha and Moses all speak to you in Korean?'
> *A*: 'It happened in a spiritual relationship and in such relationship you communicate not in words but you can communicate each other. [*sic*] Of course, some words can be exchanged but the mind communication was much more important because we communicate with heart to heart... Since I was a Korean at the time I communicated in Korean – but I would like to emphasise once again that the communication was beyond the word. Without your actual experimentation [*sic*], you can't understand . . . '[28]

Since the UC distinguishes between what it calls '*The Principle*' and what it calls '*Divine Principle*' or '*The Divine Principles*', one can assume that there is a process taking place of organising the 'raw' religious experiences of Sun Myung Moon into a satisfactory verbalised form. If this is the case, then verbalisation can only take place by using the already existing vocabulary which is employed within the religions with which one is familiar. In Korea, these would inevitably be the religions which I have named.

In identifying sources of doctrine, it should be made clear that I am not doing to Unificationism anything which academics are not prepared to do to any other religion, including in many cases their own. To claim that John's gospel is influenced by Greek thought is not to declare it invalid, or to imply that scripture is not 'revelatory'. Scholarship puts revelation into its context for the Christian. Just as it would not have been possible for John to Hellenise the gospel without drawing on Greek concepts, likewise Unificationism cannot be a Korean indigenisation of Christianity without the introduction of specifically Korean concepts. The quest for the unification of all religions must entail that there are elements found in all religions which are capable of being brought together in one unified *oikoumene*. Indeed some Unificationists hold that the affinities between some of the teachings of Sun Myung Moon and those of other religious figures indicate that there is a common truth which is revealed by God in various degrees to men and women of diverse faiths. I do not propose to settle the question of the credentials of the Rev Moon's revelation. It is sufficient to note that my treatment of Unificationism is not intended to endorse these, but I do not believe it undermines them.

## THE PATH OF THE RESEARCH

Some remarks about how my research into the Unification Church began and progressed may be of interest. I had been aware of the presence of the Unification Church since its earliest days in England, but had paid it little attention. My attitude towards the UC was generally negative, and I resisted buying candles from them at my front door and purchasing copies of *One World* in the city centre. I can recall feeling acute embarrassment when one of my students who had undertaken to give a class presentation on the theme of 'Science and Religion' turned out to be a 'Moonie' and propounded Unificationism at my seminar. On another occasion, a UC member came to see me in my office. I was surprised to learn that he was a philosophy graduate from Stirling University. I was asked if I would speak at one of their meetings, but I declined the invitation.

It was some ten years later that I became Consultant on New Religious Movements to the United Reformed Church. At that time the URC had produced a booklet entitled *Who Are They? New Religious Groups*.[29] UC leaders in London obtained a copy and asked if I would discuss it with them. I was pleased to do so, and my meeting at the UC headquarters proved to be the first of many.

My real introduction to the *Principle* occurred in 1984 when an organisation called the New Ecumenical Research Association (New ERA) invited me to Athens for a week's seminar on 'Unification Theology and Lifestyle'. A condition of attendance was that participants read *Divine Principle* in its entirety plus one other UC text: I chose *Outline of The Principle Level 4*. New ERA, like other UC-related organisations, is often criticised for being a 'front name' concealing the UC's true identity. However, the correspondence made it abundantly clear that Sun Myung Moon was the founder and that New ERA operated from the Unification Theological Seminary in Barrytown, New York. Since New ERA is an ecumenical organisation whose directors are mainly non-Unificationists, it would be grossly misleading if it were described as 'The Unification Church'.

The seminar altered my previously negative perception of the UC in several ways. Reading *Divine Principle* made me sense that there were numerous strands of religious tradition in it: there was biblical exegesis (albeit with a difference), there were explicit references to eastern writings, and some parts looked like mainstream missionary sermons. Whatever *Divine Principle* was, it could not be regarded as the insane outpourings of a megalomaniac with messianic ambitions.

The speakers at the seminar fell into two categories. There were Unificationists, nearly all doctoral candidates at US universities. (I had not realised that 'Moonies' could hold their own at such a high level in theological circles.) Then there were non-UC academics who had been asked to give critiques of elements of Unificationist teaching. Unificationism, then, was not a closed sect, but one which apparently wanted to develop and make itself more doctrinally sophisticated in the face of some very incisive, sometimes hostile, criticism.

A number of friendships were made at that seminar, and inevitably some were with UC members. It was about a year later, when I visited the British headquarters again, that I was shown some testimonies of Korean members, transcribed and translated from Korean into English, which revealed some important information about the Korean religious climate in which the UC had emerged. Further meetings with UC leaders were accompanied by the production of more material. I decided to pursue the area, but clearly no competent researcher could rely solely on materials which were selected and brought to his attention exclusively by the UC, particularly in view of the common criticism that there is a hidden body of teachings reserved exclusively for its inner coterie. I put the point to UC leaders. It was then agreed that I should be granted open access to its archives, which are situated in the basement. The preliminary work was in part the result of many days sifting through this stock of miscellaneous material.

Academics are often criticised for accepting travel and hospitality from the UC to attend international conferences in attractive surroundings, such as Athens. I therefore felt that it was important to further my understanding of Unificationism by attending more modest seminars in Britain, which the general public may apply to attend, and where attenders pay for their board and lodging. While it is held that academics are pampered at the international conferences, criticisms of 'brainwashing', inadequate diet and sleep deprivation are more frequently levelled against the more homely workshop-seminars. Accordingly, I spent two days at Stanton Fitzwarren near Swindon, and subsequently, at the suggestion of UC members, who were not completely satisfied with my understanding of the *Principle*, I completed two further seven-day seminars, one at Chislehurst in Kent, and another at Cleeve House in Wiltshire. I felt that it was valuable to allow the Unification Church to explain its teachings in its own way, rather than to present myself intermittently at its London headquarters with new sets of questions which required answers. It was also instructive to draw conclusions from first-hand observation about whether seminar leaders really 'brainwash' enquirers or whether they simply provide thorough and detailed instruction. In addition to the seminars, I have also attended worship services and evening celebrations of some of the festivals of the UC's liturgical calendar.

Adopting the role of a 'participant-observer' raised a number of important ethical issues. Many mainstream Christians would be unwilling to take part in UC worship, for example. After all, it is asked, do not UC members worship the Rev Moon as the new messiah who has supplanted Jesus Christ, and use the word 'Father' to refer to him as an object of devotion?[30] The sharing of worship presented me with problems of conscience at first. In Athens, I went to their service of worship out of curiosity, but making it clear that I was only a spectator; I deliberately did not join in the singing or the prayers. Now I find little problem about a participant-observer status in worship. Having carefully studied UC doctrine, I am convinced that the Rev Moon is not worshipped and that the word 'Christ', when used by Unificationists, refers to Jesus Christ and not to Sun Myung Moon.[31] This has not only been explained to me by UC members; to construe worship in any other way would not make good sense theologically, as I shall show.

Participation in seminars created some problems when one lecturer addressed questions directly to me. Faced with a question like, 'What qualifications must the messiah have?', it was clear that it would be unproductive to provoke an inter-religious confrontation by proffering mainstream Christian answers: my aim was first and foremost to understand, not to refute. We quickly reached agreement, however, that I would give 'Moonie answers' to such questions – that is to say, my answers would attempt to reflect a correct understanding of the UC position, but carry no implication that I endorsed the veracity of those answers.

Inevitably there have been limits to the possibility of assuming a participant-observer stance while preserving moral and intellectual integrity. For example, I declined one member's suggestion of undertaking certain 'prayer conditions' which, he said, would provide me with experiences which would demonstrate conclusively to me that there is a real spirit world. It may be that western scholars should consider more seriously the possibility that spiritual discipline yields truth more reliably than critical analysis, but at least in the meantime the armoury of the researcher is intellectual rigour rather than spiritual advancement, and I have not attempted to change the rules of western scholarship. I have also felt unable to participate in higher level seminars, since these involve a certain amount of street-witnessing and fund raising. Although I have been prepared to channel my energies into maximising my understanding of the *Principle*, it seemed improper that I should act as one of the UC's builders.

There are other areas where the researcher is excluded from a participant-observer stance, since certain events are for members only. The Blessing and related ceremonies are cases in point, as is the Sunday morning Pledge

Service. To participate one would have to belong, and the account one would give would be an insider's account. Whether the 'insider' or the 'outsider' understands a religion best is a matter of discussion.[32] I believe there is no 'right' answer to the question; both stances provide a useful and complementary way of understanding a faith. Despite the fact that some parts of the present study defend the UC against prevalent criticism, the account which I offer is essentially an outsider's one, and the limits to participation have had to be compensated by the reading of instructions given to members and detailed discussions with them. I am grateful that members in the main have proved so willing to share their insiders' experiences with me, the outsider.

# 2 Unification Doctrines

Before we can analyse the origins, beliefs and practices of the Unification Church, it is necessary to provide a summary of basic UC beliefs for the benefit of those who are unfamiliar with them. This chapter summarises the teachings which a typical attender at a UC workshop might be given. The teachings more or less correspond to what is found in *Divine Principle*: sometimes further elaboration is given, and almost certainly some account of the life of Sun Myung Moon will be included. Although the Rev Moon's life is usually expounded last, I have decided, in line with much of the UC's own literature, to start with the tradition of its founder-leader.

## THE LIFE OF SUN MYUNG MOON

Although his biography is not given either in *Divine Principle* or *Outline of Principle Level 4*, Unificationists insist that the *Principle* cannot be understood independently of Sun Myung Moon's life. More of the Rev Moon's history will be related elsewhere in the book. The revelations enshrined in the *Principle* did not come to him all at once, but progressively. Unlike religious leaders such as Muhammad, to whom the angel Gabriel is said to have recited the Qur'an from heaven, or Joseph Smith (the founder of the Mormon Church), who was given gold plates to translate, the Rev Moon's revelation was not delivered from the celestial world in an almost unsolicited way. Unification members insist that the Rev Moon had to struggle to receive the *Principle*, and received it as a result of deep prayer, conversations with God, Jesus and members of the spirit world, in fierce combat with spiritual adversaries, including Satan, who did not wish certain spiritual truths to become known.

Sun Myung Moon was born on 6 January 1920, in P'yeongan Pukto[1] in North-West Korea, three miles from the coast. He was the son of parents who had converted to Presbyterianism when he was aged 10. A deeply religious boy, he used to go frequently into the mountains to pray. Ever since his family's conversion to Christianity he read the Bible meticulously, but could not understand why, if God was omnipotent, he could not eliminate evil from the world. On Easter morning, 1936, when he was 16 years old, Sun Myung Moon had an experience in which, he believed, Jesus appeared to him. Jesus explained that, through humanity's unbelief, he had been unable to complete his mission and that Sun Myung Moon was commissioned to finish his task. At first he refused, but was finally persuaded to do so.

As he continued to pray and study the Bible, he received further revelations. He had no formal training in theology, although he received a private education in which he studied the Chinese classics. He is also said to have familiarised himself with Buddhism and other religions. As a young man he used to pray deeply and tearfully (it is a common occurrence for Unification members to cry – sometimes uncontrollably – when they pray). Indeed, there is a hagiographical tale about Sun Myung Moon's tearful prayers. One day water began to come through the ground floor ceiling of the family's house. His father climbed the stairs to investigate its source and found his son in the upper storey, weeping copiously in prayer.

At the age of 19 Sun Myung Moon went to Seoul to study electrical engineering, and he continued his studies in this field at Waseda University in Japan. In Japan, he sought out many types of religious group, and also became heavily involved in the Korean Independence Movement (at that time Korea was under Japanese control). He was arrested for his political activities. Having returned to Korea in 1945, he continued to develop his religious life by seeking out many religious groups of various kinds. He believed that he had discovered, in gradual instalments, the various parts of the *Principle*, partly through prayer, but more especially by fighting with the spirits. Kwang Yol Yoo,[2] a Unificationist biographer, states that neither God nor Jesus would tell Sun Myung Moon about the Fall, and consequently he had to ask Lucifer himself. He did this by asking very indirect questions, until finally he arrived at a satisfactory conclusion.

Having finally satisfied himself that he had discovered all of the *Principle*, Sun Myung Moon set about formulating it in a more systematic way. He did not write it down immediately, however, but disseminated it by preaching. Thus in August 1945 the Rev Moon's public ministry began; he left his employment and devoted himself to the teaching of the *Principle*. Like many other Korean visionaries, the Rev Moon's message proved unacceptable to Korean Christian ministers, and, because of persecution, on 6 July 1946 he moved to Pyongyang in North Korea – a rather bold move, in view of the fact that the North was at that time occupied by Soviet troops. There were many spiritual groups there, and Sun Myung Moon made a point of exploring many of them.

Rumours began to spread about the Rev Moon: he was accused of heretical teaching and of being a spy for South Korea. On August 11 he was arrested by the Communist police and gaoled. After torturing him, the prison authorities abandoned him in the prison yard, leaving his followers to pick up the body. They did so, and their leader was restored to health once more. Some external literature suggests that comparisons are made here between Sun Myung Moon and Jesus Christ: he was betrayed, tortured by the authorities, presumed dead, abandoned by all but his closest disciples, and after three days revived, and started preaching again.[3] This interpretation is presumably designed to demonstrate that Unificationists see parallels between the Rev Moon and Jesus, but members do not stress this: some acknowledge that God may have intended that the Rev Moon should follow Jesus' course in such a way; others do not.

Five months later (22 February 1948) the Rev Moon was arrested again, the charge being that he was 'advocating chaos in society'.[4] He was found guilty, and sentenced to five years of hard labour at the Tong Nee Special Labour Concentration Camp in Hungnam. According to Unificationist sources, the average life expectation of a prisoner there was between three and six months; they were severely treated, given little rest and food, and each person was made to fill 130 bags of fertiliser every day. The ammonium sulphate in the fertiliser burned the hands of the workforce, and sometimes peeled off the prisoners' skins down to the bone. Sun Myung Moon was prisoner number 596, and this number is regarded as significant by Unification members: the Korean characters spell out the word 'sorrowful', and the number itself sounds similar to a Korean word meaning 'unfair'.

The Korean war broke out in June 1950. When the UN forces moved in on North Korea in 1950, arriving at Hungnam on October 14, they liberated Sun Myung Moon and the other prisoners. He went north to Pyongyang, where he met up with two close followers, Won Pil Kim and Jong Hwa Pak. After some 40 days they fled to the south. Jong Hwa Pak had a broken leg, and the other two, with considerable difficulty, managed to convey him alternately on a bicycle and on Sun Myung Moon's back until they reached Seoul.[5]

They departed from Seoul to Pusan in January 1951, and it was in Pusan that Sun Myung Moon met an architect by the name of Mr Aum. Sun Myung Moon also began writing *Divine Principle* in notebooks, in pencil. It is stated that he wrote so fast that his assistant, who was delegated the task of sharpening his second pencil, had difficulty in keeping up with him. Yoo writes:

Around that time Father first organized the Divine Principle theme. He wrote very fast with a pencil in his notebook. One person beside him would sharpen his pencil, and he couldn't follow his writing speed. By the time Father's pencil got thick, this next person could not sharpen another pencil, so wrote so very fast. [*sic*] That was the beginning of the Divine Principle book; also at that time Father began to teach the Principle.[6]

The draft of the *Principle* was completed on 10 May 1952. From this time on, Sun Myung Moon preached the *Principle* in Pusan: formerly his preaching had consisted of his 'principled' interpretation of the Bible. He taught in a small makeshift building, a small house under a hill, made out of rocks, earth, scrap wood and old cardboard boxes; the floor was made of sand, with mats on top, and became flooded when it rained.

Sun Myung Moon moved to Seoul the following year, and in 1954, on May 1, the Unification Church was founded – or, to give it its full and official name, the Holy Spirit Association for the Unification of World Christianity. It is important to note what the term 'Holy Spirit' means in this context, since the evangelical wing of mainstream Christianity is only too ready to assume that Unificationist terms are to be construed in an identical way, and thus constitute a travesty of Christianity as conventionally understood. Dr David S. C. Kim, one of the founder members (now President of the Unification Theological Seminary), gives the following explanation:

> We translated *Shilryung* as 'Holy Spirit', but it actually means 'spiritual'. This name is often confused with the Holy Spirit (one of the Trinity) by outsiders and theologians, but no other translation seemed adequate at the time. The name actually means, 'spiritual association to unite all Christian churches'.[7]

In the HSA-UWC, services consisted of exposition of the *Principle* and deep prayer which elicited much weeping. The bulk of the teaching was not given by the Rev Moon himself, but by Hyo Won Eu, the first President of the Church. Apparently Eu would lecture far into the night, although the lectures were scheduled to stop between 9 and 10 p.m. As midnight approached, the lecture would stop and Eu would introduce the Rev Moon to the congregation. Owing to the midnight curfew, members were now unable to go home, and consequently their shoes were often found outside the building at all hours of the night, since they were obliged to stay until the morning.

This, at any rate, is the explanation which most Unificationists give. Opponents of the church interpreted the evidence differently, and rumours spread that all sorts of immoral sexual practices were taking place.[8] The authorities were more inclined to believe the stories about sex orgies than the accounts of the lengthy prayers and teachings, and they arrested Sun Myung Moon and four others on 4 July 1954. He was charged, amongst other things, with illicit sexual practices. However, all the charges were eventually dropped, apart from one – the avoidance of conscription. After three months he was released and returned to the church, which was now on its third site.

From the period of the formation of the HSA-UWC, the Rev Moon was preparing to meet the 'True Mother', in order to accomplish the unfinished mission of Jesus. Hak Ja Han was married to Sun Myung Moon on 16 March 1960, and the event is known as the 'True Parents' Blessing'. It is from this period on that the Unification Church inaugurated what the media call the 'mass wedding', or, as the UC prefers to call it, 'the Blessing'.

Unlike most of the other minor religious groups in Korea, Unificationism is unique in having spread beyond the peninsula's boundaries. Sun Myung Moon preached the *Principle* in Japan, and a Japanese mission was set up there in 1959. In the same year Miss Young Oon Kim was sent to the USA, followed soon after by three other early leaders. There were some differences of opinion between the various missionary groups which developed, and when the Rev Moon finally visited the United States in 1972, one of his achievements was to unify and reorganise the movement in the USA.[9] During his visit the Rev Moon organised a number of rallies which began to bring the movement to public attention. Around this time, missionaries were also sent to the United Kingdom and to Europe, and by 1975 a UC presence was established in 120 different nations.

DIVINE PRINCIPLE

It is important to explain something about the central text *Divine Principle*. This work, translated and published in English in 1973, is often reckoned to be the infallible word of Sun Myung Moon. This common view, however, is far from accurate. The work was not actually written by him, but by Hyo Won Eu. It is probably a composite work, emanating principally from Sun Myung Moon's revelations, but with some additions: the section on the history of Christianity, for example, is said to have been written by one of the UC's leading theologians Dr Young Oon Kim, who died recently. The work is 'authorised' by the Rev Moon, being one interpretation of the *Principle* amongst several. A somewhat simplified version of *Divine Principle* is contained in *Outline of The Principle, Level 4*,[10] written by the Rev Chung Hwan Kwak, whom most Unificationists regard as another of their senior scholars. The Rev Moon has not personally written any of the published versions of the *Principle*; the only account of the *Principle* which he wrote was the set of pencilled notes which circulated in Korea in the early 1950s.

Unificationism makes an important distinction between the '*Principle*' and '*Divine Principle*'. The former is the revelation which was given to Sun Myung Moon in his various spiritual experiences and through his personal study, and the versions of *Divine Principle* or *The Divine Principles* are various written interpretations of this. The *Principle* is an interpretation of the Old and New Testaments. Unificationists hold that it is the ultimate, final truth[11] – indeed God's own interpretation of previous scripture and not merely that of humankind. The *Principle* is therefore the 'Completed Testament' which transcends the existing Christian canon of scripture. The summary that follows is sufficient indication of its distinctiveness. Not only does the *Principle* interpret specific scriptural passages in a new way, but in several instances passages which have vanished into oblivion in the minds of mainstream Christians (if they ever knew of their existence in the first place) assume a crucial role in explaining God's providential plan for humankind. The *Principle* falls into three main sections: Creation, Fall, and Principles of Restoration.

## (1) THE PRINCIPLE OF CREATION

*Divine Principle* starts by considering the nature of God. How do we know what God is like? How can we find out? We might, the *Principle* argues, compare this question with trying to find out what an author is like. By reading the contents of this book readers will no doubt draw certain conclusions about me, the author: am I careless or meticulous, witty or boring, fair-minded or gullible? Just as we can draw inferences about the character of the author by examining the author's work, similarly we can see God's works in creation and thus make inferences about the nature and character of God.

So what is creation like? *Divine Principle* states that everything which exists has an 'internal character' and an 'external form'.[12] A human being[13] has a body which is 'external' and a mind which is 'internal'. Animals too have an external form (body), but also an internal character in the form of an animal mind. Even at the level of plants the same is true: there is a 'plant mind' which underlies the external physical form of a plant. It is stated in the Book of Genesis that God made humanity in his own image, and therefore what is found in human beings (at least in some degree) must also be true of God. Thus God also has an internal character and an external form. ('External form' is sometimes given the technical Korean name *hyung sang*, and 'internal character' *sung sang*.)[14] The essence of God's internal character is also called *heart*, and it is very important to understand God's innermost feelings such as love, joy, and sorrow, which are in his heart, in order to understand fully how he is accomplishing humankind's restoration.

*Divine Principle* explains that humankind not only consists of mind and body, but 'positivity' and 'negativity', which are expressed in the masculinity and femininity of human beings respectively. The same polarities (positive and negative) are found in animals and plants (stamen and pistil). At the level of inanimate objects, atoms possess positive and negative ions. If humankind is created in God's image, then not only must God have an internal character and external form, but God must also have male and female aspects. (Although it is acknowledged that God has male and female aspects, it is customary for members to speak of God in the masculine gender, addressing him as 'Father'.)

'Internal' and 'external', and male and female, are not polarised opposites, however. Each contains the other. The notion of the complementarity of opposites derives from the Taoist notions of *yin* and *yang* to which explicit reference is made in *Divine Principle*.[15] *Yin* is the female aspect of the universe: maternal, yielding, intuitive, receptive and restful, and is associated with Earth. *Yang* is male, associated with Heaven: strong, rational, creative and active. If these characterisations of male and female appear to reflect western sexist stereotypes, it should be remembered that in Chinese thought these are not complete contrasts: each contains the other, although females are often regarded as possessing the former set of characteristics and males the latter. However, one can possess *yin* and *yang* elements in different degrees: the sage who spends his life in contemplation possesses more *yin* characteristics (intuitive, receptive, restful) than, say, a western feminist career woman. No aspect of the universe is totally *yin* or totally *yang*: each gives rise to the other, and interacts with it. *Divine Principle* calls this mutual interaction 'give and take action'. In Unification thought, 'give and take action' originates from God, whose external form is called 'Universal Prime Force'.

Thus we have an Origin, a Division and a complementarity of the Division's components (Union). This way of looking at creation now develops into a distinctively Unificationist doctrine, which is known as the 'Four Position Foundation'.[16] God (the origin) created every human being with a mind and body (division) which should have united to make a true or perfect individual; God (origin) created man and woman (a division), who should have united to give birth to a true united family (union);

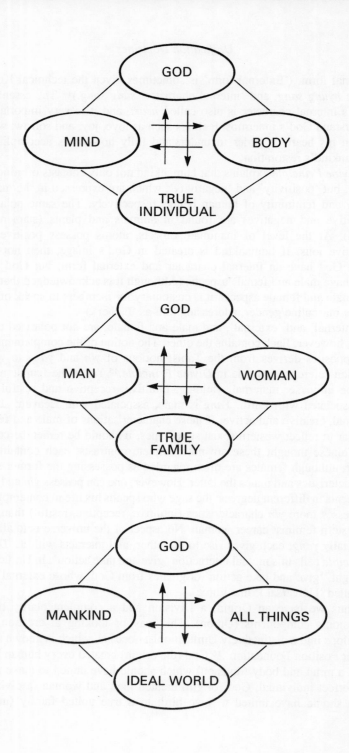

God created humankind and the rest of creation (division), and humankind should have created an ideal world (union) under God's dominion. The doctrine of the Four Position Foundation is often expressed diagrammatically in UC texts (see diagram opposite).

These three examples of 'origin, division and union' (O-D-U) are particularly important, for they constitute the three 'Blessings' which God intended humankind to establish. They should 'be fruitful, multiply, and have dominion over the earth'.[17] Being 'fruitful' means having one's mind and body in harmony so as to become a true individual. 'Multiply' means to bear children. Having dominion over the earth means creating an ideal world in which there is harmony between God, humankind and the rest of creation. From establishing a perfect family, one 'multiplies out' to achieve a perfect society, nation and world.

## THE STAGES TOWARDS PERFECTION

Nothing fulfils its purpose instantly, not even God. God is a god of order, and he has set the universe to run in accordance with consistent and absolute laws. As *Divine Principle* states, 'God cannot ignore the laws which He has set up.'[18] Many of these are physical laws (such as the law of gravity), but there are 'spiritual laws' too, through which the universe operates. These spiritual laws in their totality are known as the '*Principle*'.[19] God's purpose is that humanity should perfect itself, but this cannot be accomplished by God instantly creating perfect men and women: human beings must exercise their own free will and responsibility in order to perfect themselves. Therefore humanity is expected to grow, but this will take time, and the accomplishment of God's purpose can be retarded by lack of human co-operation.

The *Principle* teaches that there are three stages of development: Formation, Growth and Completion. According to the creation story in Genesis, after each day of creation it is stated that 'there was evening and there was morning, one day'.[20] A night, it is argued, must intervene between evening and morning, and hence we have three stages of development in creation (evening, night and morning), and one may call these 'Formation', 'Growth' and 'Completion'. (This interpretation may seem contrived, but it is worth noting that this ordering in Genesis is taken seriously by Jews and is held to justify beginning the sabbath on Friday evening rather than Saturday morning.)

Adam and Eve were expected to progress through these stages until they were sufficiently advanced spiritually to be blessed by God in marriage and bear children. If they had done this, they would have established the Kingdom of Heaven on earth, and lived under the 'direct dominion' of God. ('Direct dominion' means the situation in which God's will and humankind's will are one, and where God communicates directly with all of humankind, rather than through intermediaries such as prophets or sacred scriptures. At the moment, it is claimed, men and women need the *Principle* for God to make his will known to them.)

The Kingdom of Heaven on earth would not have been the ultimate bliss for human beings, for men and women live and die, and the physical world alone offers no promise of eternal happiness. However, since God is mirrored in his creation, the fact that God has an external form and internal character indicates that men and women too have bodies and spirits. After death they will live on in the spiritual realm, realising the Kingdom of Heaven in the spiritual world.

It is significant that Unificationists, unlike most mainstream denominations, do not typically use the word 'salvation' to describe their goal.[21] 'Restoration' is a term which is more favoured, but it should be remembered that restoring the state which existed before the Fall is only a prelude to the establishment of the Kingdom of Heaven. Adam and Eve were expected to grow beyond their prelapsarian state: if the Garden of Eden was Paradise on earth, humanity's spiritual quest must look beyond Paradise to the genuinely ultimate state which Unification theology calls the Kingdom of Heaven. This was God's 'primary plan' – that is to say, the original and ideal purpose which God had for creation. However, this was not accomplished, since Adam and Eve fell from grace.

## (2) THE FALL

The Unificationist doctrine of the Fall is distinctive. It is taught that the Fall did not occur as the result of a serpent tempting Eve to eat a fruit from a tree. UC members do not believe that the literal story-line of Genesis gives an account of actual events in human history. Serpents just do not walk and talk; hence the story must be understood symbolically. What really happened, they believe, was this. Lucifer (the serpent, also known as Satan) was originally the archangel who was closest to God, and who was created before the creation of human beings. When Adam and Eve were created, God loved them more than the angelic kingdom, and so Lucifer became jealous, even though God's love for him had not diminished. Lucifer therefore attempted to secure the love of Adam and Eve, and to this end he seduced Eve into an illicit sexual relationship. (This was not a physical relationship, but a relationship between two 'spirit bodies': angels do not possess physical bodies.) Having yielded to Satan's temptation, Eve then realised what she had done. Satan was not her husband, yet she had engaged in sexual intercourse with him. She now felt guilty and wanted to return to God: she therefore sought out Adam, whom God had destined to be her spouse, in the desire to act as a wife to him. By returning to Adam and entering into a sexual relationship with him, Eve believed that she could return to God once more.

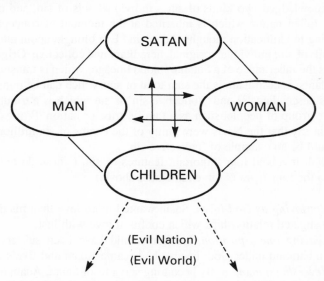

Eve's thinking was mistaken. 'Give and take' with Satan cannot simply be restored by 'give and take' with one's true marriage partner. Furthermore, God had not willed Eve to have a sexual relationship with Adam since they were not yet blessed by God in matrimony. The Fall was thus a sexual offence: Lucifer seduced Eve, who until then had remained a virgin, being only in her teens at the time. By yielding to temptation, Eve committed a three-fold sin. She should have obeyed God, remained faithful to Adam, her betrothed, and only entered into a sexual relationship when both she and Adam had reached the top of the 'Completion' stage of their spiritual development.

As a result of the Fall, Adam and Eve fell to a point below the lowest point on the 'Formation' stage, into what is called the 'unprincipled realm'. (In other words, they had fallen to a state where they had placed themselves outside God's 'principled' law. This state is sometimes called 'hell'.) God could have prevented Adam and Eve from succumbing to temptation; however, God does not predetermine the outcome of human choices, for men and women have free will and responsibility to decide whether or not to obey his laws.

By their sin Adam and Eve had put humankind under a new and false master: humanity was now serving Satan instead of God. This set up a new Four Position Foundation (see diagram on p. 29)

In this way, sin entered the world. Mainstream Christianity has traditionally acknowledged two kinds of sin – individual acts of sin, and original sin (the fallen nature which is inherited at the moment of conception).[22] According to Unification thought, Adam and Eve brought about altogether four kinds of sin: individual, original, hereditary and collective. Original sin involves the inheritance of a Satanic 'blood lineage' which is transmitted to descendants; ancestral sin is the sum total of sins which can be transmitted to one's descendants;[23] and 'collective sin' is sin which is attributable to an entire group of people, such as a family, tribe or nation. (For example, we might say that the Nazis were guilty of the deaths of six million Jews: this would be an example of 'collective sin'.)

The Fall involved four important features of sin. (These do not correspond to the four *types* of sin enumerated above.)

1.  *Not loving as God loves.* Satan wanted more love than his due and instigated relationships which confused love with lust.
2.  *Leaving one's position.* Lucifer should have been subservient to humankind under God: instead he became Adam and Eve's master.
3.  *Reversing dominion.* By becoming servants of Satan, Adam and Eve reversed the hierarchy of God–humanity–angels to Archangel–humanity–God (Satan is the Archangel), God being relegated to the lowest place.
4.  *Multiplying evil.* Satan's evil spread to Eve, who propagated further 'unprincipled' acts, such as Adam's sin, and sins of families, societies and subsequent generations.

According to the *Principle*, the Fall occurred on two levels – the spiritual and the physical. Lucifer (a spiritual being) seduced Eve, thus bringing about a 'spiritual Fall', and Eve entered into a sexual relationship with Adam (both, of course, were physical beings) before they were sufficiently spiritually developed, thus causing the 'physical Fall'. What this meant in practice was that humankind's aspirations to reach the Kingdom of Heaven on earth and the Kingdom of Heaven in the spiritual world were both forfeited.

## THE COMING OF THE MESSIAH

In order to set humanity back on the path towards restoration, the only way to deal with sin was the sending of a messiah. The messiah is an ideal sinless person whose function is to restore the universe to the state it was at before the Fall, since a completely new start is needed. If I have lost my way in unknown territory, often the only way of remedying the situation is to backtrack to the point at which I deviated from the proper route. Only then can I proceed towards my original destination. The analogy of losing one's way serves as a rough illustration of the Unificationist concept of obtaining salvation. First, the state of humanity must be brought back to the point at which sin originally entered the human condition; only then can men and women progress according to the original purpose of God. A messiah is needed because the messiah is an ideal person who is at one with God in mind and heart, and who can know God's will directly, rather than through intermediaries such as priests, temples and religions. The messiah can inaugurate a new lineage by marrying and giving birth to sinless children: by doing this the rest of humanity can be ingrafted into God's true family and thus can be freed from the parentage and dominion of Satan. (It is worth noting at this juncture that teachings about the messiah's marriage would not normally be given at a seminar, notwithstanding the fact that this was one of the first teachings with which mainstream Christians became familiar. I have included reference to the intended marriage of Jesus for the sake of completeness.)

Mainstream Christianity typically defines its goal as 'salvation': humankind has fallen into the plight of sin and has to be 'redeemed' by securing the removal of sin. Unification thought is more complex: there are two stages in the quest for the Kingdom of Heaven – first restoration (the reversal of the effects of the Fall), and second the progress towards perfection. The restoration of Eden is insufficient for the attainment of the Kingdom of Heaven, since the prelapsarian state of Adam and Eve still fell short of perfection. Restoration can only be achieved by the coming of a messiah; attaining perfection is then obtainable through men and women acting in a 'principled' way, so that they grow from their present 'unprincipled' state through the stages of spiritual development – Formation, Growth and Completion – until at the end of the Completion stage they are fully perfected individuals who are capable of establishing the Kingdom of Heaven.

Because of the Fall, human history has been sinful; but throughout history God's providential plan has been at work in order to restore his original plan of the ideal family under his direct dominion. God worked through such men as Noah, Abraham, Isaac, Jacob and Moses, until finally Jesus was sent. Jesus' mission was to restore the sovereignty of God which Satan had usurped, to restore the 'ideal' person and to establish the Kingdom of Heaven on earth.

Unificationists are emphatic that God did not intend Jesus' death to be the means of establishing the Kingdom of Heaven. If God's plan had been fulfilled, Jesus would have married and fathered sinless children. But Israel rejected Jesus: even his own disciples were disloyal and abandoned him when he was arrested. Jesus was thus led to die on the cross.

Unification Church members often find themselves foisted with the belief that Jesus' mission was a failure.[24] *Divine Principle* does not say this at any point, and UC members feel justifiably indignant when their critics persistently ignore their attempts to explain what they really believe about Jesus. They have two principal reasons for insisting that Jesus did not fail. First, Jesus himself was not a failure; other people failed Jesus (principally John the Baptist, but others too). Second, as we shall see, Jesus' mission had a significant measure of success; Jesus accomplished 'spiritual salvation', although not 'physical salvation'; he opened the gates of Paradise, but not the Kingdom of Heaven itself. (The two are distinguished in Unification thought and will be explained later.)

Jesus' death was not the end, of course, for the Bible records that he rose again. *Divine Principle* teaches that this was not a physical resurrection: Jesus' spirit was raised and his disciples saw the spirit body of Jesus during the forty day post-Easter period, but not a physical body. Yet his mission was incomplete: by being unable to open the Kingdom of Heaven, 2000 years of preparation were lost, and thus the foundation which Jesus had established had to be restored.

The lost time span of 2000 years has now elapsed, and the events in history from the time of Christ to the present day have been preparing for the new messianic age in which there is once again the opportunity to receive the 'Lord of the Second Advent'. These are the 'last days' to which Christ referred; the new messiah is now said to be on earth, and it is important to recognise him and follow him.


## (3) PRINCIPLES OF RESTORATION

What I have explained thus far may be regarded as a basic summary of UC teachings. However, it may appear to contain many logical gaps and unsupported assertions. Unification Church members often insist that the *Principle* is 'logical': indeed members have frequently told me that they accepted the *Principle* because it offered such a logical explanation of the Bible, which they believed mainstream Christianity lacked. The function of the third section of the *Principle* is to fill these gaps in, and to demonstrate systematically how the course of history has been planned by God to fulfil his purpose of sending a messiah to restore humanity's lost lineage.

At the beginning of this chapter, I mentioned that God is believed to operate through firmly established spiritual laws. The third section of the *Principle* is devoted to demonstrating how these laws have been at work throughout the history of Israel and in world events up to the present day. What follows is by no means easy material. Inevitably I have had to simplify and make some omissions, and therefore any reader who is anxious to have a fuller account of UC theology must be prepared to tackle either *Outline of The Principle Level 4* or *Divine Principle* itself. In deciding what to include and what to leave out I have borne in mind the need to be as fair as possible to the subject-matter and, more particularly, to lay the bearings for the analysis which follows in subsequent chapters. (In order to make sense of some of the particularly opaque material, I have felt it necessary to put in my own occasional explanatory gloss.)

Because of the Fall, humanity is held to be in a new lineage – that of Satan. God had therefore to restore the lineage and enable men and women to be brought once again under his direct dominion. Yet human beings cannot understand God's heart while they are under Satan's dominion: if only some ideal man could be born on earth, who knew God's heart perfectly, then he could establish a true family, bring people back to God and ingraft them into God's sinless family.

The messiah cannot simply be sent by God without preparation on the part of men and women. Humankind had become so sinful that it would have rejected the messiah and sought to destroy him. Humanity must therefore play its part in the restoration process. Just as human freedom resulted in the Fall, likewise human responsibility must be exercised to enable fallen men and women to obtain restoration after the Fall.

Humanity must therefore make due preparation to establish a 'foundation' to enable the messiah to come. Divine grace alone will not accomplish this. Mainstream Christianity has grappled with the question of whether individuals are saved by faith or by works, Protestantism being largely influenced by Paul in stressing divine grace rather than human effort, and Roman Catholicism typically stressing the need for explicit acts such as attention to the sacraments – the eucharist, confession, penance, and so on. Unificationism comes somewhere between these two positions. Salvation – or, more accurately, restoration – comes neither through faith nor through works, but through 'indemnity' (*t'ang gam*).

The word 'indemnity' is to be understood as having a technical meaning here, and not its usual sense of offering a guarantee that the indemnifier will accept the legal consequences of blame. The Korean word *t'ang gam* means the settlement of a debt and is primarily used in the business world. 'Indemnity' in this context means the making of repayment for a debt which is not necessarily equal to the original debt. If I am entrusted with, say, a rare book and I lose it, I cannot replace that book. However, common decency would dictate that I should not shrug my shoulders and proffer a feeble apology. Instead I might offer to compensate that person with a sum of money in lieu: in Unificationist terms, this would be 'indemnity'. Perhaps I can afford to pay a sum equivalent to the value of the book: this would be paying indemnity equivalent to what I owed. But perhaps I lack sufficient funds, in which case at least a repayment of a token amount would be appropriate: if I offer a sum smaller than the book's value, this will be indemnity which is less than the real debt. Alternatively, it might be argued that in such a situation I should pay the lender a greater sum than the book's value, to match the cost of the irreplaceable book and to compensate the lender as well; if I did this, I would be paying indemnity which is greater than the debt owed.

Humankind must, accordingly, pay indemnity before it is possible for the messiah to come. Men and women must make some form of repayment to expiate sin, since they must demonstrate that they have themselves made some effort towards their own restoration. Normally, God will require indemnity which is less than what is strictly needed to repay him for humankind's sin, but the exact amount of indemnity is set by God.

To make restoration possible there are two requirements for human indemnity. Two 'foundations' must be laid for the messiah to come – a 'foundation of faith' and a 'foundation of substance'. These are technical terms within Unificationist thought and are by no means easy to understand. At the Fall, two types of relationship were seriously damaged: human relationships with God (Adam and Eve disobeyed God's commandments), and human relationships with other human beings (Adam and Eve engaged in premature sexual relationship with each other). The former relationship is often referred to as the 'vertical', the latter as the 'horizontal'. Both these relationships must be restored: the 'foundation of faith' restores the first, while the 'foundation of substance' restores the second.

The foundation of faith enables certain divinely designated characters to assume the role of 'central figure'. These central figures stand at the crux of humankind's salvation history, and they must accomplish three things in order to establish themselves in the *position*[25] of a true central figure. They must be able to 'stand in Adam's position' (that is to say, they are to act towards God as an ideal man, in order to restore Adam's failure); they must make a sacrifice to God; and they must go through a period of growth. (The sacrifice is a 'symbolic offering': that is to say, it is a token gesture to appease God, paying indemnity which is less than equivalent to the full amount of the debt.) The foundation of faith establishes a correct divine–human relationship (a correct 'vertical' relationship). Only when 'vertical' relationships are satisfactory can a correct 'horizontal' relationship (a proper set of inter-human relationships) be established. The latter is called the 'foundation of substance'. When this is accomplished successfully, the foundation for receiving the messiah has been laid.

Throughout the history of the Jewish people, various central figures have appeared to lay the foundation of faith for the coming messiah. Adam was unable to establish the foundation of faith since he was himself responsible for the Fall. Adam was now in a *position* where he was serving two masters, God and Satan. (Because men and women have free will, they are never totally committed to serving Satan consistently: Adam still had free choice, although his initial sin had to be indemnified.) God therefore needed someone who could prove himself to be totally dedicated to him. A fundamental principle of restoration is that God cannot use the same figure a second time after he has failed. If a central figure has 'give and take' with Satan he cannot then be totally dedicated to God. Consequently, God's plan in history involves a continual separating out of good and evil: this is why in Unification thought there is a constant polarisation between biblical characters, particularly brothers. It was by no mere chance that Adam had two sons, Cain and Abel. One represented the satanic, the other the ideal of humanity which Adam had lost. (Incidentally, Unificationists do not hold the view – sometimes attributed to them – that Satan was Cain's genetic father and that Cain was born as a consequence of Eve's illicit sexual relationship with Satan.)[26]

The first central figure was Abel.[27] The Bible records that Abel made an offering to God,[28] and by accepting his offering, God acknowledged that the 'vertical' relationship between himself and humanity was restored; thus the foundation of faith was established. Accordingly the next set of relationships which were capable of being restored were the 'horizontal' relationships – those between one human being and another. If Cain and Abel had entered into proper ('principled') relationships with each other, then the foundation of substance would also have been laid and the messiah could have come.

However, as we read in the Bible, this did not happen. Cain, whose offering was rejected by God, became jealous and killed Abel.[29] This had a number of effects. The most obvious was that the foundation of substance was not laid. Second, the failure to build the foundation of substance destroyed the foundation of faith which Abel had already built.[30] Consequently, both the foundation of faith and the foundation of substance required rebuilding.[31] Not only was that so, but by his murderous act Cain had committed a further sin which required indemnification. The older brother (Cain) had refused to submit to the younger brother (Abel), and thus humankind had taken a further wrong turning which had to be backtracked. The failure of the elder to submit to the younger must be re-enacted in a 'principled' way.

God's will to restore humanity is unchanging, however, even though human beings do not fulfil their share of responsibility. Although Cain and Abel had failed, Adam had a third son, Seth, a less well known biblical character, but who was nevertheless the ancestor of all the famous Old Testament patriarchs, the first of importance being Noah. Noah was destined to be the next 'central figure' – 1600 years after Adam – and his 'symbolic offering' to God was the famous ark, which saved humankind from the flood. The foundation of faith was established and humankind could therefore proceed to establish the foundation of substance.

It now remained for Noah's family to lay the foundation of substance by establishing proper 'horizontal' (inter-human) relationships and to restore the proper Cain-Abel relationship. But before Noah's sons could do this, they had first to receive the benefit of the foundation of faith, and this they evidently failed to do. The failure occurred in a rather obscure incident involving Noah. The Bible records[32] that one night Noah became drunk and lay naked in his tent. In the interests of conventional decency, his eldest son Ham covered up his father's naked body – a seemingly proper act, but unfortunately one which was improper from God's viewpoint. According to Unificationist teaching, Noah's act of exposure was perfectly proper on that occasion: Adam and Eve's sin had been a sexual one and had resulted in their becoming ashamed of their nakedness. By laying the foundation of faith, Noah had restored humanity to the situation where shame at one's naked body was no longer necessary. By covering up Noah's nakedness, Ham had reversed this part of the restoration process and thus the whole restoration drama had to be re-enacted again from the beginning.

Abraham, a further 400 years later, was selected to be the next central figure. Once again Unification theology lays great emphasis on an Old Testament incident which is not widely known amongst mainstream Christians. Abraham was commanded to make a burnt offering to God, and accordingly he offered a heifer, a ram and some doves.[33] The writer of the story records that, before the sacrifice was offered, Abraham cut the heifer and the ram into two halves, but not the doves. The Bible does not explicitly state that God commanded that all three offerings should have been divided, but after this incident Abraham had a dream in which God's wrath was poured out upon him. Unification theology concludes that God was angry at the way in which Abraham had performed the sacrifice: he should have divided the doves, just as he divided the heifer and the ram. The two-fold division was important, because it would have signified the separation of good and evil, the divine side and the satanic side. Accordingly the foundation of faith was not established.

One might have expected at this point that, because Abraham had failed, the whole history of restoration must start again and that humankind would have to pay another 400 years of indemnity to secure the arrival of a new central figure. However, Abraham was the third successive central figure and there is a spiritual law relating to the number three: whoever is appointed as the third chosen instrument of God must necessarily succeed. Abraham was therefore given a further opportunity to establish the foundation of faith.

In the much more familiar story, Abraham was required by God to offer his own son Isaac as a human sacrifice.[34] Isaac, having shown himself willing to offer up his life at God's command, was now qualified to become the central figure in Abraham's place. God then commanded that the human sacrifice should be abandoned, and Abraham and Isaac together sacrificed a ram as the 'symbolic offering' to set up the foundation of faith.

The foundation of substance now had to be established. Isaac's two sons, Esau (the elder) and Jacob (the younger), had to establish true 'horizontal' relationships amongst their family. Esau and Jacob had the providential task of re-enacting the Cain–Abel situation in a principled way: just as the younger brother Abel had the responsibility to perform the indemnifying acts, with Cain – the elder – submitting to Abel, so Jacob should have played the central role in overcoming Satan, and Esau (representing Satan's side) should have submitted to his younger brother Jacob (representing God's side).

A number of incidents described in the Bible demonstrate Esau's submission to Jacob. One day Esau came home from hunting so hungry that he agreed to trade his entire inheritance for a bowl of soup which Jacob offered him.[35] Jacob ensured that this agreement was implemented by disguising as Esau when his father Isaac – now old and almost blind – was on his death bed, and thus Jacob secured his father's blessing and inheritance.[36] (This signified the transference of the lineage from the elder son to the younger, from Cain to Abel, from Satan to God.) For many years Esau bore a grudge against Jacob, but finally a reconciliation took place in which Jacob came to Esau bearing gifts and Esau acknowledged Jacob's superiority.[37]

One further incident is important in Jacob's life. At the Ford of Jabbok, Jacob met an angel who wrestled with him and was finally overcome by Jacob.[38] The angel is taken by Unificationists to be an angel of God, occupying Satan's *position*, and the story is held to demonstrate that Jacob overcame Satan. Just as Adam and Eve had submitted to the Archangel (Satan) in the Garden of Eden, Jacob restored the true *position* of man and God by forcing the Archangel to submit to him. Human beings had now obtained dominion over the angels, as God had originally intended.

Isaac had previously established the foundation of faith, and Jacob now established the foundation of substance. One might therefore have imagined that the messiah could now come at once and that the restoration could take place. Not so. When Adam and Eve sinned, they sinned as a couple, and (as we have seen) one of the effects of the Fall was to 'multiply evil' from the individual through to the levels of sinful families, tribes, nations and finally a sinful world. The foundation of faith and the foundation of substance had been laid within a family; however Israel was now a nation,[39] and foundations at family level were insufficiently substantial to permit the messiah to come to restore a nation or an entire world. This did not mean that Jacob's achievements were in vain, however: Jacob established a pattern (a 'formula course', as it is called) for subsequent central figures to follow.

A new central figure was needed, and the next was Moses. Moses had to lay a foundation of faith and a foundation of substance at national level. Spiritual laws dictated that slightly different conditions of indemnity were required to do this. The required offering was no longer a physical object such as an animal or an ark; it was a period of time in which faith in God's word could be demonstrated. Since it was no longer a family which had to be restored, but a nation, it was no longer sufficient for an elder brother to submit to the younger brother. (One might have expected, for example, that Aaron should have been required to submit to Moses.) The nation was now in the 'elder brother' *position* and had to submit to the central figure Moses who was in the 'younger brother' *position*.

In the course of laying the foundation of faith, Moses appears to have been allowed three attempts. First he spent 40 years in the Pharaoh's palace,[40] which was invalidated after Moses killed an Egyptian.[41] (Instead of supporting Moses, the Israelites spread rumours about him.) Second, Moses spent 40 years in Midian, at the end of which he broke the two tablets of stone on which the Ten Commandments were inscribed.[42] Third, there was a further 40-year period in the desert which culminated in an incident which caused Moses to forfeit his *position*. At Kadesh the Israelites lacked water; God commanded Moses to strike a rock out of which water would flow; but instead of striking it once, as God had intended, Moses struck it twice, thus forfeiting his *position* as central figure.[43]

However, Moses accomplished one important achievement: he was responsible for the creation of the 'Tabernacle'. This was the portable shrine in which God would dwell and at which religious ceremonies would be performed until such time as the Temple was built during the reign of King Solomon. This Tabernacle, and later the famous Temple built during King Solomon's reign, were to symbolise the coming messiah. The Temple is believed to symbolise the messiah since on one occasion Jesus referred to himself as the Temple.[44]

It is not easy to see why Moses appears to have been allowed three successive attempts at establishing the foundation of substance. The explanation is that the first two failures are to be attributed to the Israelites and not to Moses himself: the Israelites left their *position* (they spread rumours about Moses killing the Egyptian instead of supporting his courage, and they built the golden calf while Moses was receiving the Law on Mount Sinai).[45] Moses' loss of his *position* appears superficially to be due to a fairly trivial offence; nevertheless the Bible is emphatic that Moses' deed angered God,[46] and *Divine Principle* points to St Paul's assertion regarding the incident, that 'the rock was Christ'.[47] Thus Moses' act is interpreted as a serious insult to the coming messiah.

The role of central figure now passed to Joshua after 40 years in the desert. It is not entirely clear why Israel did not have to wait a further 1600 years for a new successor to Moses' *position*, who would once again be required to establish the foundation of faith. One possible explanation is that, up till the incident at Kadesh, Moses' *position* as central figure had been so firmly established that Joshua was able to assume it. Another possible explanation is that the Tabernacle had been successfully built and Israel by now had the 'symbolic messiah'. Whatever the explanation, spiritual laws are held to be at work; it is firmly believed that the Rev Moon knows what they are, but has not yet disclosed all his revelations to his followers.

Joshua now assumed the role of central figure and was able to complete Moses' 'third course'. He sent out twelve spies to survey the land of Canaan. The spies brought conflicting reports about the strength of the opposition, but Joshua successfully discerned between the courageous and cowardly spies, and managed to secure the Israelites' unity with him: Israel (in Cain's *position*) had submitted to Joshua (in Abel's *position*). The six days of marching around the city[48] are regarded as the 'restoration of the number six'. Adam and Eve were created on the sixth day; thus, as a result of the Fall, the number six became Satan's number:

If anyone has insight, let him calculate the number of the beast, for it is man's number. His number is 666.[49]

The conditions for receiving the messiah appeared now to have been completed, yet the messiah did not come immediately. The problem was that, although indemnity had been paid to receive the messiah on a national level, God's plan was to save the entire world, and not simply the nation of Israel. Even though Jacob and Joshua (together with Moses) had succeeded, the foundation of faith, foundation of substance and the Tabernacle were insufficient for a world-wide restoration. A further central figure was therefore needed, and thus we come to the mission of Jesus.

THE MISSION OF JESUS

It is often claimed that the Unification Church downgrades the role of Jesus and declares his mission a failure. The relatively small space given in this chapter to the mission of Jesus is not intended to endorse this popularly held view. On the contrary, the importance attached to Jesus' mission is reflected in the fact that it merits a separate chapter which gives much more detailed discussion than can be achieved in a brief summary. In Unificationist seminars the mission of Jesus is held to be one of the most important lectures, which should move the hearts of the enquirers and make them determined that the way in which the messiah was treated should not occur again in the present age.

Briefly, the account of the mission of Jesus is this. John the Baptist came as the next central figure in restoration history. It is important to note that it was not Jesus himself who was the central figure. John the Baptist had the crucial task of laying the foundation for the messiah, and preparing the Jewish people to accept him and unite with him. John the Baptist, being the son of the high priest Zacharias, had sufficient status in the eyes of the Jews to be able to accomplish this. However, John wavered, and although at first he testified that Jesus was the one for whom he was preparing, he began to have doubts. When he was imprisoned, he even sent some of his own disciples to enquire whether Jesus was the messiah or not.

John the Baptist failed Jesus, and as a consequence the Jewish people had no other authority on which to accept Jesus as the messiah. Instead, he was regarded as a messianic pretender, and was sentenced to death by crucifixion. Thus Jesus died before he was able to marry and beget a family, which would have been one of the first steps towards the attainment of the Kingdom of Heaven on earth. However, although Jesus was unable to bring about the Kingdom of Heaven, Unificationism teaches that the crucifixion achieved something, and not nothing. By offering his life on the cross, Jesus was able to accomplish 'spiritual' although not 'physical' salvation. By his death he was able to open up 'Paradise': 'Today you will be with me in Paradise,' was his promise to the dying thief on the adjacent cross. What this in effect meant was that those in the spirit world, who had thitherto been unable to progress beyond the 'formation' stage of spiritual development, could now advance to the next stage, the 'growth' stage. Paradise is not to be equated with the Kingdom of Heaven, which has remained unopened until the Lord of the Second Advent has come to complete Jesus' unfinished work.

As far as the doctrine of the Resurrection is concerned, the *Principle* does not acknowledge that Jesus physically rose from the dead. The mainstream tradition that the tomb was empty on Easter morning is denied. However, after his death Jesus is acknowledged to have appeared to his disciples, but these were not appearances of a physical body but a spirit body. After all, it is pointed out, Jesus' body could suddenly appear and vanish, and even go through closed doors: such phenomena could not be accomplished by physical bodies. The return of spirit bodies, in Unification thought, is in fact a relatively common occurrence: good and evil spirits alike can return to earth to co-operate with men and women on earth or to lead them astray. The phenomenon of a returning spirit is known as 'returning resurrection', and this was precisely what happened in the case of Jesus. (The story that the dead came out of their tombs at the time of Jesus' crucifixion is likewise construed by Unificationists as a 'returning resurrection' of spirits.)


## THE SECOND ADVENT

Unificationism teaches that, since Jesus did not fully accomplish his mission, a new messiah must come to complete the restoration process. This is believed to be necessary since, according to UC teaching, physical bodies do not reincarnate, and the messiah needs a physical body to perform his task in the physical world. Four questions must be asked about the Second Advent: How will it happen?; When will it happen?; Where will it happen?; and, finally, Who will accomplish it?

First, *how* will it happen? The Bible appears to give conflicting evidence here. Some passages talk about Christ returning on the clouds of heaven,[50] while others state, for example, that 'The Kingdom of God is not coming with signs to be observed,'[51] supposedly indicating that the Christ's second advent would come about in a non-miraculous way.

Unification theology favours the latter position, for a number of reasons. The original concept of the messiah was that of a human saviour who would be born in a normal human manner. This has been the concept of messiahship embraced by orthodox Jews, both in New Testament times and today, and this interpretation would also receive the endorsement of many Christian scholars. The apparent discrepancy in the biblical evidence is resolved by taking literally those passages which predict a non-miraculous inauguration of the Kingdom of Heaven, while regarding as 'symbolic' the references to a supernatural being descending on the clouds of heaven. *Divine Principle* notes that certain references to clouds are not to literal clouds at all: for example, the writer to the Hebrews talks about a 'cloud of witnesses'.[52]

*When* will the second coming take place? This is undoubtedly the most complicated section of the *Principle*, and I cannot hope to compress it into a few paragraphs. Suffice it to say that the calculation of the date of the Second Advent depends on a doctrine known as 'providential time-identity'. What this rather forbidding term means is that, if one looks at history, one can discern clear patterns of events which are repeated in the course of restoration. If one looks at the period from Adam to Jacob, this is stated to be roughly equal in length to the period from Jacob to Jesus; this time period is also roughly equal to the period from Jesus to the present day. This tripartite sectionalisation of history is not arbitrary, according to Unification thought: the first period culminates in the successful laying of the foundation to receive the messiah on the 'family level', the second period at the 'national level', and the third period at the 'world level'. Further, these three sections of history have within them an almost exact correspondence of events. *Divine Principle*'s analysis is detailed: I can only give a very rough outline. The second period of restoration begins with 400 years of slavery in Egypt; this is held to correspond to the first 400 years of Christian history, in which the Christians were persecuted by the Roman Empire. The next 400 year period of the Judges parallels 400 years of Christian patriarchs; 120 years of the united Israelite monarchy corresponds with 120 years of the Carolingian Holy Roman Empire; the division of Israel into the two kingdoms of Judah and Israel (400 years) corresponds to the division of Christendom into the East and West Franks; and so on. Finally the period from Malachi (the last prophet, who predicts the coming of Elijah) to the advent of Jesus Christ lasts 400 years and corresponds to the period from Martin Luther's Protestant Reformation to the present day.

Without going into the complexities of the calculations, it is sufficient to state that, according to the *Principle*, we can expect the Lord of the

Second Advent's birth to occur between 1917 and 1930.[53] Unificationism is sometimes accused of lack of precision regarding its prediction of this date and inconsistencies in its calculations.[54] The UC's answer to such charges is that there is always a leeway in predicting such dates, because the precise time at which components of God's plan are accomplished depends on human free will. Indeed, *Outline of The Principle Level 4* states:

> The year cannot be pinpointed so exactly because a difference of up to ten years was often observed throughout the dispensational history.[55]

Although it is inevitable that God's providential purpose will finally be accomplished, humankind can slow it down, or even on occasions accelerate it: humanity shares responsibility with God.

*Where* will the new messiah be born? It cannot be Israel, since God never uses the same nation or person twice to fulfil his purpose once failure has occurred. Because Israel failed God by crucifying Jesus, Israel's *position* passed to Christianity, which became known as the 'new Israel' or 'second Israel'.[56] God's chosen nation must therefore be a Christian nation. The nation cannot be a western nation, for the Book of Revelation predicts that an angel will rise from the East to 'seal' the 144 000 members of the tribes of Israel.[57] The eastern country must satisfy a number of conditions which *Divine Principle* enumerates. The chosen nation must have suffered as God has suffered, it must have many religions in need of unification, it must be on the 'front line' on which God and Satan are fighting, it must have paid appropriate indemnity, and it must have been the centre of messianic prophecies.

Korea is held to satisfy these conditions. As a nation, it has suffered much war and struggle, thus paying indemnity; as we shall see, it has several religions and many messianic prophecies (as well as claimants). Most important, however, is the fact that Korea is divided between North and South, the North being communist and the South democratic. Korea is thus the meeting place of the two conflicting ideologies. Since the Unification Church is strongly opposed to communism, which is regarded as satanic, democracy is regarded as the stage of political development into which the messiah can step.

The function of the messiah is to establish the three Blessings which God intended Adam to achieve: individual perfection, a true family, and an ideal society under God's direct dominion. The messiah himself is deemed to have achieved individual perfection; the *Principle* teaches that God has taken many generations to purify the ancestry of the messiah so that he can be free from sin.

Finally, *who* is the Lord of the Second Advent? His identity is not revealed in the body of the *Divine Principle* text, and it is a common criticism of Unificationist seminar leaders that this information is withheld from enquirers until a very late stage in their exposition of the *Principle*. UC practice on this tends to vary: while some lecturers, when asked, will state directly that they believe that Sun Myung Moon is the messiah of the present age, others will take the view that it is inappropriate to give a direct response. What is important, they will claim, is that enquirers pray and decide for themselves what is the Rev Moon's role in the restoration process. But however reticent or forthcoming the seminar leaders may be, the introduction to the 1973 *Divine Principle* leaves no room for doubt on this question:

> With the fullness of time, God has sent His messenger to resolve the fundamental questions of life and the universe. His name is Sun Myung Moon. For many decades, he wandered in a vast spiritual world in search of the ultimate truth. On this path, he endured suffering unimagined by anyone in human history. God alone will remember it. Knowing that no one can find the ultimate truth to save mankind without going through the bitterest of trials, he fought alone against myriads of satanic forces, both in the spiritual and physical worlds, and finally triumphed over them all.[58]

As the second messiah, the Rev Moon's task is to ensure that humankind gains physical salvation as well as spiritual salvation. In order to effect this, he must do what Jesus was unable to accomplish, namely restore the Fall by marrying and giving birth to children who are free from original sin. This marriage took place on 16 March 1960, when Sun Myung Moon married Hak Ja Han. The Rev and Mrs Moon are referred to as the 'True Parents' and they are accorded messianic status as a couple by members of the Unification Church.

Now that the Marriage of the Lamb – the wedding of the present-day messiah and his bride – has taken place, Unification Church members can be ingrafted into the holy family and can play their part in the restoration of the kingdom. After joining the Church they can be invited to take part in the marriage ceremony known as the Blessing – often referred to by the media as the 'mass wedding'. Marriage is not only temporal but eternal: marriage partners will continue to be bonded in the spirit world after death, and will live eternally as a couple. Indeed, it is impossible to enter the Kingdom of Heaven unless one not only is married, but has undergone the Blessing.

There is still the third Blessing to be fulfilled. The physical world must be brought to a harmonious and unified state under the direct dominion of God. It is believed that in the last 400 years there have been signs that this is being accomplished, and the *Principle* teaches that advances in science and technology in recent times, as well as moral advances, for example, in concerns for human rights, are signs that the new messianic age is dawning. Recent trends in ecumenism and inter-faith fellowship are regarded as signs of an imminent unification of religions.

However, half the world is still under a regime which is atheistic and totalitarian, and that regime is communism. If the Kingdom of Heaven is to be established on earth, communism – which represents Cain, the satanic – must be eliminated. There have already been two world wars, and these are considered to have provided humankind's indemnity for receiving the messiah; the third world war, however, will be the final battle between Cain-type communism and Abel-type democracy. It is not necessarily to be expected that this war will involve physical conflict; the *Principle* teaches that, depending on how men and women exercise their free will, this war may be fought out either through armed combat or through 'ideological conflict' – in other words through reason and persuasion, and particularly by presenting an alternative ideology which is called 'Godism'.[59] Whatever the means by which communism is defeated, its demise is believed to be inevitable, since God's purpose of establishing the Kingdom of Heaven on earth cannot ultimately be defeated.

# 3 The Korean Religious Heritage

If we are to understand Unificationism, we must understand the religious background against which it developed. There are many different strands of religious tradition, which have waxed and waned at various stages of Korea's history. The picture is by no means straightforward, for two reasons. First, there have been various attempts to unify different strands within broad traditions, as well as attempts to unify Korean religion more generally. Confrontation has been tempered with much cross-fertilisation and syncretism. For example, Yulgok, often reckoned to be Korea's greatest scholar, was brought up as a Confucian, but converted to Buddhism, which he later formally abandoned but yet allowed to influence his neo-Confucian philosophy.

Second, westerners often find it difficult to cope with the typically eastern practice of pursuing several religious traditions simultaneously. Judaeo-Christianity's essentially uncompromising character which permits no rivals stands in sharp contrast to most other religious climates, not least Korea, where the religious seeker uses whichever of the available religions will best fulfil his or her current purposes. As early as 1902, the Christian missionary, the Rev George Heber Jones noted:

> [The Korean husband] personally takes his own education from Confucius; he sends his wife to Buddha to pray for offspring; and in the ills of life he willingly pays toll to Shamanite Mu-dang and Pansu. The average Korean is thus a follower of all three systems, in the hope that by their united help he may reach a happy destiny.[1]

In this chapter I hope to disentangle some of the complexities of Korean religion and philosophy and show how some of their ideas and debates find their way into Unification thought.

Two popular religious myths are known to most, if not all, Koreans. The Korean people regard themselves as the descendants of the great ancestor Tangun. According to Korean legend, Tangun was the grandson of the supreme God Hwan-in and son of the divine spirit Hwan-Ung. Hwan-Ung obtained permission to descend from heaven to live on earth and establish the Kingdom of Heaven there. He came to Korea, and discovered a tiger and a she-bear who wanted to learn how they might become human. Hwan-Ung gave each of them sacred food, which they had to eat in a prescribed manner. The bear obeyed and was transformed into a woman; she then wedded Hwan-Ung. The tiger did not obey and remained a beast. Tangun was born as the offspring of the she-bear and Hwan-Ung. In the year 2333 BCE he came to Pyongyang, established his royal residence and gave the name 'Choson' to his new kingdom.[2]

The notion that a divine emissary should descend to establish a family and thence the Kingdom of Heaven on earth has some resemblance to Unification theology. The parallels are not exact, of course, but it is significant that the components of the myth include the divine aim of establishing the Kingdom of Heaven on earth, the sending of a divine emissary, the themes of obedience and disobedience to the supreme God with the resultant contrast between quasi-messianic and quasi-satanic figures.

A further Korean religious myth illustrates the theme of sexual misconduct by celestial beings and its possible influence on humankind. The theme of the serpent is highly significant.

A legend of the Namwon area says that a man convicted of adultery in heaven became a serpent as he fell onto the earth. The serpent became a maiden and as she tried to seduce a young scholar she suddenly realized her sin and ascended to heaven again.[3]

## FOLK SHAMANISM

At a popular level, the prevalent religion in Korea is a kind of shamanism. Although this folk religion has encountered fierce opposition from the authorities, who wished to impose a neo-Confucian culture, folk shamanism is still prevalent, and shows no signs of decline in a technological era. Estimates of the number of shamans vary: a conservative estimate suggests that there is one shaman for every 1500 members of the South Korean population, while other authorities indicate that the statistic could even be as high as one in every 316.[4]

A shaman (or *mudang*, to use the appropriate Korean expression) is one who is believed to be able to make contact with the spirit world on behalf of the laity. In Korea, shamans are usually, although not exclusively, female. She is an oracle who can summon the spirits of the dead to provide information or guidance, for example about a coming harvest, an imminent epidemic or a possible calamity. She is believed to provide cures for illnesses, generally held to be the work of malicious spirits; she performs sacrifices on behalf of the people to placate the pantheon of spirits who may, if not suitably appeased, prove troublesome.

Although the shaman is believed to be guided by spirits, spirits are not held to provide invariably appropriate advice. There are malevolent as well as benevolent spirits, and the former will attempt to deceive or misdirect the shaman. The shaman is supposed to have acquired the necessary skills to discern the spirits. In contrast with the Siberian shamans who are believed to make heroic journeys into the spirit realms, engaging in combat with malevolent ghosts and rescuing wandering wraiths, the Korean *mudang* is more usually held to be visited or possessed by members of the spirit world who come to her. On account of this pronounced difference from the shamanism of other cultures, some writers have preferred not to use the term 'shamanism' at all in the context of Korea, but to talk about 'mudangism' or 'mu-ism'.[5]

The shaman does not only provide a service for the living, but for the dead also. When required, the shaman can provide guidance to the spirits of those who have recently died, so that they can find the appropriate passage through the world of the dead. Humans who die often have unfulfilled desires, and such desires can hamper the passage of spirits in their after-death existence. It is not uncommon for such desires to include the desire to marry, and in such circumstances the shaman can conduct a ceremony in which spirits of the departed are married in the spirit world.[6]

The placation of evil spirits and the invocation of the benevolent spirits is generally done through elaborate ritual, which may take as long as two or three days. Elaborate colourful robes are donned to transform the ceremony into an aesthetic as well as a religious experience, and the shaman commences incantations and performs sacred dances which take her into a state of trance.

The role of the shaman is generally a hereditary one. However, it is possible for women who have non-shamanic mothers to assume this role. Such a calling is not a matter of choice, but is grounded in compelling spiritual experiences. Dreams are accorded great importance, and it is common for aspiring shamans to dream that they are visited by spirits, and in some instances to claim that they experience sexual relationships with spirits. If such signs of calling are resisted, it is common for the woman to fall sick and to be found incurable through normal medical means. Such illness is known as *sinbyong* ('possession sickness'), and it is only through accepting her calling that the shaman, once initiated, recovers her health.[7]

## SHAMANISM AND UNIFICATION THOUGHT

It has been suggested that the Rev Moon himself is a shaman.[8] Much
depends on the definition of 'shaman': certainly the Rev Moon is believed
to travel into the spirit world and be visited by spirits who offer revelations;
however, unlike the traditional shaman, Sun Myung Moon cannot be commissioned by patrons to perform ceremonies on their behalf in exchange for
payment. The Rev Moon is also reputed to have his own personal shaman
(possibly two, one in Korea and one in New York) and the Korean shaman
is believed, amongst other things, to prepare the ingredients of the Holy
Wine used at the Blessing Ceremony.[9]

It takes little acquaintance with the Unification Church to discover the
tremendous importance which is attached to the spirit world and the
continued interaction between the living and the dead. The Rev Moon,
as we have already noted, is believed to be visited frequently by spirits,
ranging from Jesus Christ to Satan himself, from the Buddha and Lao Tzu
to spirits of ordinary mortals recently deceased.

Such experiences have proved decisive in the Rev Moon's own spiritual
history. Most notably, there is the account of his visitation from Jesus
Christ on Easter morning 1936. Less known, however, is the story of
the divine vindication of the *Principle*. Interestingly, this story, which
follows, implies that the Rev Moon's relationship with the spirit world
is not passive but active: unlike the typical *mudang*, Sun Myung Moon is
believed to travel into the spirit world to receive some of his revelations,
more in the style of the Siberian shaman.

After the end of the Second World War, Sun Myung Moon had satisfied
himself on all of the *Principle*, except for one part: why should God have
permitted the Fall if he was truly omniscient? Why could not God create
humankind so that it was unable to sin? It was finally revealed to Sun
Myung Moon that humankind's perfection must be accomplished by their
own efforts, without God's help, so as to pay indemnity for their past
failures.[10] With this discovery the Divine Principle was now complete,
and Sun Myung Moon took it to the spirit world for ratification. The
Buddha, Confucius, and Jesus Christ amongst others were present. None
of them would accept it. Sun Myung Moon took the Divine Principle
to God, who also rejected it. However, Sun Myung Moon persisted and
presented the Divine Principle a second time. Again it was rejected. He
persevered again, and at the third presentation Jesus bowed his head in
acknowledgment, and Satan turned back in anger and walked away. Even
the most advanced spirits bowed to the Rev Moon.[10]

Some reference to miraculous healing is worth mentioning. The Rev

Moon does not perform any healing ceremonies, and spiritual healing forms no obvious part of the practices of the Unification Church. However, many members will vouch for the fact that they possessed certain physical ailments before joining, only to find that these disappeared after they committed themselves to the movement. Miss Young Oon Kim, who joined the UC in its early years in Korea, is reported have have suffered incurable diarrhoea until she decided to join the newly formed Holy Spirit Association for the Unification of World Christianity, whereupon her ailment vanished almost instantly.[11] Perhaps such phenomena are to be regarded as parallelling the 'possession sickness' of the aspiring shaman who has still to accept her vocation.

Finally, the shamanistic idea that everyone is entitled to marriage, even spirits, finds its way into Unification thought. Not only is there a firm belief that only married couples may enter the Kingdom of Heaven, but the marriage of spirits is undoubtedly part of Unificationism's religious practices. Although the media image of the 'mass wedding' (the Blessing) conveys the impression of youthful couples being wedded, less known is the fact that the Rev Moon marries the dead as well as the living. One Unificationist couple to whom I spoke had already been married before joining the church, and therefore participated in a smaller scale ceremony than those which involve hundreds or thousands of members. At that ceremony, they informed me, the Rev Moon blessed some elderly single members, bonding them in eternal marriage with spirit partners. One of the Rev Moon's sons, Heung Jin, was involved in a car crash in December 1983 and died early in 1984. He was then unmarried, but at a subsequent Blessing ceremony he was wedded to a bride who is currently alive on the earth.

## TAOISM AND NEO-CONFUCIANISM

Although folk shamanism has much popular support, the official state religion of Korea is Confucianism. However, to claim that Korea is Confucian is potentially misleading; Confucius lived in the sixth century BCE, and inevitably his thought has been developed by later writers, both in China and Korea. As Chinese and Korean thought developed, the ideas of Confucius became intertwined with Taoism and in particular the ideas expressed in the now well-known oracle the *I Ching*. Something must therefore be said about Taoism.

Explaining what is meant by the Tao is problematic, to say the least, since the Tao is held to be inexpressible and indefinable. As Lao Tzu's classic text, the *Tao Te Ching* puts it:

> The way that can be spoken of
> Is not the constant way;
> The name that can be named
> Is not the constant name.[12]

If we can say anything about the Tao at all, it is the source of the universe and of the entire natural order which flows through it. It is not a separate being which exists beyond space and time, but the ultimate principle which governs what takes place within the universe. The course of the universe is like the flow of a river: the water is soft and yielding, yet it is strong and often irresistible. The sage who is in tune with this 'watercourse way' is the one who is attuned to the natural flow of the universe, yielding, and spontaneously adapting to its course. Although this natural flow is irresistible, Taoism emphasises spontaneity rather than adherence to fixed and externally imposed laws: the laws which the sage must follow cannot be expressed in words, and therefore those who follow the course must find their way in it for themselves.

The Tao represents the oneness of nature, but it gives rise to pairs of opposites. The universe contains light and darkness, beauty and ugliness, mountains and valleys, male and female, and so on. These opposites reflect the two fundamental concepts of *yin* and *yang* described in the *I Ching*. As noted in Chapter 2, *yang* is the masculine, light, active principle within the universe, while *yin* is the feminine, dark, passive. *Yin* and *yang* are not totally irreconcilable opposites, for each contains and generates the other. Even the male anatomy contains its surrogate female elements, and vice versa.

It may be asked how such an apparently flexible, spontaneous and inexpressible philosophy could run side by side with Confucianism, which defined a system of government which relied on firm unalterable heavenly laws. However, as one writer has pointed out,[13] the essence of Taoism is that every concept generates its (complementary) opposite and hence spontaneity must inevitably be counterbalanced by law. Taoism certainly does not entail an antinomian ethic of 'anything goes'.

Confucius' writings were concerned mainly with ethics and government, and are expressed in short aphorisms. His thought aimed at establishing a perfect harmony between heaven and earth. There were fixed and unalterable 'Mandates of Heaven', and it was incumbent on human-kind to act in accordance with them. Later Confucian thinkers main-tained that the Way of Heaven involved a progression from the imper-fect physical world towards a perfect state of affairs in three stages of development: (1) a past era of disorder; (2) a present era of relative peace; and (3) a future utopia (*ta-tung*), the coming Age of Grand Unity.[14]

The notion of these fixed and unalterable divine laws does not imply that humans are not able to exercise free choice; humankind may act in accordance with or in contradiction to the Heavenly Way. In order to act in accordance with the Way of Heaven, it was incumbent on the Chinese emperor, who was accorded the status of the son of God, to carry out the ritual which was required by Heaven in the appropriate manner. Heaven and Earth existed in a bi-polar relationship, and it was important that each must be kept in its correct *position*, with Heaven as the prevailing power.

It was not merely the emperor who had to act in accordance with the Way of Heaven. The one who acted in accordance with the will of Heaven was the ideal man (often translated, somewhat quaintly, as 'gentleman'). Relationships within the human realm more generally were instrumental in establishing a right relationship between Heaven and Earth. In particular, *The Doctrine of the Mean* (an important Confucian text) identified five 'right and harmonious relationships' which it was incumbent on humankind to establish: king–subject, father–son, husband–wife, elder brother–younger brother, friend–friend.[15]

These right relationships within the physical world were necessary prerequisites for establishing a right and harmonious relationship with the Way which transcended the physical world. It should be noted that four out of the five relate to the family – a supremely important concept in Confucian thought. According to Confucius, it was preferable to be condemned to hell than to die without a descendant, thus terminating one's blood lineage.

Confucian philosophy was developed by the Chinese philosopher Chu Hsi (1130–1200) beyond the ethical maxims and principles of government. Chu Hsi combined Confucius' aphoristic teachings with a metaphysic derived from the *I Ching*. Lao Tzu's classic, the *Tao Te Ching*, told of a mystical Way, inseparably connected with the physical world, yet penetrating beyond it. What is important is to recognise those situations which are 'bendable' and those which contain a current so strong that resisting them is futile and perverse. The *I Ching* (the Book of Changes) is believed to enable the consultee to recognise the characteristics of the situation. It is an ancient book of divination, possibly predating Confucius, although this is not altogether certain. Superficially, the consultee is offered advice in accordance with the tossing of coins, or the casting of yarrow sticks. By such devices one constructs a 'hexagram' – a set of six lines, each of which represents either *yin* (female) or *yang* (male). Depending on the permutations of *yin* and *yang* lines, the consultee is directed to the relevant hexagram, which gives a 'judgement' relevant to the situation.

The *I Ching* is no mere fortune telling device, however. Heaven continuously interacts with the Earth to produce a constantly changing continuum. If I am to act in conformity to heavenly law, I must be able to locate the point in the continuum at which I stand. When the lines of the hexagram are viewed as pairs rather than trios, the top two line-combinations are said to represent Heaven, the bottom two Earth, and the middle two human beings as the connecting link. The consultee thus locates his or her *position* in relation to that of Earth and Heaven.

Because one's *position* is a constantly changing one, one must establish one's proper *position* by acting in a manner which is timely for the changing situation in which one finds oneself. Critics of Chinese oracle consultation will sometimes point out that a consultee can put the same question twice to the *I Ching* and receive contradictory answers. This is to be expected: at the second consultation, the consultee's *position* may have changed, and hence a different response is appropriate. Although everything is subject to change, there is a constancy in change, since everything which occurs does so in accordance with these unalterable heavenly laws. Despite apparent counter-currents, the Principle will assert itself within human history. Also, since *yin* contains *yang*, each situation has within it the seed of the new one: consequently one must constantly adapt, since what is oppressive in the present can become transfigured or preserved in the future situation. There are thus frequent references in the *I Ching* to 'moving with the time', 'harmony with time', 'missing the time', and so on.

In order to effect any enduring change, any earthly movement requires a leader. The *I Ching* identifies this person as the 'hero', 'king', or 'great man'. In Chinese thought there are key figures who appear at crucial points in human history. A common motif associated with such appearances is the shedding of blood. As Richard Wilhelm explains:

> From time to time such a man appears, appropriating to himself and molding, according to his image, larger and smaller areas, by allowing his body to be eaten and his blood to be drunk. Here emerges the esoteric aspect of sacrifice. 'To bring great offerings creates good fortune.' In barbaric times the king, in whom God manifested himself, who was man and god or the son of God, was immolated at the height of ecstasy. He was the sacrifice for his kin, and his overflowing blood expiated those who belonged to him. Chinese culture long ago transformed this into symbol. The representative of the Creative must somehow sacrifice himself, and his spiritually flowing blood is used to nourish those who belong to his community.[16]

In Chinese alchemy various methods were devised for purifying the blood, and numerous secret religions arose in the Orient which claimed to have produced such a substance. Various meditative techniques were devised to obtain similar results. Blood, being the seat of the soul, must be freed of all impediments and obstructions, so that it could flow continuously and 'never fall behind the times'.[17]

We can see that many ideas from neo-Confucianism and the *I Ching* find their way into Unification thought. The importance attached to the family is paramount in Confucianism, and the notion of great leaders who come to effect important changes parallels the *Principle*'s concept of 'central figures' who appear at various stages in human history. The notion of changing *positions* and locating one's true *position* is a further feature of both systems of thought, as are the concepts of blood and blood lineage. The importance of these references to blood and blood lineage will become clearer later. In the meantime it is necessary to return to a concept which, until now, has only been mentioned in passing, but which is crucial to any explanation of Unification thought. That concept is the concept of 'Principle'.[18] The material which follows is not easy, but it is fundamentally important in placing *Divine Principle* in its cultural and intellectual context.

Chu Hsi regarded the Mind as a miniaturised form of the cosmic Principle. Thus, when a person's relationships are right and harmonious with family, society, nature and the cosmos, that person is in harmony with the self and with the Way, and experiences equilibrium of the forces of *yin* and *yang*. Principle was not separate from everything in the physical world (called 'Material Force') but was that on which everything (Material Force) depended, and from which everything originated. As Chu Hsi wrote:

> Before heaven and earth existed, there was after all only principle. As there is this principle, therefore there are heaven and earth. If there were no principle, there would also be no heaven and earth, no man, no things, and in fact, no containing or sustaining (of things by heaven and earth) to speak of. As there is principle, there is therefore material force to operate everywhere and nourish and develop all things.[19]

## CONFUCIANISM IN KOREA

When Confucianism came to Korea, there were two principal subjects of philosophical debate. One was the question of the relationship between Principle and Material Force, initiated by Chu Hsi; the other was known as the 'Four–Seven' controversy which can be traced back to Mencius (c.371–289 BCE). These debates require some explanation.

The most important exponent of both these subjects was undoubtedly T'oegye (1501–70). According to T'oegye, human nature is comprised of 'Four Beginnings' and 'Seven Emotions'. The Chinese classics (notably *The Book of Rites* and *The Doctrine of the Mean*) had propounded a thesis known as the 'Four Beginnings'. Mencius had stated that human nature possesses four cardinal virtues: (1) compassion *(jen)*; (2) righteousness *(I)*; (3) propriety *(li)* and (4) wisdom *(chih)*. In addition to these 'Four Beginnings', the *The Book of Rites* enumerated 'Seven Emotions': (1) joy, (2) anger, (3) sorrow, (4) fear, (5) love, (6) hate and (7) desire.

It is not easy for westerners to see immediately what the classical 'Four-Seven' debate is about. The first problem is understanding why the two lists ('Four' and 'Seven') should be kept separate and not merged to form an eleven point list. One way of explaining it is this. If someone were to ask what kind of nature I had, I could sensibly (maybe even truly) describe myself as 'compassionate', 'righteous', 'upright' (a suitable adjective relating to 'propriety') or 'wise'. However, there would be something slightly odd about describing myself as 'a joyful person', 'an angry person', 'a sorrowful person', a 'fearful person', and so on. Sometimes I am joyful, at other times not: it all depends on my current state of affairs, which often changes, and I can only be joyful, angry, sad or fearful *about* these states of affairs, not *simpliciter*. In contrast, the four virtue concepts can only describe me *simpliciter*: I am not wise *about* subjects; I am simply wise (or maybe not so wise!). Another way of putting this is to say that feelings need an object, whereas virtues do not.

It follows from this observation that the four virtues are aspects of my nature which are displayed as emotions (in whatever degree they exist) when certain situations arise. If I am compassionate, then I will feel sorrow if I hear that a friend has had an accident; if I am wise, I will ensure that desire is kept in check by channelling my energies into researching this book rather than going to a party every night.

So far, this may seem uncontroversial. However, controversy arose when the 'Four-Seven' distinction was related to the two crucial philosophical concepts, 'Principle' and 'Material Force'. The concepts of 'Principle' and 'Material Force' might be said roughly to correspond to Aristotle's distinction between 'form' and 'matter': Principle is the rational power which is said to underlie all that exists; Material Force, by contrast, is what gives rise to the physical, and to physical sensation. In neo-Confucian thought, Principle is ultimate and immutable, whereas Material Force is the motivating power of things in the physical world which are subject to change. Because Principle is changeless it is purely good, and hence undergirds everything that it is good or virtuous; Material Force, on the other hand, is capable of giving rise to both good and evil.

It is important to note, incidentally, that the classical debate about Principle and Material Force was not a debate about which came temporally first. No neo-Confucian philosopher ever maintained the thesis that there was a time when there was Principle without Material Force or vice versa. The Principle–Material Force controversy was about inter-dependence. Which depended upon which? Was it possible to think of Material Force without presupposing the existence of Principle? If there were no changing objects in the world, and hence no 'Material Force' which initiated any changes, would Principle also vanish into oblivion? Which of the two was the more fundamental? According to T'oegye, Material Force depended on Principle.

T'oegye held that the Four Beginnings and the Seven Emotions were related to Principle and Material Force respectively, and his reasoning was as follows. The classical Four (compassion, righteousness, propriety and wisdom) are the conditions inherent in human nature, while the Seven only arise from contact with the physical world. Thus I can have a sense of propriety (one of the Four) even when I am not faced with situations in which my desire might get out of control, but I cannot have desire until I encounter objects in the physical world which generate feelings of desire. Consequently, the Four are the conditions for displaying the traditional virtues, while the latter are not in themselves either morally commendable or reprehensible; their moral worth lies in their relationship with the former. For example, if I experience joy because I have been loyal to my friend, that is good; if, on the other hand, I am joyful that my parent has died and I will now receive a legacy, that is morally deplorable. The Four Beginnings, then, appear to have an existence apart from the senses; they emanate from Reason rather than feeling. The Seven Emotions, on the other hand, can only arise in the context of Material Force – when events change in such a way as to provide a condition for manifesting joy, anger, sorrow, fear, love, hate or desire.

It was this line of reasoning which caused T'oegye to assert that the Four Beginnings issued from Principle, and the Seven Emotions from Material Force. The image which T'oegye used to explain this was that of a man riding a horse. The man cannot move forward unless the horse moves, but the reverse is not necessarily true. Thus, movement of Material Force emanates from Principle and not vice versa. As T'oegye put it, '*ch'i* [Material Force] rides on the back of *li* [Principle].'[20] It also follows from this line of thinking that what underlies human (and other) behaviour is basically good. It is only through contact between the human mind and physical reality that evil arises.

T'oegye's account of the Principle–Material Force relationship did not go unchallenged, and T'oegye himself was obliged to modify his own position in the light of subsequent criticism. Kobong (1527–72), a contemporary of T'oegye, contended that the Four-Seven Thesis should not be explained in terms of Principle and Material Force respectively; instead, the Four Beginnings and Seven Emotions should be regarded as merely opposite sides of the same coin. For example, it is inconceivable that there could be compassion without the existence of living beings to whom compassion might be shown, and their existence (being physical – at least in part, if not in whole) must result from Material Force. Equally, the Seven Emotions actually contain the Four Beginnings: hatred or desire cannot exist apart from one's sense of right and wrong. When we use concepts like 'desire' and 'hate' they normally presuppose value judgements: 'desire' and 'want' usually have negative moral connotations (such as lack of propriety or wisdom) while concepts such as 'love' or 'sorrow' are more likely to be morally commendable (they are ways of displaying compassion, for example). Hence, Kobong argued, Principle cannot be separated from Material Force. The Four and the Seven equally involve both; Principle is simply more evident with regard to the Four, and Material Force with regard to the Seven.

The philosopher Yulgok (1536–84) went even further in his criticism of T'oegye. If Principle is changeless, how can anything emanate from it at all? If one thing emanates from another, there must be some change in the latter which causes the emanation of the former. Indeed, if Principle gives rise to Material Force, is not the activity of giving rise to Material Force a change which Principle undergoes? Principle-issuance is itself a form of change: if Principle is immutable, it cannot give rise to anything at all, and cannot result from anything either.

Yulgok denied that Principle was primordial either with respect to the Four or to the Seven. His reasoning was as follows. If Principle cannot be present without Material Force, then why not say that everything issues from Material Force? This would be much more consistent with the idea that Principle is changeless and Material Force potentially changing. T'oegye's theory of Principle-issuance was therefore superfluous, according to Yulgok; Material Force issues, he contended, and Principle rides on it.[21] By claiming that Material Force was primordial, Yulgok was contending that anything that exists depends for its existence on the physical rather than anything which is beyond or more than the physical. Principle is thus supportive of Material Force rather than causative. Yulgok is often described as a materialist on account of his emphasis on Material Force;[22] however, it should be noted that Yulgok did not deny the existence of Principle, but rather the concept of Principle-issuance. Indeed it might plausibly be contended that Yulgok, unlike T'oegye, maintained the perfection of Principle by preserving its immutability, a point on which T'oegye's thesis did not appear to be wholly consistent.

What we have considered thus far is the mediaeval debate. Confucianism became further developed in the philosophy of Tasan (1762–1836).[23] Confucius had spoken of 'one thread' which bound all things, and Tasan's central task was to identify this one thread. As we have seen, the mediaeval scholars had tended to regard this single thread as Principle, and from thence to construct a metaphysic which defined the relationship of Principle to Material Force. By so doing, these philosophers found themselves engaging in somewhat abstruse metaphysical debate at the expense of practicality. By contrast, Tasan proposed that this single thread was *shu* (the Way), which was the means of realising *jen* (virtue). Confucius himself had emphasised ethics rather than metaphysics, and thus Tasan's philosophy may be viewed as an attempt to return to the spirit of Confucius. Although Confucius had referred to the Mandates of Heaven (a metaphysical concept), Tasan held that it was only by the Way of Humanity – the ethical way – that the Mandates of Heaven could be followed. Thus the realisation of *shu* was dependent on *jen*; the attainment of the goal was dependent on humankind's efforts. Ethical practice involved the cultivation of one's own self by ensuring that human relationships were right and harmonious between oneself and others. As Confucius had said, do not do to others what you would not wish for yourself.[24]

## CONFUCIANISM AND UNIFICATION THOUGHT

In the light of the summary of Unificationist teaching in Chapter 2, much of the material on Confucianism has obvious affinities with the teachings of *Divine Principle*. First, the ideal of the family in Confucian thought permeates the teaching of the *Principle*. For the Unificationist, as for the Confucian, the ideal is the ideal family. The notion of ensuring that one has a lineage is of paramount importance in Confucian thought, and we can readily detect clear dependence on Confucian ideas in the UC notion that one's lineage needs to be purified and restored from the satanic to the divine. The Confucian ethic of family relationships also finds obvious expression in Unification thought, especially in the 'two brothers' theme which recurs throughout the *Principle*. The Unificationist doctrine of divine providence and human responsibility has an obvious precursor in the Confucian's acknowledgement that there can be discrepancies between the Way of Heaven and the Way of Earth: the Will of Heaven is a moral and social requirement, not an inevitable necessity.

Of crucial importance is the concept of Principle. It would be a gross misunderstanding of Unification thought to construe the term 'Principle' in a merely colloquial sense, or to assume that it merely means a set of divine precepts. The Unification *Principle* is fundamentally about how it is possible for humankind to follow the divine pattern which undergirds the universe and its history. Thus when *Divine Principle* describes actions as 'principled' and 'unprincipled' it is referring to their degree of compatibility with the Way of Heaven which undergirds everything in the physical world. The idea that the Way of Heaven has a three-stage development finds parallels in the Unificationist notion of the three stages of Formation, Growth and Completion.[25] It is possible, although not certain, that the *Divine Principle*'s insistence that a 'foundation of substance' must be laid before a 'foundation of faith' is possible harks back to the debate about whether Principle can exist without some physical Material Force: if God's will is to be manifested, this must be preceded by some physical token, even if this is merely symbolic.

The idea that Principle combines the two polarities of *yin* and *yang* (an idea found explicitly in *Divine Principle*) is scarcely surprising. As we have discovered, this is very traditional Taoist teaching. Indeed, *Divine Principle* explicitly equates God with the Korean notion of the T'aeguk (the origin of the universe). The Taoist notion of male–female complementarity finds expression in Unificationism's claim that God has a male and a female nature, and that there are two present-day messianic personages, one male and one female.

*Divine Principle*'s references to the *I Ching* are not only explicit acknowledgements of philosophical dependence, but have great explanatory powers regarding much that follows. For example, the UC's concept of the 'central figure' parallels the ancient Chinese notion that at strategic points in history there would appear the appropriate hero, leader or great man. *Divine Principle* is dominated by the idea that the central figures in the restoration drama (Jacob, Moses, John the Baptist) occupy 'positions'. As events change, *positions* change, and thus these figures can find themselves ousted from the *position* which they have been divinely commissioned to occupy.

Finally, the relation between Principle and virtue is worthy of comment. Just as Tasan concluded that acknowledging Principle was not merely a matter of intellectual understanding or debate, Unificationists too will insist that *Principle* is no mere piece of abstruse theorising. The *Principle* is lived, not merely believed, and notions such as 'occupying one's position' are not abstract metaphysical ideas, but moral requirements: to live the *Principle* I must ascertain my own *position* in the constantly changing set of events in the earth world, and, having found it, I must not leave it until my role in the salvific process is accomplished.

The parallels which I have drawn between neo-Confucianism and Unification theology are not the result of mere speculation. As I have noted, some of these parallels are themselves acknowledged in *Divine Principle*, and it should be remembered that the Rev Moon himself was educated in the traditional Chinese classics before his own family converted to Christianity. It is scarcely surprising that such ideas find their way into Unificationism's interpretation of Christianity, and indeed it would be surprising if such notions were singularly absent.

## BUDDHISM

Buddhism originated in North India in the sixth century BCE. It was brought across the Himalayas, through Mongolia and China, before finally reaching Korea, where it began to take its root between the third and fifth centuries CE, when Korea was still divided into three separate kingdoms. Having come to Korea through the 'northern route' rather than the southern (Sri Lanka, Burma, Thailand), the form of Buddhism which arrived in Korea was Mahayana rather than Theravada. The Mahayana tradition typically proved to be more adaptable than that of the conservative Theravadins, with the result that it established itself by accommodating many of the ideas and customs of the countries into which it came.

Traditionally Buddhism has been a world-renouncing religion, preaching escape from the realms of constant birth and rebirth (*samsara*) by attaining the goal of nirvana. The Buddha's Four Noble Truths highlighted the unsatisfactory nature of existence,[26] the cause of unsatisfactoriness (ignorance and craving), the elimination of unsatisfactoriness and the Eightfold Path which led to its elimination (perfect view, aspiration, speech, conduct, livelihood, effort, mindfulness, 'absorption').[27] Buddhist tradition has generally made it clear that 'perfect conduct' and 'perfect livelihood' involve refraining from the taking of life.[28] The adaptability of the Mahayana tradition in Korea can be seen in the transformation of the five traditional lay precepts. The original list is:

1.     To avoid the taking of life.

2.   To avoid taking what is not given.
3.   To avoid unchastity.
4.   To avoid incorrect speech.
5.   To avoid intoxicating liquor and drugs which give rise to careless-
     ness.[29]

An early Korean statement of the lay precepts, however, runs as follows:

> There are ten commandments in the Bodhisattva ordination. But since
> you are subjects and sons, I fear you cannot practice all of them. Now,
> here are five commandments for laymen: serve your sovereign with
> loyalty: tend your parents with filial piety; treat your friends with
> sincerity; do not retreat from a battlefield; be discriminating about the
> taking of life. Exercise care in the performance of them.[30]

The more conventional precepts enjoining the abstinence from taking life
give way to the prescription of courage in a just war, and the reference
to filial piety is, of course, straightforwardly Confucian. Buddhism thus
became a religion aimed at national protection, and it was hoped that
it would unite the three kingdoms which eventually came together to
form the nation of Korea. Its aims were 'this-worldly', and the concept
of *kong* (*sunyata* or ultimate reality) was not recognised as something
which was super-mundane. The pagoda at the Hwangryong Temple was
built to invoke the aid of spirits and to subdue neighbouring countries, 'to
open wide heaven and earth and unify the three kingdoms'.[31]
    When the three kingdoms were unified under the Silla dynasty (668–935
CE), Buddhism gained momentum, and Buddhist scholars visited China,
returning with important scriptures. Uisang, a Buddhist monk, returned
from China in 669 CE, bearing the *Avatamsaka Sutra* (the 'Flower Garland'
Sutra), which is the story of a young man's quest to realise *dharma-dhatu*,
that is to say 'totality' or 'universal Principle'. The teaching of this sutra[32]
is that the components of the world cannot exist independently; the one
who sees the harmonious totality of everything is an enlightened being,
a Buddha. Already we can detect the 'unity' theme in Korean Buddhism.
During the Koryo dynasty (935–1392 CE) Buddhism was at its zenith, only
to experience a decline in the subsequent Yi dynasty (1392–1910 CE) when
it was overtaken by neo-Confucianism.
    At a popular level, the Confucian notion of filial piety was devel-
oped within Buddhism with the cult of the bodhisattva Kshitigarbha.
(A bodhisattva, in the Mahayana tradition, is an enlightened being who
renounces entry into final nirvana in order to help other living beings.) On

a literal interpretation of Confucian teaching, filial piety extends to two people only – one's mother and father. However, since Buddhism teaches that beings are constantly born and reborn, many living beings have at some time in the past been one's parents, and many more will be one's parents at some future point in time. Thus all living beings come within the scope of parenthood and one's duty is therefore to extend one's compassion to all and to rescue them from their predicament of unsatisfactoriness. The bodhisattva Kshitigarbha, who is popularly revered in Korea, vowed that he would not himself experience the pleasures of nirvana until such time as all living beings had been rescued from hell: 'If the hells are not empty I will not become a Buddha; when living beings have all been saved, I will attain to Bodhi [enlightenment].'[33]

Kshitigarbha's vow made his own enlightenment conditional upon universal liberation. The idea of universal salvation was very much part of the Korean religious consciousness, and was difficult to adapt to the preaching of those Christian missionaries who, influenced by Calvinism, taught that God had only elected certain men and women to salvation and that others were predestined to be eternally damned. It is therefore not surprising that numerous New Christian groups, including the Unification Church, have adopted a universalist stance. Indeed, Unificationism holds that even Satan himself will finally gain entry into the Kingdom of Heaven.

Some attention must now be given to the various schools of Buddhist thought which impinged on Korea. There are two main Buddhist sects: Seon Buddhism (more widely known as Ch'an or Zen), and an 'indigenous' form of Buddhism, known variously as 'Han Buddhism' (*han* meaning 'one'), or 'Tong Buddhism' (the 'Buddhism of Unity'). The founder of this school of Buddhism was Wonhyo (617–686 CE): few people in Korea have not heard of him, and he is popularly regarded as a buddha. Wonhyo composed 99 written works, over 240 volumes, the most important of which was the *Critique on the Synthesis of the Ten Schools*. Since Buddhism originated from outside Korea, of course no form of Korean Buddhism can be strictly 'indigenous', but this description refers to the fact that, unlike the majority of eminent scholar-monks, Wonhyo never succeeded in reaching China to learn from the celebrated Ch'an teachers there.

Wonhyo made two attempts to visit China, together with his contemporary, Uisang. On the first occasion he failed, having been arrested on suspicion of being a Korean spy attempting to infiltrate China. On the second occasion, the two scholars encountered a fierce storm, and were forced to take refuge in a cave. Being thirsty during the night, Wonhyo picked up what he thought was a gourd, and drank out of it, only to discover in the morning that it was not a gourd but a skull, and that they had slept in a burial ground surrounded by skeletons. They were forced to spend a second night there, haunted by frightening apparitions of demons.

Unlike Uisang, who finally reached China, Wonhyo turned back, not out of cowardice, but because he believed his experience in the cave had enabled him to become enlightened. As he said:

> Last night I slept at ease because I thought this place was an earthen cave; but tonight all are confused because I know that this is a home of devils. Now I understand this. When Mind works, various events happen; when Mind does not work, the distinction between an earthen cave and an old tomb disappears. The whole worldly events spring from One Mind (*eka-citta*) and all events are of consciousness only (*vijnana*). Therefore one should not seek after truth outside the Mind.[34]

It may not be immediately obvious how such an experience enabled Wonhyo to become enlightened. The point is this. It is the mind which creates divisions: when Wonhyo did not reflect on the question of whether the vessel from which he drank was a gourd or a skull, the distinction between the two was not present. Such distinctions (gourd/skull, cave/tomb) are artificial constructs of the mind, which an enlightened being – a buddha – transcends. This also applies to concepts such as truth and falsity, good and evil, love and hate, mercy and vengefulness.

Wonhyo extended this analysis to the prevailing Buddhist schools of thought which vied with each other at the time. The school which contended that the mind only was real (the Yogacara) and the school which claimed that neither mind and matter were appropriately described as 'real' (the Madhyamika) were simply complementary ways of regarding the same ultimate reality:–

> The previous interpreters failed to express the points of their arguments in an open-minded manner; they only touched branches while forgetting the trunk.[35]

A further philosophical dispute – to which I have already referred – was whether nirvana lay beyond this world or whether it was to be found in the physical world. If it were the former, then it was unclear how Buddhism could perform the function of achieving national unity, which was a 'this-worldly' goal; if, on the other hand, Buddhism had a 'this-worldly' goal, how was this consistent with the Buddhist notion of 'non-attachment'? The famous second century Buddhist philosopher Nagarjuna had contended that things in the world had no independent existence, and hence any attempt to describe them must be denied. However, since denials are themselves descriptions, the denial must be denied also, and thus everything reduces to negations of pairs of opposites. Accordingly, things in the world are:

> Without cessation, without origination, without annihilation, without eternity, without unity, without diversity, without coming and without going.[36]

However, Wonhyo's method was not negation, but absorption. If two contradictory ideas laid claim to truth, they were equally different ways of viewing the same phenomenon: the final truth had to absorb what was true in both pairs of opposites. As Wonhyo stated:

> As the Dharma is elucidated more or less with the passage of time, there arise many disputes and much confusion. If one says that he is right, another will refute him, and there ensues the formation of many sects and sub-sects. In the foundation, however, there are not many but only one. To think of them as separate is like looking at individual trees without seeing the dense forest which they comprise. In a similar way, blue and green are essentially the same. Water and ice, in the original sense, are not separate things. Again, it is like all kinds of things being reflected in one single mirror.[37]

If Wonhyo had continued his journey to China, he would have been enabled to study one form of Buddhism only (Ch'an), which would have provided only one sectarian way of viewing reality, when in fact the various Buddhist schools offered complementary ways of viewing reality. What Wonhyo proposed therefore was one great Buddhism arising from various schools asserting different points of view. Buddhism must sort out, organise and add to these points of view, mediating rather than confronting. Wonhyo's aim was to eliminate sectarian arguments and to integrate Buddhism to achieve universal peace and harmony. From the standpoint of the mind there was only a relative contradiction between a pair of opposites: this applied to concepts such as truth and falsity, good and evil, love and hate, mercy and vengefulness. In the conventional way of looking at things, these contradictions prevail, but ultimately anyone who is enlightened must transcend these contradictions.

The average Korean citizen may not be familiar with the subtleties of

Wonhyo's philosophy, but it is more likely than not that he or she will know some of the stories of his attempts to give his teachings a practical application. Many anecdotes about Wonhyo illustrate his quest for unity between samsara (the cycle of birth and rebirth) and nirvana, and his insistence that faith was to be embodied in everyday life. For example, Wonhyo viewed the monastic and the secular life as one. In addition to instructing other monks, he would go out into the secular world to preach, sometimes dressed as a monk, at other times as a beggar or as a soldier. He frequently visited taverns and brothels, and his meditation was done in the open air rather than in the monastery.

Although Wonhyo had originally taken up the monastic life, he nevertheless asked the king's intervention to find him a wife. Wonhyo was directed to a widowed princess in Yosuk Palace, and on his way fell in a river. His clothes were not dry until after dark, so he had to stay the night. He slept with the princess, who subsequently became pregnant. Buddhist tales such as this often shock westerners, but what the story *means* is more important than whether Wonhyo appeared to behave in a morally responsible way. While sexual misconduct is a violation of a monk's precepts, Wonhyo is held to be a buddha, and hence omniscient. Wonhyo would therefore have been able to foresee all the consequences of his action, and in fact his son Sol Chong became one of the great figures of Confucian scholarship.[38] The function of such stories is to illustrate Wonhyo's insistence that there should be no sharp division between the monastic meditative life and engagement in worldly activity. Wonhyo had the state of mind of a buddha, but his body still lived in the ordinary world, separating these apparent dichotomies: 'One must be detached from everything, and, on one straight path, escape birth and death.'[39]

Like many Mahayana Buddhists, Wonhyo had considerable interest in 'Pure Land' teachings. Particularly in the Theravada tradition, there had been stress on the expected coming of Maitreya, the Buddha of the next aeon, but the emphasis shifted from the cult of Maitreya to that of another buddha, Amitabha, the Buddha of infinite light. According to Pure Land teaching, a buddha (usually Amitabha) after reaching enlightenment creates around himself a celestial paradise or 'Pure Land' (*sukhavati*), into which those who pay sufficient devotion to the Buddha may enter. The Pure Land is not normally held to be nirvana itself, but is a penultimate religious goal, from which there will be no falling back into samsara. In the Pure Land, buddhas and bodhisattvas instruct the devotees and show them the way to nirvana. Wonhyo saw the concept of the Pure Land as a means of mediating between Buddhists who advocated mundane and those who advocated super-mundane goals:

Both the Pure Land and the mundane land were originally products of One Mind; the Sakyamuni Buddha taught in the mundane world, while Amitayus leads all men to the Pure Land because it is not easy for them to return to the origin of the One Mind.[40]

## BUDDHIST INFLUENCES ON UNIFICATION THOUGHT

When we turn to *Divine Principle* we can, I believe, detect some influences from extant Korean Buddhist teachings. Some of these are explicitly acknowledged, such as the belief in the coming Maitreya coinciding with the Unificationist eschatological expectation of the Second Advent. The notion of unity is another major theme which is clearly held in common between Han (Tong) Buddhism and Unificationism.

At certain points in Unification thought one can find stories which are overtly Christian, but, I believe, covertly Buddhist. For example, there is a story that at the age of twelve Sun Myung Moon prayed to God for wisdom greater than that of Solomon, and compassion greater than that of Jesus. The selection of Solomon as a kind of counterpart to Jesus may seem strange to mainstream Christians, who, if asked to pick out the two most significant figures from the Judaeo-Christian tradition, would surely think of Moses, Elijah, King David or indeed St Paul before alighting on Solomon. While Solomon's reign was marked by the building of the Jerusalem Temple, it is possible that the pairing of Solomon and Jesus is the result of Buddhist influence: Solomon and Jesus are used to represent to two Mahayana Buddhist ideals of wisdom (*prajna*) and compassion (*karuna*), which are the characteristics of enlightenment.

The emphasis on Pure Land teaching is also noteworthy, since the Pure Land occupies an almost identical role to the Unificationist concept of Paradise. Just as the Pure Land is the penultimate stage in the attainment of nirvana, so Paradise is the penultimate stage of the spirit's entry into the Kingdom of Heaven. The 'Heavenly Kingdom of God' has not yet been attained, since this can only be accomplished after the attainment of the Kingdom of Heaven on earth, which requires the fulfilment of all the three Blessings. However, since Jesus on the cross promised the dying thief that he would be with Jesus in Paradise that very day,[41] it is clear that Jesus had accomplished something significant. Jesus had opened Paradise, 'the region of the spirit world where those spirit men who have attained the "life-spirit" stage by believing in Jesus while on earth go after death, and stay until the gate to the Kingdom of Heaven is opened.'[42] (There are three stages of development in the spirit world, according to Unificationist teaching: 'form spirit', 'life spirit' and 'divine spirit'.)

The practice of having undisclosed teachings is also a possible derivation from Buddhism. According to the Mahayana tradition the Buddha only taught 'provisional teachings' which were geared to the level of intellectual and spiritual attainment of his listeners. As humankind became more ready for fuller teachings, these were revealed. This is particularly the case in certain Tibetan traditions, where portions of esoteric teaching are transmitted from guru to disciple when the disciple is ready. The *Lotus Sutra*,[43] the principal scripture of the Nichiren sects which have flourished in Japan, teaches that Gautama, the historical Buddha, was already enlightened many aeons previous to his experience under the bo tree at Bodh Gaya: he only pretended to become enlightened there, since this was a 'skilful means' of imparting the *dharma* (the teaching) to his first disciples. The *Lotus Sutra*, it is held, supersedes all previous teachings.

Although it may be argued that the notion of 'progressive revelation' is something which many mainstream Christians believe to occur within Christianity, it is generally held that undisclosed revelations are held by God and not by any human intermediaries. It is 'the Lord' who 'hath yet more light and truth to break forth from his word', as the popular hymn puts it. The notion of a clergyman, a prophet or a visionary deliberately concealing part of the Christian message until hearers are ready is something which is not found in mainstream Christianity, and if there is an extraneous source for this aspect of Unification thought, it must be found elsewhere.

Buddhism, I believe, provides such a source, and it is to remembered that in one place *Divine Principle* accords the Lord of the Second Advent the status of a buddha.[44] 'Skilful means' is a concept which is frequently found in Mahayana Buddhism, and one discussant has compared the Buddhist concept of 'skilful means' with the practice of 'heavenly deception' attributed to the Unification Church.[45] Although I believe there are parallels between Unificationism and Buddhism in this area, I think it is misleading to use the term 'heavenly deception' in this context. 'Deception' implies passing off falsehood for truth: this is certainly not done in Buddhism, since the 'provisional teachings' are not actually false but merely incomplete. Similarly in Unificationism the publicly disclosed teachings, such as those found in *Divine Principle*, are not subsequently contradicted by new revelations given by the Rev

Moon: they are simply new revelations which complement those which have previously been given.

It was against a background of this variety of religions, with their cross-fertilisation and quests for 'unity', that Christianity arrived in Korea. It was therefore hardly surprising that at least some Koreans viewed this new faith as yet another religion which had to be merged into this universal synthesis. The methods by which Christianity was introduced and the effects on Korean religious thought form the subject of Chapter 4.

# 4 The Advent of Christianity

It was amidst this complex religious climate in Korea that Christianity arrived. On the whole, it was the Protestant missionaries rather than the Roman Catholics who were more influential on the Korean population. The reasons for the appeal of one type of Christianity rather than another in any particular culture is a matter for speculation. Roman Catholicism, for example, was more able to take root in Latin America, whereas Protestantism proved more popular in the far East, and certainly in Korea. Part of the explanation no doubt lies in the methods of evangelism which were used, but the indigenous religious and cultural climate has also played its part. Protestantism enjoyed greater popularity in Korea for both sets of reasons: it was propagated more openly, and the Protestant emphasis on the Bible message struck more of a chord with the Korean populace than the Roman Catholic concepts of the sacraments as the means of salvation.

Protestant missionaries were permitted to enter Korea after its frontiers were formally opened to the rest of the world in 1882. Before then, Roman Catholic missionaries had infiltrated the country secretly: one nineteenth-century Roman Catholic missionary, for example, succeeded in entering the town of Wuju by climbing through a sewer. When such subterfuges were discovered, those who were responsible faced severe penalties, and public antagonism increased. The under-cover nature of Roman Catholic evangelism necessitated a very sporadic propagation of the gospel rather than a sustained official presence.

In 1883 Korea established diplomatic relations with the United States, and this paved the way for the advent of Protestant missions. In 1884 Presbyterians and Methodists arrived, followed by the Church of England in 1890, the Seventh Day Adventists in 1905, and the Jehovah's Witnesses in 1912. The year 1907 marked the setting up of the Oriental Missionary Society, which became the Holiness Church of Korea. The Salvation Army, which arrived in Korea in 1908, can also be regarded as a Holiness movement, although not itself part of the Holiness Churches.

The 'Holiness Churches' are perhaps unfamiliar outside the USA, and a brief explanation is therefore in order. The Holiness Churches developed from Wesleyism, and emphasised 'sanctification'. This term, originally used by St Paul,[1] contrasts with 'justification by faith', which is St Paul's term for the conversion experience. Justification is the receiving of Jesus

Christ, whereas sanctification is the working of the Holy Spirit which continues to purify believers after conversion, making them more sinless or holy in God's sight. Justification, the Holiness Churches taught, was the 'first blessing'; sanctification was the 'second blessing'. Christianity has consistently taught that receiving the Spirit should follow the receiving of Jesus Christ,[2] although the expectation of precisely how the Spirit comes has differed from one denomination to another. While the Pentecostalist Churches have equated the receiving of the Holy Spirit with the experience of members 'speaking in tongues', the Holiness Churches have typically denied being Pentecostalist, and have viewed sanctification as the cultivation of spiritual and moral purity.

'Justification by faith' was nonetheless important, and the missionaries laid great emphasis on sin and forgiveness. The Methodist Board required missionaries to have had a personal conversion experience for which they had to provide substantial credentials. Personal and public devotion was emphasised, and missionaries were trained to preach in a way which combined careful preparation of their sermon material with identified places at which they would extemporise in order to imbue their sermon with directness and feeling. They presented their message in a way which contained an urgency, using aggressive, militaristic images. Men and women had to fight, to combat, to compete; humankind was engaged in a battle between righteousness and sin, light and darkness, God and Satan. Unless the heathen could successfully engage in this combat, they were lost.

## THE MISSIONARIES AND THE BIBLE

The content of the missionary message, of course, was Bible-based, and the task of Bible translation was predominantly a Protestant undertaking. Between 1875 and 1887 the New Testament was translated from Chinese to Korean. By 1911 the entire Bible (excluding the Apocrypha[3]) had been translated: this was known as Ross's Version, and was a rather crude, undignified rendering. In 1937 a second completed version superseded that of Ross, and this 1937 version remains the one most commonly used by Korean Christians today.

The missionaries' decision to use the Korean language was not as self-evident a choice as may appear. The normal language of the educated élite was Chinese, and the choice of Korean was a conscious attempt by the missionaries to target their message to the lower classes and the less educated. Women were a particular sector of the population who were targeted for evangelism. The missionary and Bible translator James Gale wrote, 'Korea's native script is surely the simplest language in the world . . . Why, yes, even women could learn it in a month or a little more . . . '4

The art of Bible translation is never a mechanical process of pairing off words and phrases by means of a dictionary. It cannot be theologically neutral, and any attempt to translate the Bible for a new readership leaves open the possibility of syncretism. For translation to be possible, translators must assume the existence of shared concepts between themselves and the readers. If the missionary lacked shared concepts, he or she would be like the fictional traveller in H. G. Wells' *The Country of the Blind*. In that story, the traveller possessed sight, but, since everyone else in the country was blind, he had no means of communicating to the inhabitants the meaning of words like 'see'. By the same logic, if any missionary had a message with totally novel concepts, this would be incommunicable to the indigenous population. If translation is possible at all, then it can only be done by finding concepts which already exist within the language of the target audience, with all their connotations, and perhaps with only an approximation to the intended meaning of the translator. (All of us who have learned a language are familiar with the situation in which there is no exact fit in one language for an expression from another.)

A number of examples illustrate the problems confronted by the Bible translators in Korea. Problems arose on account of the structure of the Korean language itself.[5] For example, Korean verbs have suffixes which indicate the degree of politeness or rudeness employed by the speaker – something which is not found in the original Greek and Hebrew texts, or in English translations. In order to translate the Bible into Korean, Ross had to decide how politely Jesus spoke on each occasion to his parents, to his disciples, to the scribes and Pharisees, or whoever. Obviously no dictionary can adjudicate on such matters: a translator can only conjecture from the scenarios which the gospel writers describe.

A further problem was how to translate the word 'God'. The options which lay open had definite theological significance. To use the word 'T'aeguk' would be to equate God with an impersonal cosmic force; to introduce a quasi-Hebrew term like 'Jehovah' would have defined the Christian God as a different God from that of the Koreans, as well as hampering effective communication. Ross's choice of the word 'Hananim' quite consciously equated Jehovah with the Korean personal God of the Tan'gun legend: the Christian missionaries were thus acknowledging a point of contact rather than claiming to import a new deity to the

Korean people. A directly confrontational approach between the Christian missionaries and the indigenous religions was thus avoided.

Just as the translation of the word 'God' indicated the degree to which the missionaries wished to distance themselves from indigenous Korean religion, there were similar implications in the way in which words like 'unclean spirit' were to be rendered. The chosen Korean equivalent was *sagwi*, a word used within the context of Korean shamanism. *Sagwi* means 'demon', but the word denotes a specific type of being in the shamanistic world view. The missionary scholar Heber Jones[6] defined *sagwi* as a 'tramp spirit', and referred to such spirits as 'the criminals of the Shamanic spirit-world': they are spirits who have been evicted from their former spiritual position, and are condemned to wander the earth, having no fixed abode in which to rest. Thus, the choice of word for 'unclean spirit' immediately imported a shamanistic concept, together with much of its associated cosmology, into the Christian gospel.

Finding such points of contact between Christianity and shamanism was in no sense a dilution of the gospel and a capitulation to Korean folk shamanism. On the contrary, the Korean view of a world which is populated by spirits and demons, arguably, is nearer to the biblical way of thinking than to that of the more liberal Christians. When faced with the New Testament accounts of Christ's exorcisms, the more liberal camp is inclined to take the view that the supposedly demon-possessed were suffering from illnesses such as epilepsy, and that talk about demon possession is a merely rather quaint way of describing such conditions. The followers of shamanism have no need to demythologise in this way: demons are real, and belief in their reality is corroborated by the Bible.

## MAKING THE BIBLE ACCESSIBLE

Propagation of the gospel not only demanded policies on translation. Once the Bible was translated, a policy was also needed on how to make it physically accessible to the Korean population. The fact that the Bible was translated did not mean that it was freely available to all. The missionaries' aim was for each member to possess his or her own Bible, and they appear to have been largely successful in achieving this. But transmitting the gospel message to the unconverted could not be accomplished by making Bibles available to all, since this was too costly and in any case the literacy rate in Korea was not high. The missionaries' physical distribution policy therefore was to employ colporteurs – itinerant book distributors – who would travel within Korea distributing religious literature: this was seldom an entire Bible, but more generally tracts or individual gospels such as Luke. This policy enabled the missionaries to circulate Christianity's central proclamation more widely, being less expensive than distributing entire Bibles. However, by virtue of his itinerant role, the colporteur served to encourage independent Bible study rather than instruction which was supervised by a resident trained missionary who could answer questions and define the dividing line between orthodoxy and heresy.

What was more, the missionaries had been trained in doctrine; the indigenous population by contrast was theologically unsophisticated and tended to be less concerned with biblical theology and more struck by the appeal of the Bible stories themselves. The concrete was of more interest than the abstract, and, once the colporteur had come and gone, those who wished to try their hand at theological explanation had no resources at their disposal other than the shamanistic world view to which they had been acclimatised.

The completion of Bible translation by 1911 was considerably later than in most other countries in which Christian missionaries operated, and it is therefore unlikely that its contents would be widely known in the time of Sun Myung Moon's childhood, and certainly not the more obscure passages (such as the sin of Ham, the story of Tamar, or the circumcision of Gershom) which assume in Unification thought a much greater significance than they would for mainstream Christian missionary preaching. Although some missionaries adopted a 'full Bible' approach, the missionaries would more typically preach from the basic Old and New Testament stories with which western Christians are most familiar.

One is forced to conclude that Sun Myung Moon's knowledge of scripture was derived from personal study of the Bible, rather than from missionary sermonising or organised Bible study and prayer groups of the mainstream Christian churches. Indeed, Unificationist sources state that the Rev Moon studied the Christian faith with his own copiously annotated copies of the Bible in Korean, Japanese and English.[7]

## THE MESSAGE OF THE MISSIONARIES

We have seen how the process of biblical translation required points of contact between the world views of the Koreans and the Christian missionaries. The biblical stories, arguably, had ready-made points of contact too. In his study of Christianity in Korea, Spencer Palmer[8] notes that biblical and Korean customs were in many respects remarkably similar. Salutations of peace, for example, are common to both: 'Go in peace,' or

'Be in peace' are the most common forms of greeting in Korea, in common with the Hebrew salutation '*shalom*', meaning 'peace' or 'prosperity'. The ceremonial bowing (kow-towing) of the Koreans corresponds to the biblical accounts of Joseph's brothers coming to Egypt and bowing before him,[9] Saul bowing in front of Samuel,[10] and so on. In the accounts of the healing miracles, Jesus' instruction is 'Take up your bed (i.e., mat) and walk';[11] as Palmer points out, the Koreans have typically slept on bed-rolls which are taken up in the morning and unrolled at night. Again, the biblical custom of wearing sackcloth and ashes to symbolise repentance or mourning[12] is mirrored in the Korean practice of wearing coarse hemp for long periods after a death. Finally, the proliferation of devil posts and statues provided a first-hand reminder of the idolatry which the Bible so vehemently condemned.[13] Such points may seem trivial, but conversions are seldom accomplished by wholly rational persuasion: religions must touch the heart and the imagination rather than secure mere intellectual acceptance. A necessary prerequisite therefore for conversion is that the convert must in some way 'feel at home' within the world of the Bible.

Protestant mission in Korea was not merely an interaction between Protestant biblicism and folk shamanism, but it was an interaction of the Korean world view and the distinctive way in which the missionaries had studied the Bible. As Donald Dayton suggests, it is more than likely that they would be familiar with the Scofield Reference Bible, which was highly popular in the USA.[14] The original Scofield Bible contained notes and a system of cross-referencing for the King James edition. (Modern Scofield Reference Bibles now offer the same introduction and referencing system for more recent translations also.) The Scofield introduction sets out a number of assumptions about scripture: for example, there are stated to be several 'dispensations' within the Bible, demonstrating the 'increasing purpose' of God. It asserts that the whole Bible centres on Christ, the Old Testament being 'preparation', the gospels 'manifestation', the Acts 'propagation', the epistles 'explanation' and St John's Revelation 'consummation'.[15] The history of Israel is divided into seven distinct periods,[16] the last of which (the 'dispersion') continues into the present. Prophecy is regarded as predictive and relates to the present dispensation which will lead to the divine consummation. This approach to the Bible bears a certain resemblance to *Divine Principle*'s sectionalisation of history into discrete compartments which are then re-enacted as part of the restoration process.

The idea that contemporary events were re-enactments of biblical events was certainly perpetuated by the missionaries to Korea. One particular exegetical device which the missionaries employed was 'typological' interpretation. This involved asserting the relevance of a biblical text for a later time period by establishing points of analogy between the events mentioned in the text (the 'type') and the events which it supposedly foreshadowed (the 'anti-type'). Thus, Noah's ark (the type), being made of wood, has been said to foreshadow the cross of the Christ (the anti-type), which was also wooden; the waters of the flood in Noah's day (the type), from which humankind was saved, foreshadow the waters of baptism (the anti-type) which bestow salvation from sin. This method of exposition of scripture involves imagination and creativity rather than the more conventional tools of contemporary biblical criticism. If it seems far-fetched, it should be remembered that it was used fairly liberally by the biblical writers themselves as well as the early Church fathers, and indeed the comparison between the flood and the baptismal waters can be found in the first Epistle of Peter.[17]

It appears that such methods were not simply confined to relating Old Testament material to Jesus Christ's atoning work. Although the missionaries stopped short of claiming that their presence in Korea was actually foretold in scripture, nonetheless comparisons were made between biblical events and their own situation. A Korean who studied secretly by night with Appenzeller (the first Methodist missionary to Korea) was referred to as 'Nicodemus',[18] for example. In an address to his home church, Appenzeller used the story of Joshua and the capture of Jericho as a vehicle on which to describe his own experiences of evangelising in Korea: although he did not claim that the passage foretold his arrival, at least he construed it as enjoining something which he was to fulfil.

The sufferings of the Korean nation, or of Christians undergoing persecution, were frequently compared with the trials of the Old Testament patriarchs. It was quite common for missionaries to tell their members that the Korean independence leaders were analogous to Moses, the Korean people to the Israelites and the Japanese to the Egyptians. The Koreans were told that their sufferings were like 'Abraham's course', or 'Jacob's course'.

No doubt many of the parallels were drawn by the missionaries without strict theological intent. The Korean seeker 'Nicodemus', one imagines, was so named semi-jocularly. Nevertheless, the overwhelming missionary belief that they, together with the Korean nation, were acting out a role in a divine salvation drama entailed that contemporary occurrences were not merely coincidental, but part of a divine providential plan. Given the prevalent Protestant belief in predestination, it would not be surprising for a missionary to hold that his situation was divinely foreknown, if not in some way foreshadowed.

The missionaries' typological exegesis undoubtedly paved the way for the interpretation of scripture which we find in *Divine Principle*. Those who protest that the Unificationist interpretation of the Bible is bizarre are often oblivious to the fact that many of its pairings between 'type' and 'anti-type' are already given in the Bible. *Divine Principle* compares Jesus Christ with Moses' bronze serpent,[19] the stone Moses struck at Kadesh[20] and the Jerusalem Temple;[21] and it claims that the manna and quails which were eaten by Moses and the Israelites prefigure the body and blood of Christ. These are all analogies used in the New Testament.[22]

Other typological interpretations in *Divine Principle* appear to be innovatory, for example that Jesus was prefigured by the Tree of Life,[23] that Moses' tablets of stone represent Jesus and the Holy Spirit,[24] and that Joshua's battle with the Amalekites is the 'type' representing Jesus in combat with Satan.[25] Nevertheless, however much one may dislike these particular typological renderings, few mainstream Christians who accept the legitimacy of typological interpretation would contend that the biblical writers should have a monopoly of it. Typology is innovative, and if Unificationism's typology is called into question, it is not evidently more prolix or implausible than that of the Christian missionaries. If the theory of 'providential time-identity' seems contrived, it must be remembered that the theory had its obvious precursor in the missionaries' application of biblical history to current events.

## METHODS OF EVANGELISM

So far I have considered the content of the missionaries' message. It is now necessary to say something about the policies which the Christian missionaries used in their evangelisation of Korea.

The Protestant missionaries used what are known as the 'Nevius methods',[26] so called after missionaries to China called Dr and Mrs Nevius. The methods were are as follows. First, converts would continue to live where they resided: they were not themselves required to live at a mission station or to become itinerant preachers or colporteurs. Second, the church would be built up as the indigenous population itself was able to manage it. It was believed that the Christian leadership should be prominently Korean rather than western. Third, the church, when it was able, would provide the means for training the most promising converts for ministry and evangelism. Fourth, the indigenous population would provide their own buildings, with native architecture and through their own finances.

At first sight it looks as if mission was well planned, and indeed, according to the accounts given by some of the early missionaries to Korea, standards of evangelism and training in the Christian faith were very high.[27] Christianity grew from small beginnings at such a phenomenal rate that one set of membership statistics provided by Christian denominations in 1973 suggested that Christianity had almost as much support as Confucianism.[28] Not only were numbers impressive, it has been said, but converts to Christianity were not accepted on any terms whatsoever: they had to be strictly scrutinised and had to pass a number of tests set by the clergy.[29] Enquirers had to renounce idols and fetishes, undergo instruction for a period, pass an examination on the principles of Christianity, and undergo examination for admission to the Church. They had to adopt an appropriate life-style: no drinking, smoking, or gambling, with compulsory sabbath observance, including twice weekly attendance at church. A convert had to be literate and to have taught literacy to his or her family. But, above all, the convert already had to have started witnessing, and to have preached the gospel to at least one other person.

Alas, these contentions are little more than missionary propaganda. While it is certainly true that Christianity grew rapidly in Korea, it is doubtful whether foreign religions ever secured more than 11 per cent of the population's support,[30] and the missionaries' methods of propagating the gospel gave serious cause for concern both inside and outside Korea. Indeed when the first World Mission Council met in Edinburgh in 1910, the theological inadequacy of the Korean church was raised as a major concern.[31] The truth of the matter is that the missionaries' stated and consciously chosen policy was to ensure that the clergy were not too advanced educationally, lest they should arouse the envy of their congregations. Since the initial converts were from the lower classes and were not sufficiently well educated to read the Bible critically, this effectively ensured a poorly trained clergy, whose lack of theological training was rationalised by the anti-intellectualism which was typical of the American fundamentalism which formed the basis of much of the Korean missionary activity.

Further, although the missionaries demanded high moral integrity from the catechumens, the required standard of intellectual understanding was not particularly high. The notion of undergoing examination may seem to suggest a safeguard of orthodoxy on the part of the catechumen. However, Blair and Hunt,[32] prominent turn-of-the-century missionaries in Korea, report that typical questions to be put to candidates for baptism were: 'How long have you been a Christian?', 'Who is Jesus?', 'Why do you believe in Him?', 'Have you kept the sabbath faithfully?', 'Do you have daily family prayers?', 'Have you brought anyone to Christ?' These questions, put one year after conversion, and nine months after the convert had been received as a catechumen, may have ensured a high degree of commitment on the part of the new convert, but they did not confirm that the candidate had even a rudimentary grasp of Christian teaching.

The requirement that each catechumen should first preach the gospel to someone else was significant to the way in which Christianity developed in Korea. On the surface, this may have appeared an astute policy (based on the second point of the Nevius plan), given the proselytising objectives of the Christian missionaries and their very small presence (at least initially) within Korea. However, the policy of 'each one teach one' was somewhat misjudged. Newly converted Christians have often lacked sufficient knowledge or experience to proclaim the gospel in an acceptable and orthodox form, and this missionary tactic has given rise to problems in various cultures in which it has been employed. A former missionary once told me of an incident in Africa, where a recent convert was still illiterate, but nonetheless had been impressed by the missionaries' practice of flaunting a Bible as they preached the gospel. He managed to acquire a book which he then waved in front of his audiences as he preached his newly-found faith. Unbeknown to the preacher and most of his listeners alike, the book he brandished was Daniel Defoe's *Robinson Crusoe*!

In fairness to the missionaries in Korea, they would most certainly have disapproved if a similar incident ever occurred, since catechumens were at least required to be literate, and indeed to have instructed their families in reading skills. Nonetheless, bearing in mind that the illiteracy rate in Korea was high during the early days of Christian mission, a catechumen-preacher's audiences would probably be unable to check the veracity of the Christian message for themselves. Further, the catechumens who were preaching would inevitably be inexperienced in matters of doctrine, and often unable to locate points of misinterpretation on the part of the listeners, or to identify elements of competing faiths which were incompatible with Christianity. Indeed, Christianity was unique in demanding exclusive allegiance, whereas the indigenous faiths (as we have seen) were not viewed as incompatible with each other. It was therefore natural for many new converts to wish to accept Christianity, but to combine it with non-Christian rites. One major controversy arose because large numbers of Christians continued to venerate ancestors. Although the practice was officially denounced, the very fact that this loomed large as a serious issue on which opinion could be divided indicates the scale on which syncretism was occurring.

These problems were compounded by the somewhat gentle manner in which Christianity was introduced. Christianity was propagated by the persuasiveness of the missionaries, not by any political imposition of the Christian faith, as happened to the Spanish in Mexico and the Byzantines in Bulgaria. Where Christianity has been imposed by political power, the Church has successfully exerted fairly strict controls on what was orthodoxy and what was heresy. The internal political life of Korea did not involve, nor could it possibly have involved, a political take-over on the part of the Christians. One early Roman Catholic convert who wrote to the Pope, requesting gun boats to secure freedom for Christian worship, found his request denied (perhaps predictably)!³³ In matters of religion, then, the Korean people were largely left to their own devices.

There was no sure way for the missionaries to know how Christianity was being filtered into Korean culture, how it was understood, and how it was allowed to develop. The policy of 'each one teach one' resulted in the preaching of the gospel going outside the complete control of the Christian leaders. Who was to tell what a catechumen was preaching in the name of Christianity, particularly in a religious climate where, apparently, it was characteristic to comment that Christianity and shamanism were basically identical? As one Korean recently remarked, 'Missionary activity enabled the propagation of shamanism in Christian guise.' There is reason to doubt whether many Koreans who supposedly embraced the Christian faith actually understood the differences between Christianity and shamanism. One early Unification member states in her testimony that 'Christianity is very close to shamanism in Korea.'³⁴ It was not uncommon for someone to accept Christianity because the *mudang* (shaman) predicted that he or she would do so. Christianity, clearly, was perceived through shamanist-tinted spectacles.

No missionary message is transmitted exclusively by preaching and Bible distribution. Methods of worship can teach attenders in ways which complement more overt missionary preaching. Hymns, prayers, ritual (or lack of it) have a didactic function too. Although it is difficult to determine precisely which hymns proved the most popular in the early days of Korean mission, Sankey and Moody's *Sacred Songs and Solos*, first published in 1873, was immensely popular amongst American fundamentalist Christians in the early part of the twentieth century, and indeed today.

Several of these hymns take up themes which are of particular relevance to the way in which Unification thought arose. Of particular interest are those hymns which speak of the blood of Jesus: although Unificationism rejected the traditional Christian belief that the blood shed on the cross had complete salvific power, nevertheless they reinforced the notion that blood was the bearer of power – a notion which had considerable affinity with neo-Confucian thought. For example:

Would you be free from your burden of sin?
There's power in the blood, power in the blood;
Would you o'er evil a victory win?
There's wonderful power in the blood.
There is power, power, wonder-working power
In the blood of the Lamb;
There is power, power, wonder-working power
In the precious blood of the Lamb.[35]

Interestingly, another hymn from the same hymnary juxtaposes the themes
of blood and marriage:-

When the Bridegroom cometh will your robes be white?
Pure and white in the blood of the Lamb?
Will your soul be ready for the mansions bright,
And be washed in blood of the Lamb? [36]

## THE 'KOREAN PENTECOST'

I mentioned that prayer could contribute to the way in which the Christian
message was propagated. One particular incident is worth mentioning in
this connection. It occurred in Pyongyang during the winter of 1907, and
left its mark on the history of Korean Christianity. The Presbyterian winter
Bible classes were usually regarded as great occasions for the outpouring of
the Spirit, but one Saturday night the meeting was subdued and solemn. The
meeting on the Sunday night was dead. On Monday, the missionaries met to
pray, and that night the church seemed filled with an incredible presence.
A Mr Lee, the preacher, led the customary 'chain prayer': this is a form of
prayer where members of the congregation pray in turns after the prayer
leader, so that the contributed prayers form a 'chain'. On this occasion
so many of the congregation wanted to pray that Mr Lee had to instruct
them all to pray at once. The missionary writer W. H. Blair describes the
incident thus:

. . . the whole audience began to pray out loud, all together. The effect
was indescribable - not confusion, but a vast harmony of sound and
spirit, a mingling together of souls moved by an irresistible impulse
of prayer. The prayer sounded to me like the falling of many waters,
an ocean of prayer beating against God's throne. It was not many, but

one, born of one spirit, lifted to one Father above. Just as on the day of Pentecost, they were all together in one place, of one accord praying, 'and suddenly there came from heaven the sound as of the rushing of a mighty wind, and it filled all the house where they were sitting.' God is not always in the whirlwind, neither does He always speak in a still small voice. He came to us in Pyengyang [*sic*] that night with the sound of weeping. As the prayer continued, a spirit of heaviness and sorrow for sin came down upon the audience. Over on one side, someone began to weep, and in a moment the whole audience was weeping.

Blair proceeds to quote Lee, who wrote at the time:

Man after man would rise, confess his sins, break down and weep, and then throw himself to the floor and beat the floor with his fists in perfect agony of conviction. My own cook tried to make a confession, broke down in the midst of it, and cried to me across the room: 'Pastor, tell me, is there any hope for me, can I be forgiven?' and then he threw himself to the floor and wept and wept, and almost screamed in agony. Sometimes after a confession, the whole audience would break out in audible prayer, and the effect of that audience of hundreds of men praying together in audible prayer was something indescribable. Again, after another confession, they would break out in uncontrollable weeping, and we would all weep, we could not help it. And so the meeting went on until two o'clock a.m., with confession and weeping and praying.[37]

This revival was not confined to a single congregation: it quickly spread to Protestant churches throughout Korea and is therefore known as 'the Korean Pentecost'.

The event left its legacy to Unificationism also. When Unificationists are praying together, they frequently pray 'in unison', each member praying out loud, simultaneously. It is quite common to hear members weep freely when this is taking place. This style of prayer has a clear precedent in the revivalist activities of the mainstream Christian missionaries.

## CHRISTIANITY AND NEO-CONFUCIANISM

In the main I have dwelt on how Korean Christianity was interpreted in the light of the prevailing shamanism. However, the neo-Confucian environment must not be overlooked. We have seen that one of the fundamental 'right and harmonious relationships' was the relationship between brothers: the proper role of the younger brother is to submit to the elder brother. There are many stories about brothers in the Bible – Cain and Abel, Ishmael and Isaac, Esau and Jacob, Aaron and Moses, and so on. Yet when these are examined it becomes apparent that God's favour seems to rest with the younger rather than the elder, and the younger establishes his superiority over the elder. As the Bible itself affirmed, 'The elder shall serve the younger.'[38]

Unification theology lays great emphasis on this theme. Certain events in Old Testament narrative are regarded as decisive in the restoration of the true lineage; the right of inheritance must pass from the older (representing Cain) to the younger (representing Abel). This teaching is not to be found in *Divine Principle*, but it is taught to members and found in some of the Rev Moon's sermons.[39] Since the origin of human life is in the mother's womb, Unification thought holds that the restoration of the birthright must occur there. The Bible records that before the twins Esau and Jacob were born, they appeared to struggle within their mother Rebecca's womb.[40] The struggle appears to have been simply a sign of things to come, and we have to look to a further incident in the Old Testament to find the restoration of the birthright.

The birthright was restored in a rather obscure story concerning a woman called Tamar.[42] Tamar disguised as a prostitute in order to have sexual intercourse with Judah, her father-in-law. (The Bible deems Tamar to have acted justly: she was concerned to propagate the lineage, and Judah was effectively preventing this.) As a result of her deed she became pregnant with twins. At the moment of birth, one of the twins, Zerah, put out his hand, which the midwife marked by tying a scarlet thread to it. Zerah withdrew his hand, and his brother Perez pushed forward and was born first. Thus Zerah, who was technically the elder brother, was ousted from his *position* by Perez, the younger, and so Perez, representing the 'Abel-type' lineage, triumphed over Zerah, who represented the 'Cain-type' satanic lineage. In this way, the lineage was restored. There was of course no immediate change in the history of Israel at that point: it is explained that God's plans take time to enact. Rebecca was told that 'two nations' were in her womb, and thus the process of restoration could only be accomplished when the offspring of Rebecca – and subsequently Tamar – had multiplied into nations.

A further Old Testament incident confirms the 'brothers' theme. Jacob, now in his old age, blessed his two grandchildren, Manasseh and Ephraim; however, he crossed his arms when giving the blessing in order to reverse the *positions* of elder and younger brother. It is the younger who must have the inheritance.[41] Indeed, the Unification Church views itself as the younger brother to mainstream Christianity: it regards itself as having the inheritance which will enable the Lord of the Second Advent to fulfil his work, and it believes that mainstream Christianity, as the 'elder brother', should acknowledge his messianic status.

## CONCLUSIONS

It is difficult to draw firm conclusions about the influence of the missionaries on the Unification Church for several reasons. First, there are linguistic barriers which make much of the potential evidence inaccessible. Second, without ascertaining the precise history and topography involved in the events of the Unification Church it is difficult to establish precisely which Christian churches the Rev Moon had contact with. The Rev Moon himself has refused to give any further interviews (the last was with Professor Frederick Sontag in 1977)[43] and mainstream Christian churches are extremely reticent about providing information which might suggest that they have had links with the Unification Church or had some responsibility for its inception. However, notwithstanding these limitations, I believe it is possible to draw the following conclusions.

First, the message of the missionaries suggested a particular form of Christianity which influenced the Unification Church and some other newer Korean religions. Typological interpretation and emphasis on a dispensational history involving a fierce struggle between God and Satan paved the way for the UC's doctrines of providential time identity, and certainly the God–Satan confrontation. The Holiness Churches' teaching that personal conversion only marked the commencement of the redemptive process and that there were two 'blessings' may have been instrumental in suggesting the UC's doctrine that the restoration involves a plurality of 'blessings'. Finally, as we have seen, some specific points of Unification practice, such as unison prayer, can be traced to events which occurred in the history of mission.

Such conclusions must remain tentative. What is certain, however, is that the policies employed by the missionaries to proclaim the gospel resulted in many second- and third-hand versions of Christianity being propagated. This is no new phenomenon: the Mormons, the Rastafarians, the Aladura, the cargo cults and Peyote cults of America, arguably, have developed in a similar way. All of these religious groups result from the interaction between Christian mission and the indigenous religions of the countries in which they arose. In Korea, what was mainstream Christianity and what was folk shamanism, popular Buddhism or Confucianism were not always clearly distinguished. As a result, a number of small religious groups which combined these various religious strands began to take their rise. Their influence on the founding the Unification Church is fairly firmly accredited, and to these we must now turn.

# 5 Korea's New Christians

The various religious traditions of Korea had been constantly intertwining and it was inevitable that when Christianity arrived it would also become part of the amalgam of the Korean religions. Although Protestantism made more of an impression than Roman Catholicism, the Roman Catholics had made their mark too, and Roman Catholicism was one ingredient in an important new religion which grew up in Korea, namely the Ch'ondogyo. Unlike some of the other syncretistic movements I shall consider later in this chapter, Ch'ondogyo was not directly involved in the founding of the Unification Church. Nevertheless it was a fairly popular and influential movement, boasting some 636 000 adherents in 1970, and it would undoubtedly have been known to Sun Myung Moon and the early Unification members.

The Ch'ondogyo religion was originally a political movement, founded in 1860 by Ch'oe Che-u, a former aristocrat and a scholar. Ch'oe Che-u had studied Buddhism, Taoism and Confucianism, and was also familiar with the form of Christianity which had been propagated by Roman Catholic missionaries. At the age of 37, Ch'oe Che-u received a vision that he was commissioned by Heaven to establish a new religion which would relieve the oppression of the people.

The movement Ch'oe Che-u founded was originally known as the 'Tonghak', which means 'Eastern Learning'. The name was intended to underline the movement's rejection of 'western learning', which at that time meant Roman Catholicism. Ch'oe Che-u and his followers did not accept the Christians' concept of a Creator God who stood outside humanity and the physical world. God was the potential which humankind possessed – the Great 'I' to which each little 'I' could aspire. The kingdoms of heaven and hell were not states which awaited mortals after death, but potential states of the present physical world. Earth could become a paradise or a hell, depending on human behaviour.

In the conviction that he was divinely inspired, Ch'oe Che-u devised a 21-character formula (*chumun*) which enshrined the doctrines of the Tonghak and which members ritually recited:

Infinite Energy being now within me, I yearn that it may pour into all living beings and created things.

Since this Infinite Energy abides in me, I am identified with God, and of one nature with all existence.

Should I ever forget these things, all existing things will know of it.[1]

God was the Totality, the ultimate energy (*chigi*) which was the source of humanity and the universe. God and humanity were one; humanity bore the essence of God within it, therefore men and women ought to be treated as God. From this it followed that all men and women were equal regardless of sex or of class. Thus the Tonghak movement had as its agenda a programme of radical social reform: the traditional class distinctions between the *yangban* (the aristocracy) and the *ssangnom* (the peasants) must be abolished.

The Tonghak movement was essentially a synthesis of the various major religions of Korea. It acknowledged the five cardinal relationships of Confucianism; from Taoism it derived the notion of a Way to be followed which sustained the world but was not separate from it; from Buddhism it derived the notion of cleansing one's heart; from Roman Catholicism came some of the organisational and ritual elements (as in Christianity the Ch'ondogyo meet for congregational Sunday worship); and from shamanism it inherited its rituals to placate departed spirits and its belief in geomancy: building altars on mountains, for example, was very much in accordance with the practices of the shamanists. The Tonghak laid emphasis on a work entitled *Ch'amwisol* – 'The Theory of Interpretation of Divinations'.

The *Ch'amwisol* had predicted that the Yi dynasty would fall after 500 years of existence – in other words in 1892. Chou Pong-jun, Ch'oe Che-u's successor, believed that he was the one who was destined to fulfil this prophecy, and accordingly he led a large uprising which amassed great support from the peasants who had been exploited through heavy taxation. The Tonghak Rebellion was eventually quashed, but not until the Tonghak army had advanced as far as Seoul, after the assistance of Japanese and Chinese forces had been sought to crush the rebellion.

Although defeated, the Tonghak movement lived on, and in 1905 Song Pyong-hi, who was now the leader, ordered that the movement's name should be changed to 'Ch'ondogyo' – the Religion (or Society) of the Heavenly Way. He proclaimed eight principal doctrines:

1. God and humanity are one. (*In Nae Ch'on*);
2. The unity of mind and matter;
3. The consistency of religion and politics;
4. The doctrine of the transmigration of the Spirit;

5.    Sacrifice of the physical for the spiritual (i.e., humanity should live for the ideal rather than for the desires of physical body alone);
6.    Uniformity of discipline;
7.    Uniformity of faith;
8.    'Definition of religion' (religion can only be pursued through knowledge, love and will).[2]

The fourth and seventh of these points require particular comment. By the time of the inception of the Ch'ondogyo there had been three successive leaders – Ch'oe Che-u, Chou Pong-jun and Song Pyong-hi. It is held that, although separated in time and space, their spirits form a complete unity, and the energy of the spirits of the dead lives on in posterity: an individual's energy is everlasting. There are obvious affinities here with the Unificationist belief that spirits can return to co-operate with men and women in the physical world, and it is also basic Unificationist teaching that an individual's spirit, once created by God, can never be destroyed.

Turning to seventh point, Song Pyong-hi believed that while there had been a plurality of different religions in the world, when the nature of the Heavenly Way was rightly understood, men and women would follow this and there would be only one faith. Just as the rising sun obscures lesser lights, so the one true faith (Ch'ondogyo) would obscure the lesser faiths, and humanity's religions would become unified. The quest for unification is thus a fundamental theme of Ch'ondogyo.

Something should be mentioned about the role of Ch'ondogyo in the Sam'il Independence Movement. Korea had been annexed by Japan in 1910, and this colonisation was resented by the Korean populace. On 1 March 1919 a Declaration of Independence, prepared jointly by the Ch'ondogyo, Protestant Christians and Buddhist monks was publicly read. The signatories were arrested, but in Seoul and elsewhere cheering crowds demonstrated as the independence leaders were arrested and led to the police station. The independence movement had sparked off a national uprising. Thus we can see that followers of the Ch'ondogyo are nationalistic, 'this-worldly' in their aim, and unificatory in their ability to unite themselves with Protestants, Buddhists and the rest of the Korean population in a quest for a Kingdom of Heaven which is to be found within the present physical order.

## KOREA'S MINORITY RELIGIONS

Ch'ondogyo regards itself as an independent religion and, particularly in its early stages, positively rejected any claim to be a form of Christianity. In contrast, however, numerous smaller religious groups arose in Korea which were strongly influenced by the indigenous Korean faiths, but claimed a Christian identity which was vigorously challenged by the mainstream churches.

We need a term to characterise those new groups which have regarded themselves as Christian but have not secured general acceptance by mainstream Christianity. The term 'Christian-derived' is inadequate, since I believe that groups such as the Unification Church derive from the indigenous religions of Korea also. To describe them as 'semi-Christian' is pejorative, and my suggestion to the UC that 'neo-Christian' might be a suitable compromise proved equally unacceptable. I have therefore employed the description 'New Christian', which has several advantages: it is suitably ambiguous to leave unresolved the question of Christian orthodoxy, yet it differentiates these religious groups from the less controversial forms of mainstream Christianity. In addition, it proved an acceptable term to Unificationists, who acknowledge that their own interpretation of scripture is indeed a new one.

It is estimated that there were at least 170 such groups which emerged in Korea after the Second World War. Teachings and practices varied from group to group, but their principal features were that they were syncretistic, had messianic expectations, laid emphasis on communication with the spirit world, practised healing and prophecy, and aimed at transforming the existing socio-political system. The quest for a unification of Korea and of religions generally was also a typical theme.

The Unification Church (or T'ongil-gyo, as it is known in Korea) is therefore not unique. It is not even the largest of Korea's new religions: that distinction can be claimed by the Olive Tree Movement, founded by an Elder Pak, and which has established two entire 'Christian towns' near Seoul, with populations of 50 000 and 20 000 respectively.[3] What is unique about the Unification Church is that it has exported its distinctively Korean New Christianity beyond Korea's frontiers, to become an international movement.

In common with the many new Korean religions the Unification Church proclaims a 'this-worldly' (or 'earth-worldly') goal, centred on a messiah who emerges from Korea to unify and save the world. The 'messianism'[4] of the UC and the other New Christian movements comes equally from the Buddhist notion of Maitreya and the Confucian notion of *Jin-In* (the 'True Man'), and from Korean books of prophecy, such as the *Chung Gam Nok*.[5] This last-mentioned work predates Christianity's arrival in Korea, having been written during the Yi dynasty, some time after 1740 CE.

On its own evidence, *Divine Principle* draws on these messianic notions which were prevalent within Korea before the UC was founded and in particular the *Chung Gam Nok*. As *Divine Principle* states:

> . . . the Korean nation, as the Third Israel, has believed since the 500-year reign of the Yi Dynasty the prophecy that the King of Righteousness would appear in that land, and, establishing the Millennium, would come to receive tributes from all the countries of the world. This faith has encouraged the people to undergo the bitter course of history, waiting for the time to come. This was truly the Messianic idea of the Korean people which they believed according to "Chung Gam Nok," a book of prophecy . . . Interpreted correctly, the King of Righteousness – Chung-Do Ryung (the person coming with God's right words) – whom the Korean people have so long waited for, is a Korean-style name for the Lord of the Second Advent. God revealed through Chung Gam Nok, before the introduction of Christianity in Korea, that the Messiah would come again, at a later time, in Korea. Today, many scholars have come to ascertain that most of the prophecies written in this book coincide with those in the Bible.[6]

The *Chung Gam Nok* is an apocalyptic work, blending together prophetic utterances with geomancy – the art of discovering auspicious pieces of ground, especially for the purposes of burial or for the establishing of a capital city for a new dynasty. The blend of prophecy and geomancy resulted in a prediction of a new dynasty with a new capital, in accordance with the dictates of heaven. The 'Herald of the Righteous Way' would appear from the 'Southern Ocean' (that is, Korea), and after the apocalyptic catastrophes which would signal the end of the old dynasty, he would establish a new capital in South Korea. This paradise on earth was variously located by different versions of the *Chung Gam Nok*, but two places were popularly identified: one was Chong Up, and the other Mount Kyeryong, which accordingly became the seedbed of many new religious groups.

The Ch'ondogyo expressed the theme of the coming golden age in the following way:

> Then will be the time for Chongdoryong to come to Mt Kyeryong and to unify all nations, all laws, and all teachings by decreeing the Right Way (*chongdo*) for the new heaven on earth . . .
>
> In this new world there will be no cold or hot weather, no poor harvest, no flood, no typhoon, and no diseases. Man will live as long as he wants at the maximum, till 500 years of age at medium, and till 300 years of age at the minimum . . .

There will be things to eat and clothe ourselves, there will be no poor and rich, there will be no need for money and all transactions will be made by barter. The international language will be the Korean language and its alphabet. There will be no other kind of international languages and all dialects will be gone within two or three years. There will be only two hours of day and two hours of night . . .

At Mt Kyeryong there will be built a palace of precious stones and a bank of all nations. In the new world there will be no tax.[7]

It is not clear what advantage accrues to a world which has only two hours of day and two hours of night! The other details, of course, reflect the aspirations of those Koreans who sought for an ideal earth world. In the following passage, Pak Chungbin (also known as Sot'aesan), the founder of Won Buddhism,[8] describes humankind's coming Paradise with even greater precision:

In the coming world . . . more employment agencies will serve those who are looking for jobs, and marriage offices will assist those who wish to get married; a day nursery will be established in many places so that mothers can go out to work without any concern for their children; old people without a protector will live comfortable lives without anxiety at homes for the aged which will be established by the government, by organisations, or by social and charitable workers . . . Life in even the remotest place will be surrounded by the most convenient cultural facilities, a quick cafeteria will provide us with food adequate for our needs, so that we may not have to cook all the time at home; there will be many tailors, dressmakers, and laundries to help people in making their clothes and in doing their laundry.[9]

Kim Minsok, the founder-leader of a small group known as the Eden Cultural Institute, made the following proclamation:

The Lord of Judgement will rule a population of 144 billion people who will be servants to 144,000 electi especially chosen by him. He will rule the world from a palace by television aided by his 12 Apostles and by 12 representatives of the 144 kings of the 144 nations . . . Since all electi will live eternally, reproduction will no longer be needed and the potential members of this elite have to prepare themselves for their function by sterilisation. In the future world all religions will be united and any resistance against unification will be suppressed by supernatural power.[10]

In terms of ideas, the requirement of sterilisation as a means of preparation for a spirit world without reproduction is not without a rationale. It is presupposed that the spirit world in which one will participate at a future time is a mirror-image of the earth world. This belief has its parallel in Unificationism, where it is firmly believed that there are spirits with bodies which are apprehensible with five 'spiritual senses' which are spiritual replications of the five physical senses which we employ in the earth world. Unificationists in fact insist on describing the spirit world as 'the invisible *substantial* world',[11] thus indicating that it is not a semi-real world of ephemera. Members will often describe events and beings in the spirit world in very precise detail.

Like the Eden Cultural Institute, Unificationism discusses the sexuality of spirit bodies and the consequences of sexual acts.[12] Clearly, it is important to claim that sexual activity is possible on the part of spiritual beings, since the Fall is attributed to a sexual relationship between an archangel (Lucifer) and a human (Eve). If it is possible for sexual activity to be performed with spirit bodies, then it is not unreasonable to ascertain the extent to which such activity mirrors sexual relationships in the physical world. *Divine Principle* defends the contention that angels and humans can have sexual encounters,[13] and indeed cites biblical evidence of such occurrences.[14] Unlike the Eden Cultural Institute, sterilisation is, of course, not recommended as a means of preparation for the spirit world. On the contrary, the emphasis on the family entails that members are encouraged to procreate. The Rev Moon strongly encourages members not to practise unnatural forms of contraception:[15] contraceptive measures might prevent the birth of a person whom God has appointed to assume an important role in humanity's restoration.

These new religions' extremely detailed descriptions of the restored earth world must be viewed against the political and cultural background of late nineteenth- and early twentieth-century Korea. After two centuries of imperialist rule and a move into the industrial and technological revolutions, Korean history was scarred by the devastating effects of political struggle and armed conflict. Following closely after the bombings of Hiroshima and Nagasaki, the possibility that the Korean War of 1950–53 would escalate into a nuclear conflict was a very justifiable fear.

It is understandable that some of Korea's religions reflected the fear of wide-scale war, and offered the hope of an era of peace, heralded by a divine emissary, who would establish a righteous government or else collect together a chosen few who had survived general annihilation by a nuclear holocaust. Significantly, Korean messianism does not offer a purely supernatural escape from the earth world: the Kingdom of Heaven is not the

Christian heaven, the Chinese *t'ien*, or the Buddha Amitabha's Pure Land, despite the fact that all three ideas were familiar to the Koreans. On the contrary, the respective messiahs would appear in order to better the present physical world. This betterment would involve a nationalism which sought a recovery of Korea's old identity; yet although technology had created its problems for the Koreans, those religions looked to technology to solve the problems of the age, culminating in an eschaton in which science and technology became 'unified' with religion. Unification became a major theme, and the quest for the unification of all religions became a dominant feature of the messianic movements.

It is clear that Unificationism has affinities with those new religious groups which I have mentioned. Although more theologically sophisticated than the Eden Cultural Institute, it nevertheless offers a similar hope of a new era when God will rule, religions will be unified and a unity of science and religion achieved. As Young Oon Kim wrote in her early version of *The Divine Principles*:

> In this Golden Age, the highly advanced scientific achievement of the Occident will serve to make the external life of the New World convenient and pleasant. And the highly advanced religious and metaphysical achievement of the Orient will provide the philosophy of the New Age. Thus the New Age will see perfect harmony between the cultures of the East and West. The unified one world will be fulfilled horizontally between the Occident and the Orient, and also vertically between the spiritual and physical worlds. In this unified world all nations will live in harmonious associations with all others, and share a common religious philosophy under God's direct guidance. This New Age will no longer be regarded as the 'Christian Era.' Instead, it will be known as the Cosmic Era with the adoption of a Cosmic Calendar.[16]

Thus Unificationism possesses features which are common to the new religious groups under discussion. It brings a new interpretation of scripture, and it is dissatisfied with the mainstream Christian message that Jesus Christ brought full salvation to the human situation. It proclaims a founder-leader who will herald the new age, and, above all, it proclaims the message of unification. Unificationism has been emphatic about the need for a reconciliation between science and religion, and it is significant that where it rejects the miraculous elements of mainstream Christianity it does so partly on the grounds that it is impossible for modern people to believe them, but also by reasoning that God, having established certain fixed laws, would not alter them thereafter.[17] (This last idea probably owes more to Confucianism than to Christianity.) Thus it teaches that the Virgin Birth did not literally occur, since this is contrary to the known laws of human biology; there was no physical resurrection of Jesus, since we know that bodies, once dead, do not rise; Christ will not return on the clouds, since this is scientifically impossible. The far-reachingness of the attempt to reconcile science and religion is possibly reflected in its playing down of miraculous healings, when spiritual healing is a common feature of Korea's new religions. Unificationism does not deny the possibility of spiritual healing, but healings tend to be phenomena which happen to individuals rather than actions performed through the agency of designated healers. There are no services or ceremonies in which a ministry of healing is offered. Unificationists to whom I have spoken about healing tend to view it as a phenomenon which is consistent with scientific or spiritual laws, but which awaits rational explanation.

## THE PRECURSORS OF UNIFICATIONISM

Of the many New Christian groups, five are of particular significance to the rise of Unificationism, and these must now be considered. The UC teaches that each group occupies a *position* in the restoration drama.[18] Two West Coast groups and two East Coast groups represent the sides of Lucifer and Eve respectively, with two western and two eastern groups each representing the stages of 'Formation' and 'Growth', with the Unification Church as the 'Completion' stage.[19] The various interactions which are alleged to have taken place between the groups are interpreted in terms of the East Coast groups occupying the *position* of the Archangel who goes to Eve (West Coast group). The group in the 'Eve' *position* must then find the Third Adam, the Lord of the Second Advent, who has come to Korea to establish the new restored age.

### (1) The Holy Lord Church *(Songjugyo)*

The Holy Lord Church (or 'Sacred Lord Church') was one of the West Coast religious groups. It emerged in Chulsan in North Korea, and was led by a Mrs Kim Seongdo. Kim Seongdo was converted to Christianity in the early 1920s, but was extremely disturbed when her pastor entered into an extra-marital sexual relationship. She prayed hard to find out not only the root of her pastor's sin, but the cause of sin in general. She is stated to have prayed regularly from one o'clock at night until mid-morning. Jesus himself is said to have appeared to her, and taught her that the origin of sin was adultery, not the eating of a fruit in the Garden of Eden, and that his blood shed on the cross could rectify this. These two events, the Fall and the crucifixion, were the two great sadnesses of God. However, the restoration of Eden on earth was now awaited: Korea would be liberated from Japan (the exact date of the liberation apparently was revealed to Mrs Kim), and through Korea the world would be restored by a new messiah, who would appear in physical form to complete Jesus' unfinished work. This coming Lord would establish a new blood lineage, and all who were to receive him had to purify mind and body. To do this, one had to abstain from any kind of sexual activity, even within marriage. (The Rev Moon has stated that Mrs Kim's eldest son had intercourse with his own wife, who supposedly died as a consequence.)[20] Men and women should not marry, because no human marriages are true marriages. Once Eden was restored, humankind would no longer be under Satan's dominion, and men and women would no longer be ashamed of their nakedness. Because the Holy Lord Church believed that meat-eating intensified sexual desires, members were invariably vegetarian.

The Holy Lord Church was founded in 1935. It is possible that, at least on one occasion, the notion of being naked and unashamed was incorporated into public worship. Mrs Eu, the wife of the first President of the Unification Church, gives the following testimony:

> The university and the established churches thought that we danced in the nude, because they saw that some of the important points of the Divine Principle were similar to the teachings of the Holy Lord Church, and they thought that this church had come south and was now operating in Seoul.[21]

According to her grandson, Mrs Kim Seongdo stated in her last will and testament:

> In the future when there is a group or church persecuted because of sexual accusations go there and check because it could be the place of the Second Advent.[22]

Following the Rev Moon's arrest in 1955, which was a consequence of the incidents to which Mrs Eu refers, members of the Holy Lord Church concluded that Mrs Kim Seongdo's testament referred to the Rev Moon's church. The entire congregation therefore forfeited its identity in order to merge with Sun Myung Moon's Holy Spirit Association for the Unification of World Christianity.

## (2) The 'Inside Belly' Church *(Bokjunggyo)*

The 'Inside Belly' Church (Korean name, *Bokjunggyo*) emerged in Pyongyang. The precise date of its inception is uncertain, but it was some time after 1935, and was undoubtedly in existence between 1940 and 1947. Mrs Ho Bin had been a follower of Mrs Kim, and a member of the Holy Lord Church: indeed, the Inside Belly Church was established as the Pyongyang branch of the Holy Lord Church. The Rev Moon states that the group was 1000-strong, and had prepared a bride ready for the Lord of the Second Advent, as well as 'twelve plus seventy' disciples.[23] They had bought the best house in Pyongyang to provide an appropriate environment for him to raise a sinless family.

The remarkable name of this church derives from the fact that the leader, Mrs Ho Ho Bin, felt as if she were pregnant. Although it is sometimes suggested that she believed herself to be the mother of the returning Christ, the Rev Moon has explained that her false pregnancy was no more than a sign that the Lord of the Second Advent would be born of human parentage, rather than return on the clouds of heaven. Be that as it may, whenever Mrs Ho believed she was about to receive revelations from heaven, she felt as if the unborn child was moving inside her womb.

Mrs Ho's principal revelation was that when Jesus was alive he had a particularly difficult lot compared with his brothers and sisters. This was due to a problematic relationship between Mary, Joseph and Jesus, since Joseph was not Jesus' natural father. Because of this, Jesus was not provided with sufficient food and clothing, and as a result felt deep sorrow that his family should treat him in this way; as a consequence of parental lack of provision, he did not fully accomplish his mission, which awaited fulfilment by a Lord of the Second Advent.

Mrs Ho prophesied that the returned Lord had now come and was 15 or 16 years old. This new messiah must not receive the treatment which was accorded to the first. Consequently, Mrs Ho's followers were instructed to prepare sets of beautiful garments and foods, two sets of each kind, one for Jesus and one for the new messiah who was now on earth.

Different accounts provide slightly different details, but their substance is the same.[24] Clothes were to be made for each year of Jesus' life, from birth to the age of 33 (the age at which he died), and the directions for the preparation of the garments were extremely precise. Members would pray all night, take cold showers in the morning and receive spiritual direction, sometimes from Mrs Ho, and sometimes, it is said, from Jesus himself. They were directed, for example, to go to a particular shop and be the first to enter; they must purchase a specified piece of material, without haggling. (It is unusual not to haggle in Korea.) In the sanctified work room, stitches had to be sewn in multiples of three: every three stitches would be tied together, and the seamstress would pray before resuming work, continuing throughout in similar manner. No one was permitted to stand up or to visit the toilet during a sewing session. The sizes of the garments were revealed by heaven and any mistakes which were made were believed to bring severe chastisement from heaven to the negligent seamstress.

Twice weekly,[25] festivities were held to overcome the grief which Jesus had felt at his lack of proper food. A place was set for Jesus, and it was customary to bow many times before Jesus' place on entering the room. Appropriate numbers of bows were 300 or 3000, the Rev Moon relates. It took a total of ten hours to complete 3000 bows, and some devotees reportedly collapsed in the process. One man, a Mr Hwan, out of extreme devotion, bowed a total of 5000 times in the course of one evening. He was later to meet Sun Myung Moon and to prove instrumental in his mission.

When Korea was liberated in 1945, Kim Il Sung and the communists took over the North. The police in Pyongyang raided the Inside Belly Church, arrested all its members and confiscated the sacred garments. The members were imprisoned at Pyongyang. Sun Myung Moon, at this time also in prison, shared a cell with Mr Hwan, amongst others. Mr Hwan felt drawn to Sun Myung Moon, although he had not entertained the belief that he was in the presence of the Lord of the Second Advent. Mr Hwan told him about the Inside Belly Church, and Sun Myung Moon instructed Mr Hwan to renounce his beliefs and thus secure his (Hwan's) release. Learning that Mrs Ho was also in prison, he attempted to pass a note to her, using a fish bone as a pen, an old piece of cloth for paper, and a mixture of dust and saliva for ink. He asked Mrs Ho to pray about the nature of the author of this note, to renounce her faith and so secure her freedom. Apparently she did not pray: the note was discovered, Mrs Ho was shot, and Sun Myung Moon was severely tortured.

## (3) Paek Namju and the *Jesugyo* (East Coast)

Meanwhile, other New Christian groups were paving the way for a new messiah. In the Wonsan area in the East, Paek Namju, a professor at the Women's Seminary in Wonsan, had become renowned as a charismatic preacher. We know little of his religious group, except that it was apparently instrumental in setting up the Inside Belly Church and a group called the New Jesus Church. Paek Namju was given a revelation that he must go to Chulsan to meet Mrs Kim and follow her. He obeyed the vision, and, according to one testimony,[26] made a pilgrimage barefoot of no less than 130 miles. (Mrs Hong, the mother of Hak Ja Han, the Rev Moon's wife, apparently belonged to Mrs Kim's congregation.) Paek Namju and Mrs Kim met, and the former began to believe Mrs Kim's revelations.

The relationship between these two religious leaders was not to last, however, for it seems that Paek Namju quarrelled with the members of the Holy Lord Church and parted company with them. His place as leader was taken by Mr Lee Yongdo, a Methodist pastor. In 1932, Paek Namju had invited Lee Yongdo to Wonsan, and thus the 'New Jesus Church' (*Jesugyo*) was established.[27] It is reported that Paek Namju engaged in sexual practices which were given religious significance. One woman in Mr Paek's group reportedly received a revelation that Mr Paek was the new Lord and that he would beget a child by means of a virgin. The arrival of this child, understandably, was a matter of some embarrassment, and Mr Paek, formerly taken to task by Christian orthodoxy exclusively on doctrinal matters, was now the subject of accusations of sexual misconduct. An alternative explanation of his 130–mile journey to meet Mrs Kim is that it was an attempt to flee from the ensuing scandal.

## (4) The Mysticism of Lee Yongdo (East Coast)

A special significance is attached to Lee Yongdo, since he is said to have died of tuberculosis at the age of 33, the same age at which Jesus was crucified. Lee Yongdo was a famous Korean mystic and a revivalist preacher who undertook evangelical tours throughout Korea. Until the last year of his life, when he began to incur charges of heresy, he was afforded a platform by various Christian denominations. According to one mainstream Christian source, Lee's congregation engaged in ritual nudity during public worship and Sun Myung Moon participated as a regular attender.[28] As we shall see, however, there is cause to doubt this testimony.

Lee suffered from constant ill-health, and at the age of 25 developed a serious lung disorder. While convalescing at the home-town of a friend, he accepted the invitation from the local population to preach in the village church. When he came to preach the sermon, however, he was unable to speak and could only weep in the pulpit. Overcome with emotion, the congregation wept also. Lee believed that words could not encapsulate the mystical relationship which he experienced with God; as he once said, 'Speak not: that is my motto.'[29] The relationship could only be described as one of unity, or else expressed in erotic imagery which employed the symbol of a bride's sexual desire for her bridegroom.

The following words of Lee Yongdo exemplify these respective ways of expressing his relationship with God.

> O, the principle of unity, wherein I am engulfed in the Lord's love, and wherein the Lord is swallowed in my faith! O my eye, look only at my Lord with your whole heart. Let us simply concentrate our whole heart and mind on our Lord, without gazing around. The Lord, captured by my sight, will live peacefully in myself.[30]
>
> Lo, seek and search for the Lord's love, through deep thought and desire day and night. In this way, enter the inner room of love. That is the holy place of love. There, discern the true identity of the Lord. There, make songs about love, in the place which is splendid and bright, like Solomon's brocades.[31]

Lee, however, subsequently developed a new metaphor for describing his mystical relationship with God, the metaphor of 'blood blending with the Lord', and identified himself with the suffering Christ:

> Cry, holy man! Cry, holy woman! Where is Gethsemane? It is waiting for my tears of blood . . . O, the person who is making a red robe for me, . . . who is making a crown of thorns for me . . . [32]

Lee's apparent identification of himself with Jesus incurred the censure of the mainstream churches, and it was possibly on account of such opposition that he reluctantly had to found his own religious group. This was done together with another Korean mystic called Hwang Kukju, who had led his own New Christian group. According to Kyong Bae Min, a mainstream Christian historian, this religious leader grew his hair and beard in an attempt to look like Jesus and claimed that his neck (*sic*) had been cut and replaced by Jesus' own neck. He claimed, 'My head is Jesus' head, my blood is Jesus' blood, and my heart is Jesus' heart . . . I have been completely transformed into Jesus Christ.'[33] Hwang had claimed that there was a similarity between religious trance-experience and sexual ecstacy, and, Min comments,

> he established a prayer house in Samgak mountain, and taught the change of neck and of blood, in doctrine and in practice; the process of these changes was called the realisation of the exchange of spiritual body, but the reality of it was adultery.[34]

Notice, incidentally, that Min, being a mainstream Christian, finds himself unable to distinguish between a practice of ritualised sex and the promiscuous sex of adultery.

When these New Christian mystics founded the *Jesugyo*, Lee Yongdo co-operated, but only under protest:

> 'I am ready to die. But please don't let this thing (the foundation of a new church) come to pass. How can the beloved people be separated from one another, and how can the Church of Your body be divided?'

> 'O how painful it is for my name to be called that of the founder of a new Church!'[35]

Although it is clear from this account that the religious groups of Paek Namju and Lee Yongdo were in effect the same, the UC's treatment of them as two separate groups clearly lends credence to the theology of history which they wish to develop with respect to the position of the UC. According to the Rev Moon, it was God's will that Lee Yongdo's *Jesugyo* should unite with the Inside Belly Church, signifying a re-enactment of the Archangel going to Eve. This did not occur: ' . . . by failing to accomplish the unification of these two groups, God had to have a new movement, and pioneer a new field.'[36] Thus Sun Myung Moon tells us that when Lee died in 1932, his spirit passed to one Kim Baek Moon, who began a new group, known as the Israel Monastery.[37]

## (5) The Israel Monastery

Situated on the west coast of Korea, near Seoul, the Israel Monastery is still in existence, although now known by a different name, the *Ch'eongsugyo* ('Pure Water Church'). Kim gave substantially the same teachings about the Fall as the Unification Church subsequently embraced, namely that the Fall was the result of a sexual act between Lucifer and Eve, and that restoration could take place through blood purification.

Kim Baek Moon wrote two books, *Theology of the Holy Ghost (Sungshin Shinhak*, 1954) and *The Basic Principle of Christianity (Kidokkyo Keunbon Wolli*, 1958).[38] The latter work is a collection of lectures delivered over a period of three years. It has been alleged that the original *Divine Principle* of the Rev Sun Myung Moon is plagiarised from the writings of Kim Baek Moon.[39] Unificationists claim, on the other hand, that Kim Baek Moon received a revelation of the contents of Sun Myung Moon's thought, but did not act upon them. In view of the fact that Sun Myung Moon had completed his first version of the *Principle* in 1952, and Kim's writings were not published until after the UC's formation, the accusation of plagiarism, I think, can be discounted. However, Sun Myung Moon was himself a member of the Israel Monastery during the period 1945–46, and any similarities can no doubt be explained by the close relationship between the two men. Sun Myung Moon was commissioned to head a branch of the Israel Monastery in Pyongyang; previously the Israel Monastery had existed as a retreat in the countryside. It was this branch of the Israel Monastery which is sometimes referred to as the *Kwang Hae* Church',[40] often translated as the 'Church of the Ocean of Light'. I am informed that this translation rests upon a misunderstanding: the church had no official name, it appears, and the word 'Kwangya', meaning 'wilderness', was used simply to indicate that the church did not have official buildings and that members met out in the open.

It appears that within the Israel Monastery Sun Myung Moon expected to be accorded a higher status than he was given.[41] Kim had the opportunity to testify to his messianic status, acting in the *position* of the new John the Baptist.[42] Kim did not testify, and just as John the Baptist was untrue to Jesus and doubted his messianic mission, the Israel Monastery is held to have done the same with respect to the Rev Moon. Sun Myung Moon was therefore unable to continue within the Israel Monastery.

## RELATIONSHIPS TO THE UC

It can be seen how these New Christian groups culminated in the formation of the Holy Spirit Association for the Unification of World Christianity. All of them based their teachings on visions, dreams and revelations from the spirit world. They offered a new interpretation of the Christian scriptures, and construed Adam and Eve's Fall as a sexual crime which demanded restoration, involving blood purification. They claimed that Jesus Christ did not completely accomplish this restoration, and that a second messiah was needed, who would herald an earth-worldly utopia in which unification would be accomplished. Humankind must play its part in this restoration process, and in many cases stringent demands were made of their followers, in order to restore the wrongs which fallen humankind had done. Thus, in the case of the Inside Belly Church, the sewing of garments and preparation of meals for Jesus is not viewed by UC members as obsessive fanaticism, but rather as an attempt to make amends ('pay indemnity') for the shameful treatment which Jesus received during his lifetime; only by appropriate deeds on the part of humankind is restoration possible. Since the Fall was physical as well as spiritual, external as well as internal acts are required to accomplish a restoration.

The close association between the Unification Church and those movements which practised ritual nudity gave rise to allegations that the UC itself engaged in similar practices, or used sexual intercourse as a means of blood purification. In the early days of the Unification Church, in 1954, the Rev Moon and his followers resided in a small house in Seoul, which had only two very small rooms with a small kitchen. The house was popularly called the 'House of Three Doors' and it was rumoured that at the first door one was made to take off one's jacket, at the second one's outer clothing, and at the third everything else, whereupon the entrant was expected to commit adultery or fornication in the inner apartment. A story is told of one female seeker who, mindful of such rumours, went along wearing no less than seven layers of clothes, with copious undergarments securely pinned together, in order to frustrate any attempts which might be made to undress her. [43]

## CRITICAL APPRAISAL

Having outlined the received tradition of the emergence of the Unification Church, some critical appraisal of the evidence is required. The material we possess concerning these precursors of Unificationism comes from a variety of sources, and it is difficult to determine the extent to which these derive from eye-witnesses and members, or whether they merely reflect the tradition which has grown up within the Unification Church itself. The sources are these. First, we have testimonies from members: the giving of testimonies is regarded as an important spiritual activity in Unificationist circles, and many Korean members have set on record their early days of seeking amongst various spiritual groups and their initial contacts with the HSA-UWC. Particularly when these are early UC members, their testimonies have been transcribed by amanuenses, who in some cases have simultaneously translated the testimony from Korean into English. Second, we have the speeches of Sun Myung Moon, who has given an extended account of these groups, together with the theological significance they bear for the UC. Sun Myung Moon was not himself a member of the West Coast groups, but had access to Mr Hwan's testimony in prison, and it is a reasonable supposition that his wife, Hak Ja Han, and Mrs Hong, her mother, who belonged to the Holy Lord Church and subsequently the Inside Belly Church, could furnish him with information. [44]

The sources appear to be intertwined, however. Mr Son Deh Oh, in giving his testimony, cross-refers to a testimony (which is not available) by Mrs Hong, regarding the Inside Belly Church. Other testifiers incorporate Sun Myung Moon's theologisation about the significance of these groups and thus reveal that their testimonies are coloured in hindsight by the UC tradition. One testifier is the grandson of Kim Seongdo, the leader of the Holy Lord Church: his testimony is therefore highly valuable, but it contains similar colouration. The theological significance accorded to such groups may therefore cause UC members to portray them in the most favourable light possible, and we have to bear this in mind.

All the evidence regarding the Holy Lord Church and the Inside Belly Church comes from Unificationist sources, and appears to have no external corroboration. None of the testimonies are eye-witness accounts, although at least some of the early members and Sun Myung Moon himself had direct and sustained connections with leaders of the Holy Lord Church, and, in the case of the latter, the Inside Belly Church. The evidence concerning the church of Paek Namju, the *Jesugyo* and the Israel Monastery fares better: orthodox Christian sources refer to the first two of these movements, and the Rev Moon was certainly directly acquainted with the Israel Monastery. One should not give automatic credence to mainstream Christian sources, however: although free from any risk of pious legend which enhances the T'ongil movement,[45] conversely, they may well be biased against Unificationism and prone to display it in the least favourable light. Unification members are insistent that these Christian sources are less than reliable, and point to inaccuracies and inconsistencies which they generate.

The testimonies on which I have drawn do not support the view that Unificationism was originally a sexual cult and that initiation of female members into the UC involved a ritual sexual relationship with its founder-leader. The practice of sexual initiation, which may have been practised by certain New Christian groups, was known as *p'i kareun*, which means, literally, 'blood purification'. Essentially, the practice consisted of a female neophyte engaging in ritual sexual intercourse with the messianic leader, in order to restore – either literally or symbolically – the sexual purity of the woman. The woman would then have intercourse with her husband, thus restoring his sexual purity and hence the purity of their progeny. The practice appears to be based on the notion that the Fall was a sexual crime, and that restoration can only be accomplished by re-enacting the Fall in the correct ('principled') manner, the female partner representing Eve and the messianic male partner the new Adam. The first sexual act could be interpreted as a re-enactment of the Spiritual Fall, with the leader in the *position* of Lucifer and the woman in the *position* of Eve. The restored Eve would then go to her husband, who occupied the *position* of Adam, and restore the Physical Fall by initiating a 'principled' sexual relationship.

None of the sources which attribute this practice to the UC can claim to be first-hand sources, and the UC's founder-members emphatically deny such allegations. One of the founder-leaders to whom I spoke described such testimonies as 'Christian lies'! There are few testimonies which could conceivably appear to associate the UC with these ritual sexual practices. One is that of Mrs Eu, which has already been cited, but Mrs Eu describes ritual nudity, not a sexual initiation rite, and insists that it was practised within the Holy Lord Church and not the UC. A second testimony concerns Sun Myung Moon's possible involvement with Lee Yongdo's New Jesus Church which I mentioned earlier. It comes from the testimony of Mr Young Bok Chun:

> It is said that Moon was 16 years old when he received the revelation that he was the prophet raised up by God. At that time (1936) there were several ecstatic and messianic movements in Korea, and especially a Methodist pastor called *Young Do Lee* seems to have influenced Moon. I often went to these meetings when I was young. The pastor was an enthusiastic and eloquent preacher and advocated a peculiar interpretation of the Bible. During the meetings he used to roll up a newspaper and go around saying, 'Satan, get out! Satan, get out!' while the congregation was praying in a state of ecstatic shaking.
>
> This movement advocated the so-called 'restoration of the original state' before the fall of Adam and Eve. The congregation was dancing around and crying for the return of Eden. And when the pastor cried, 'Adam and Eve were naked before the fall! Take off your clothes!' the men turned to the women and stripped off their clothes, and they danced around naked.
>
> His doctor had predicted that Mr. Lee would die of tuberculosis within a short time, but he continued his evangelistic work for more than ten years and had a considerable impact on the churches in Korea. Moon came to him in 1936 and was deeply influenced by him and other charismatic leaders. The movement was suppressed and the leaders were scattered, but Moon, who was a member of the group, brought with him the idea of the return to Eden.[46]

Chun's testimony creates problems, not least of which is his chronology. Chun gives 1936 as the approximate date of Sun Myung Moon's contacts with the *Jesugyo*, naming Lee Yongdo as the pastor, despite the latter's statement that Lee died in 1932, and the overwhelming agreement amongst other sources (UC and mainstream Christian) that Lee Yongdo died in 1933. If Lee died in 1933, Sun Myung Moon could only have been 13 at the most when he met Lee, and it is surprising that Chun should have noticed his presence in the congregation, since he would not have achieved public recognition at that stage. Chun's claim that Lee lived after 1936 is implausible: although it might be suggested that the story of his death at the same age as Jesus was a pious legend created in his memory, to deny it is to contradict the overwhelming testimony of both Unificationist and mainstream Christian sources.

There is some difficulty, however, in reconciling the 1933 date of Lee's death with the UC belief that God willed the *Jesugyo* to unite with the Inside Belly Church. The year 1933 is an implausibly early date for the existence of the latter. Mrs Ho's revelation, that the Lord of the Second Advent was now 15 or 16 years old, sets the commencement date at around 1936. This is the *terminus ante quem*, however, and other evidence suggests a later date: for example, the Rev Moon states that their preparations of clothes lasted seven years, and we know that the leaders were in prison together with Sun Myung Moon in the period 1947–48. This would make the early 1940s a much more plausible date for its existence.

It is difficult to be sure where the truth lies here. Since Lee Yongdo probably did not live to witness the rise of the Inside Belly Church, the claim that God willed a union with the *Jesugyo* must refer to the continuation of this 'Jesus movement' after Lee's death: as we have seen, Lee was only one of a number of co-founders of this organisation, and indeed Kim Baek Moon's 'Israel Monastery' is sometimes referred to as *Jesugyo*.

Mrs Eu's testimony is much less of a problem than Chun's. Being a Unificationist, her testimony attributing ritual nudity to a religious group which had historical connections with the UC seems likely to be true. Having said this, however, it is necessary to clear up some important confusions regarding ritual sexual practices. Because ritual sexual practices are unknown in mainstream Christian circles, Christians tend to view any sexual relationship outside matrimony as adultery or fornication. However, *p'i kareun* is not to be equated with promiscuity, and, for any group that practised it, it was a once-only rite effecting or symbolising restoration; it was certainly not a sex orgy. *P'i kareun* is also to be distinguished from ritual nudity, a practice of the Holy Lord Church and possibly the *Jesugyo*. Neither Mrs Eu's nor Chun's testimony concerns ritual sex.

Other writers who assert connections between the UC and *p'i kareun* appear to rely on second- or third-hand sources which they do not evaluate. Thus the evangelical writer James Bjornstad writes:

> Rev. Won II Chei [*sic*], a leading Presbyterian minister in Seoul, says, 'If we believe those who have gone into this group and come out, they say that one has to receive Sun Myung Moon's blood to receive salvation. That blood is ordinarily received by three periods of sexual intercourse.'[47]

Bjornstad is in fact quoting another anti-cult writer, William J. Petersen,[48] who quotes 'Won II Chei' but cites no source. Neither writer discusses whether the blood was real or symbolic (as in the Christian eucharist), whether the sexual act was with the messianic leader or with one's spouse, or whether the latter rite was congregational or private. We are left to assume the worst. Chei claims no first-hand knowledge or access to eye-witness testimony, and it is likely that he is relying on no more than rumours relating to the Rev Moon's arrest in 1955. He ignores the point that the sexual charge against the Rev Moon was dropped, and the fact that the single charge which was brought to court was violation of the national draft law, for which Sun Myung Moon was acquitted.[49] The same must be said of Kyong Bae Min's allegations.

Which groups, if any, practised *p'i kareun* is unclear. Rainer Flasche asserts that the Israel Monastery engaged in this practice,[50] but offers no supportive evidence. Although Chun accuses the Unification Church of *p'i kareun*, we have seen reason to doubt his testimony, and he presents only unsubstantiated allegations at best. Professor Kyong Bae Min suggests that Lee Yongdo's notion of 'blood blending with the Lord' is 'the historical source of the so-called "blood changing" (*p'i kareun*) of Korea',[51] yet the Church is merely reported to have practised nude dancing during worship, not sexual initiation.

Allegations concerning the practice of *p'i kareun* have been made variously, as we have seen, against, the Holy Lord Church, the *Jesugyo* and indeed the Unification Church itself. Although it is impossible to identify which groups engaged in this practice, it is clear that *p'i kareun* was a religious practice, otherwise it is difficult to see why the name should exist at all in the Korean language. It seems unlikely, however, that the ritual was particularly prevalent.

Any connection between Unificationism and the practice of *p'i kareun* seems initially surprising in view of its absolute prohibition on any sexual relationships outside matrimony. Indeed, the UC can more plausibly be criticised for being sexually repressive than for sexual licentiousness, especially in view of the long separation period for 'purification' between the selection of marriage partners by the Rev Moon and the consummation of the marriage.[52] It is certainly not plausible to suggest that the Unification Church today attempts to secure the restoration of humanity through sexual intercourse with its leader: not even a messiah could have sexual relationships with 8000 brides!

It is important to realise that *p'i kareun* is (or was) a religious ritual, and is not be construed as resembling the feudal practice of the lord's statutory right to possess a servant's bride on her wedding night. Precisely which, if any, of the New Christian groups practised *p'i kareun* will continue to be a subject of controversy, but there is no evidence to support the allegation that the UC ever engaged in this practice. It is a fundamental principle of justice that an accused party is presumed innocent unless proved guilty.

It is more likely that the practice of *p'i kareun* was known to Sun Myung Moon and the founder members of the Holy Spirit Association for the Unification of World Christianity, and that the Rev Moon shared the underlying belief that the changing of blood lineage was a prerequisite for salvation, teaching that the lineage is restored through sexual activity. This, I believe, is one reason for the UC's strong emphasis on the centrality of the Blessing and its accompanying ceremonies. However, the restoration process entails 'principled' sexual relationships solely within the confines of marriage. It is possible that the UC's accusers are simply malicious; a more charitable explanation is that early rumours about the UC conflated the practice of *p'i kareun* (which involved a sexual act between the neophyte and the leader) with a prescribed set of sexual practices which are only carried out by husband and wife after they have been blessed in marriage.

Bearing in mind the problematic nature of the sources, it is possible to draw the following firm conclusions. First, there were numerous New Christian groups in existence prior to the formation of the Unification Church, and there is no reason to doubt that Hak Ja Han's mother and Sun Myung Moon had contact with some of them, particularly the Israel Monastery. The New Christian groups were characterised by an attempt to present an understanding of Christian teachings, but in a form which was not wholly acceptable to mainstream Christianity. The new teachings were said to come through revelations, either directly from Jesus himself, or from other members of the spirit world; accordingly, great emphasis was placed on contact with spirits, and also on dreams and visions. In particular, they claimed that Jesus Christ had not fully accomplished his mission, that a new messiah was needed and his imminent arrival in Korea was to be expected. Members endeavoured to prepare for the messiah's arrival, both internally and by external religious practice; and they emphasised the need to restore humanity's past acts of omission which they believed had caused the first messiah's mission to be incomplete. When this Lord of the Second Advent came, he would herald a restoration of Eden, and restore the fallen nature of humankind, which had resulted from Adam and Eve's sexual misconduct.

One final point deserves mention. In the last three chapters I have attempted to show how Unificationism developed from the interaction between the various indigenous faiths of Korea and the advent of Christianity and how this interaction led to the formation of various New Christian groups which appear to draw on several sources for their teachings. The Unification Church is particularly sensitive about being characterised as 'syncretistic', and of course it is certainly not the case that the Rev Moon deliberately created a faith which is no more than an amalgam of the existing religious ideas which were locally available. There is certainly material in *Divine Principle* which is new: for example, the concepts of *hyung sang* and *sung sang* are not simply new names for *yin* and *yang*; the doctrine of the Four Position Foundation does not have an obvious precursor; the finding of historical parallels running from biblical history through to modern Christian history is, as far as I am aware, a new doctrinal development. There is therefore a significant amount of creative innovation within Unification thought. Unificationists themselves, of course, would even question the appropriateness of the phrase 'creative innovation', for this implies that the theological creativity was solely the work of the Rev Moon. What appears to be creative innovation to the outsider is for them new revelation, for the *Principle* is held not to come from the Rev Moon, but rather from God himself.

# 6  Jesus in Unification Thought

We have seen how the New Christian groups in Korea looked to a new messiah to establish the Kingdom of Heaven on earth. It is therefore appropriate to examine how the Unification Church regards the respective roles of Jesus Christ and Sun Myung Moon. How is the role of Jesus understood in Unification thought? What gives the Unification teaching about Jesus the credibility which it possesses in Unificationist circles? What comparisons and contrasts are to be drawn between the UC's interpretation of Jesus and that of mainstream Christianity?

A story is told of an early Korean seeker whose deep faith caused her prayers to be answered immediately. The Rev Moon instructed her to ask God whom he loved more – the whole of humanity, or Sun Myung Moon. The woman hesitated, but, having great respect for the Rev Moon, did so. Much to her surprise, God replied, 'I love Sun Myung Moon more than all of humankind together.' She reported her answer to the Rev Moon, who gave her a further instruction: she must pray, asking Heaven whom God loved more – Jesus Christ or Sun Myung Moon. Thinking this an even more improper subject for prayer, she hesitated even further. This time she fell ill, and concluded that her hesitation was the cause. She prayed as instructed, and received a vision by way of an answer. The Rev Moon and Jesus were standing in front of her, with God, present in spirit, standing between them. God began to move towards Sun Myung Moon, and, as he got closer, merged into him and disappeared.[1]

In actual fact, relatively few stories of this kind circulate in Unificationist circles, but they are alighted upon with alacrity by the anti-cult lobby as conclusive evidence that the UC holds that Sun Myung Moon has supplanted Jesus Christ. It is popular belief that the role of Jesus is downgraded in Unification thought: the usual outsider's interpretation of UC theology is that Jesus' mission was a failure, ending in crucifixion, and that Sun Myung Moon has supplanted Jesus' role, succeeding where the former has failed. It is often believed that in UC circles the word 'Christ' refers to Sun Myung Moon, and it is therefore a plausible leap to conclude that the Rev Moon is an object of devotion: the formula, 'In the name of the True Parents', which concludes members' prayers can easily be regarded as an act of devotion towards the Rev and Mrs Moon. Such an interpretation of UC theology has a superficial plausibility, but it is based on external speculation, and

108

those who impose such interpretations on Unificationism seldom, if ever, take the trouble to check this understanding of the respective roles of Jesus and Sun Myung Moon with the Unification Church's own explanations of its theology.

I have explained how, in Unificationist thought, humanity's situation can only be restored through the sending of a messiah. A messiah, it is stated, must have certain specific qualifications: he must be free from original sin, he must come from a chosen nation, he must have good ancestors, he must have a natural disposition for the task, he must make specific preparation ('setting conditions') for his mission during his lifetime, and he must be the person who is best suited to accomplish God's purpose.[2] There may be several candidates whom God prepares simultaneously, and from whom God will select the one who will perform the messianic mission: human beings can fail, and therefore it is necessary for God to make contingency plans to compensate for human error. Some Unificationists to whom I have spoken believe that around the time of Sun Myung Moon's birth God prepared a total of twelve potential messiahs in Korea, and that the Rev Moon was the one who was in the best *position* to accomplish the messianic task.

According to Unification theology a messiah is a human being and is not to be identified with God himself. Nevertheless it is taught that Jesus is 'one body with God' and (at least until the death of the Rev Moon's son Heung Jin) a unique son of God. It may readily but wrongly be concluded that Jesus' state of perfection is not qualitatively different from the state towards which all humanity should be striving. The Rev Moon himself sometimes seems to interpret his own messianic status in this way, as Mose Durst, the President of the UC in America, records:

When Reverend Moon was asked, 'Are you the Messiah?' he said, 'Look, you be the Messiah, I'll be the Messiah, let the man next to me be the Messiah, let's all work to be the Messiah. Let's all take seriously the messianic calling, for God is looking for someone to respond to His vision . . . . We want to be the sons and daughters of God by sharing God's suffering, by sharing his desire, by sharing His hope, by sharing His will, and by sharing His love.'[3]

As I understand it, the situation is this. Jesus attained the highest state of individual perfection which was possible. When it is stated that Jesus Christ opened Paradise what is meant is that his death made it possible for humans and spirits to advance beyond the 'Formation' stage of spiritual development into the 'Growth' stage. Corresponding to the three stages of growth through which God intends humanity to pass there are three stages of spiritual development in the spirit world: 'form spirit', 'life spirit' and 'divine spirit'. Below these three stages are spirits who occupy the 'unprincipled realm' or 'hell'. Mainstream Christianity has often spoken of hell, Paradise and the Kingdom of Heaven as if these were spiritual places: people 'enter' the Kingdom of Heaven, or are 'cast into' hell. However, it would be inaccurate to view the Unificationist account of these states in the spirit world as some kind of spiritual geography. The various states refer to degrees of spiritual development, not to separately compartmentalised sections which the various spirits inhabit. However, it is believed that there is a spiritual 'law of attraction': it would be natural for form spirits to wish to associate with other form spirits, life spirits with other life spirits, and evil spirits with other evil spirits. Thus segregation of different levels of spirit is something which is believed to happen naturally within the spirit world. When Jesus opened up Paradise, what is understood by Unificationists is that he made it possible to attain the status of 'life spirit', and led the way for the rest of humanity to attain this status. Thus what Jesus attained is to be attained by everyone, and in this respect Jesus is not regarded as unique. Unlike other mortals, however, Jesus Christ was born without original sin, being of a 'purified blood lineage', and although such a state is not equivalent to godhead, it is nevertheless a state which is not shared with other human beings.

Jesus was thus a man, and not God himself. He was not born of a virgin: Mary had experienced a sexual relationship with another man before marrying Joseph. One UC source names Zacharias as the father,[4] but this is not generally agreed by members. Whatever is believed to have happened, several things can be stated with confidence about the UC's position. First, Jesus was conceived under the guidance of the Holy Spirit, and was not the progeny of a casual promiscuous relationship which Mary subsequently regretted.[5] Second, it is held that Jesus' illegitimate birth caused strained relationships within his immediate family, as will be explained. God's intention was that the messiah would take a bride when he reached the appropriate age, 'restore' her, marry her, and beget sinless children.

## THE MISSION OF JESUS

Although God uses the course of history to make careful preparation for the coming of the messiah, divine providence alone cannot restore humanity. The success of the messiah's mission is believed to depend significantly on humankind's fulfilment of its responsibility. In the life of Jesus, it is the human effort of other individuals which fails. Indeed, from the very moment of Jesus' birth, we see human failure. It is commonly taught in the UC that the members of Jesus' family failed to fulfil their task. We have seen how the tradition arose in Korean New Christian groups that Jesus was maltreated and underprivileged during his lifetime. This belief is shared by the UC, and, although not written in *Divine Principle*, it is taught orally and is widely known. The Rev Moon states that he has not declared publicly all the details he has received about Jesus' maltreatment because they would be more than humankind could bear;[6] this, apparently, is why the New Testament is relatively silent about the period from Jesus' birth to the beginning of his public ministry.

The failure of others to fulfil their responsibilities to the messiah began at the time of Jesus' infancy. The story of Mary and Joseph finding no room in the inn[7] is held to afford evidence of conflict within their wider family. Mary and Joseph must have had relatives in Bethlehem, it is argued, and they ought to have offered them hospitality and cared for them in their desperate predicament. The fact that Jesus was born in a manger reflects their total lack of concern for the holy family. The story of the Magi also receives a new interpretation. The Magi did not come merely to bring Jesus gifts of gold, frankincense and myrrh. Being intellectuals from the East, God planned that they should take Jesus away to provide him with an outstanding education. Although God provided them with the vision which took them to Bethlehem, they had the wrong expectation of a messiah, and sought him in Herod's palace. Their departure by a different route in order to avoid King Herod[8] indicates that they knew of Herod's intentions, yet made no attempt to rescue the infant Jesus from danger.

Having been denied the opportunity of a palace education, Jesus was brought up in a poorly educated family which was unsupportive of his messianic mission. Being illegitimate, he was never accepted as part of the family by his siblings or by Joseph. Jesus' family did not provide him with sufficient food and clothing;[9] the one childhood incident which the New Testament records indicates that Mary and Joseph were negligent: they lost him in the Jerusalem Temple, and made an entire day's homeward journey before becoming concerned about his absence.[10] Above all, in accordance with Jewish practice, they should have arranged his marriage when he was eighteen years old.

The New Testament is held to afford evidence of constant tension between Jesus and his family. Jesus' words to his mother at the wedding in Cana are considered impolite.[11] Jesus' family interfered with his mission, wanting him to return home, and relationships were so strained that Jesus on one occasion refused to see them.[12] Jesus' family, it is inferred, did not understand that God had appointed Jesus to bring about God's ideal within his own lifetime. Unification members do not simply dwell on the empirically observable aspects of their account of Jesus: it is even more important to them to imagine – indeed feel within themselves – the frustration and sorrow which they believe Jesus must have experienced from this constant rejection.

Despite his deep sorrow, Jesus continued to propagate his teachings. His message, expressed notably in his parables, was about an imminent Kingdom of Heaven, which, according to UC teaching, means the raising of perfect individuals, families, societies and nations. Jesus was also destined to fulfil the role of the mediator between humanity and God. As a result of the Fall, humankind's direct relationship with God had been broken. Only someone without sin can have a perfect relationship with God; hence the messiah, who is free from sin, can provide the means of restoring the divine–human relationship.

## JOHN THE BAPTIST AND THE JEWISH PEOPLE

The Old Testament had predicted that the messiah's advent would not be accomplished unannounced, but would be heralded by a return of the prophet Elijah.[13] The Old Testament prophet Elijah (c. 850 BCE) had been taken up miraculously into heaven by God, thus escaping physical death, and it was Jewish belief (and still is) that a return of Elijah would herald the advent of the messiah. John the Baptist came to fulfil this role. However, even someone in the role of Elijah had his own proportion of responsibility to perform. John had an important task, because – according to UC theology – he had authority and was held in high esteem by the Jewish people, to such a degree that he was even asked if he himself was the messiah. John's authority lay in the fact that his father, Zacharias, was the high priest; Jesus, by contrast, was the son of a lowly carpenter, and had no credentials apart from his own charisma. The *Principle* teaches that if John had testified that he, John, was the returned Elijah and that Jesus was the awaited messiah, the Jews would have believed and the foundation to receive the messiah would have been established.

John the Baptist occupied Elijah's *position*, at first achieving success, but subsequently failing abysmally in his mission. John the Baptist, accordingly, emerges as the villain of the piece – even more so than Judas Iscariot. As the Rev Moon has stated,

> There can be no doubt that John the Baptist was a man of failure. He was directly responsible for the crucifixion of Jesus Christ.[14]

It is a matter of speculation amongst UC members as to whether Jesus and John grew up together, being half-cousins. Some like to think of them as intimately related, while others hold that relationships were strained between Mary's household and the household of Zacharias (who should have looked after Mary during her pregnancy), and contend that they did not know each other well at all. Certainly, John and Jesus knew each other sufficiently well to secure mutual recognition at the early stages of their respective ministries. John became a prominent religious ascetic, and continued to fulfil his mission as the returned Elijah; he baptised Jesus, thus receiving a sign from God that Jesus was the messiah whom he should follow.

Yet even at Jesus' baptism, according to the *Principle*, John had a wrong concept of the messiah. He thought of Jesus as unapproachable when he claimed unworthiness to fasten his sandals. Although John initially established a foundation for Jesus,[15] there is no record of his acknowledging Jesus' messianic status after he had conducted Jesus' baptism; he thus failed to testify to Jesus. He began to doubt that Jesus was the messiah. The New Testament records that John sent his disciples to Jesus asking if he was the one who should come or if they should look for someone else.[16] He heard rumours that Jesus was illegitimate, and, mindful of his assertion that 'he [Jesus] must increase and I must decrease',[17] became jealous of Jesus, since Jesus was beginning to attract many more disciples than himself. John feared the lessening of his own role in contrast with the ascending status of a man of lower social origins. Indeed, John the Baptist effectively ensured the Jews' non-recognition of Jesus' messiahship by explicitly denying that he was Elijah who had come to usher in the messianic age.[18]

Faced with this crumbling foundation, Jesus temporarily had to leave the *position* of messiah and occupy John the Baptist's *position* in order to rebuild it.[19] This he did by the 40–day period of fasting in the desert. Nevertheless, without the testimony of John the Baptist, the faith of the Jewish people was lost. If John had accomplished his mission, the Jews would probably have accepted Jesus, since John was a highly respected figure, being the son of the high priest and a popular preacher. Jesus would then have travelled throughout the eastern nations, bringing 'Godism' first to the Jews, who would have united behind him, then to the Zoroastrians in Persia, the Buddhists in India and the Confucians in China. Having united their thoughts, he would then have come to Rome, persuaded the senators and thus achieved the unification of Graeco-Roman and eastern thought, establishing the Kingdom of Heaven on earth on a world-wide level.[20] Instead, Jesus was led to the cross, an event which was contrary to God's original purpose. He had died without restoring a bride, marrying her and begetting sinless children; humankind had not been restored and the Kingdom of Heaven on earth was not established.

Jesus' mission, however, was not a failure. The anti-cult exponents are often deterred at this point by the sheer complexity of the Unificationist position, and react violently and negatively to the statements that Jesus' body was 'invaded by Satan'[21] and that Jesus was 'giving his physical body to Satan, through the cross'.[22] However, what *Divine Principle* says must be seen in its proper context, which is as follows.

> Satan thus attained what he had intended through the 4,000–year course of history, by crucifying Jesus, with the exercise of his maximum power. God, who thus handed over Jesus into Satan's hands, could, at that price, set up the condition to save the whole of mankind, including the Israelites.
>
> How, then, did God come to be able to save sinful men? Since Satan had killed Jesus by exercising his maximum power, the position for God now to exercise His maximum power was created, according to the principle of restoration through indemnity. The exercise of maximum power on God's part was to bring the dead back to life, while that of Satan was to kill man. Here God exercised His maximum power as the condition of indemnity against Satan's act of killing Jesus through the exercise of His maximum power, and He brought Jesus back to life. By grafting the whole of mankind into the resurrected Jesus (Rom. 11.24) and giving them rebirth, God intended to save all mankind.[23]

It is important to note that the handing over of Jesus' body to Satan does not signify failure, but rather a condition of salvation. God had no further substance on which to lay a foundation for restoration: the central figure of John and the Jewish people had gone over to Satan's side, and the messiah was about to be killed. God therefore permitted Satan to take Jesus' physical life in exchange for the spiritual life of humankind.

What happened here has to be understood in terms of the spiritual laws which are held to operate in the universe. By offering Jesus' body in return for humankind's spiritual life, God provided himself with the only possible means to secure the future possibility of humanity's perfection. Satan, equally, is believed to have benefited from the corresponding counter-effect: the messiah was infinitely more valuable than the whole of humankind, and Satan is said always to grasp at whatever is most valuable to himself. Thus Satan gained Jesus' body, while God recovered the nation of Israel, and Jesus' spirit continued to live, offering humankind spiritual (but not physical) restoration. The resurrection appearances of Jesus are

1. (*above*) The hut in which the *Principle* was first recorded. It was built by Sun Myung Moon in 1951. (*HSA-UWC/New Future Photo*)

2. (*below*) The Rev Sun Myung Moon speaks at Madison Square Garden, New York, 18 September 1974. (*UPI/Bettman*)

3. The 'True Parents'. Each member owns a copy of this definitive photograph, and it is displayed in all shrines and official premises. (*HSA-UWC/New Future Photo*)

4. (*above*) Sun Myung Moon addresses the Assembly of the World's Religions, McAfee, New Jersey, November 1985. (*International Religious Foundation*)

5. (*below*) The Rev and Mrs Moon at the Assembly of the World's Religions, McAfee, New Jersey, 1985. (*International Religious Foundation*)

6. The Youth Seminar on World Religions, 1984, arrives at Seoul, Korea. (*International Religious Foundation*)

7. Participants at a conference of the Council for the World's Religions, a subsidiary of the I.R.F. (*International Religious Foundation*)

The text on the banner in the image reads:

Council
For the World's
Religions

Interreligious Dialogue and Peace
in the Middle East

March 15 – 17, 1988

Toledo, Spain

8. 'Victory of the Second Generation'. Shrine to Heung Jin Nim at Cleeve House, Wiltshire, dedicated by the Zimbabwean. The tree trunk depicts the Four Position Foundation and bears the motto 'Be Responsible!' (*Author*)

9. During breaks in the seminars, members pray at Heung Jin Nim's shrine. (*Author*)

10. Inside a UC Centre, a lecturer explains the *Principle* to participants. The theme is 'Providential Time-Identity'. (*Author*)

11.  The 'True Parents' and their family in eastern attire. (*HSA-UWC/New Future Photo*)

12. A blessed couple in Holy Robes. (*Unification Church, UK*)

13.  Blessing couples await their turn to process into the Jamsil Gymnasium, Seoul, Korea, for the 5837 couple Blessing, 14 October 1982. (*Camera Press*)

14.  The 'True Parents' officiate at the Blessing Ceremony, Madison Square Garden, 1 July 1982. (*UPI/Bettman*)

15. Holy Water is sprinkled on the Blessing couples as they enter. The Rev Moon and his wife Hak Ja Han preside over the ceremony. (*UPI/Bettman*)

16. The 5837 couple Blessing, Seoul. The ceremony, together with the marriage of 2075 couples in Madison Square, New York (1 July 1982) is sometimes referred to as the '8000 couple Blessing'. (*Camera Press/C.K. Kim*)

統一教会 國際合同結

THE UNIFICATION CHURCH HOLY W

17. A blessed couple who participated in the 5837 couple ceremony. (*Camera Press/ C.K. Kim*)

interpreted by Unificationists as appearances of the spirit body of Jesus, and it is not believed that Jesus' physical body left the tomb on Easter morning. Jesus was able to secure spiritual salvation, as is evidenced by his words to the dying thief, 'Today you will be with me in Paradise.'[24] Paradise, however, is not the Kingdom of Heaven, which was to remain unopened until the Lord of the Second Advent accomplished the unfulfilled part of Jesus' mission.

It is not altogether true to say that the crucifixion was not God's will. It was not God's primary purpose for Jesus: Unificationists insist that, if that were so, then Judas Iscariot would have been hailed as a hero, not as a villain. Jesus' death was not a triumph but a disaster, and UC members have little sympathy with those Christians who extol the 'blood of the lamb' as God's intended means of salvation. Nevertheless God was able to achieve something by the crucifixion, and the account given by the UC is as follows.

The crucifixion formed part of God's 'secondary', not 'primary' plan. Because humankind has free will, God at times has to change or modify his plans to accommodate men and women's co-operation or lack of it. Although the terminology may be novel, we make primary and secondary plans quite frequently. For example, we might invite friends to dinner. However, suppose they telephone to say that they can no longer come; we now cannot fulfil our 'primary plan' to entertain them, so we will then (no doubt with disappointment) implement a 'secondary plan' such as going to the cinema or spending an evening watching television.

It is worth noting that 'secondary plans' achieve something and not nothing: our evening at the cinema (the secondary plan) may have secured enjoyment although perhaps not as much as entertaining our hypothetical dinner guests (the primary plan). It would certainly be better than preparing a meal for four, and sitting with two empty places, pretending that our guests had arrived (a thoroughly disastrous plan)!

Similarly, the crucifixion, God's secondary plan, achieved something, although not as much as his primary plan. When it became inevitable that Jesus was not going to be acclaimed as the messiah, Jesus had two options: he could accomplish God's secondary plan, or else he could enact a thoroughly disastrous plan which would have achieved nothing at all. Thus, Jesus could have fled into the desert and hidden himself, or else he could remain and be crucified. The former course of action would have achieved nothing in the restoration process, but God could see that crucifying the messiah could accomplish something. Jesus' self-sacrifice was sufficient to secure humankind's spiritual life, and Satan accepted the offering because the death of the messiah was more important to him

than the rest of humanity. Jesus' physical body died, but his spiritual body
continued to live and indeed opened up Paradise, as Jesus promised to the
dying thief on the cross.

It is worth mentioning at this point that 'Paradise' is not to be construed
as synonymous with the 'Kingdom of Heaven'. Before Jesus' death, spirits
existed in the spirit world either in the 'Formation' stage, or else in
the 'unprincipled realm'. Paradise is that level of spiritual attainment
equivalent to the 'Growth' stage of those in the spiritual world; the
Kingdom of Heaven will be the 'Completion' stage, and will only be
attained by spirits when the Lord of the Second Advent accomplishes his
mission.

The crucifixion, accordingly, was part of this secondary plan. On the
occasions when the Rev Moon has said that the crucifixion was a 'murder'
and 'contrary to God's will', Unification members insist that he is speaking
in terms of God's primary purpose. According to Unificationist teaching,
Jesus successfully accomplished the role of 'spiritual messiah' and is the
spiritual True Parent. As *Divine Principle* states:

> On this foundation, Jesus could establish the position of the spiritual
> Messiah from the position of the spiritual mission-bearer of John the
> Baptist and restore the Holy Spirit. By doing this, he became the spiritual
> True Parent and came to perform the work of rebirth. That is, as it is
> written in the Bible (Acts 2:1–4), after the advent of the Holy Spirit at
> Pentecost, the resurrected Jesus became the spiritual True Father and,
> working in oneness with the Holy Spirit as the spiritual True Mother,
> spiritually grafted the saints to them, thus beginning the work of spiritual
> rebirth. By doing this, Jesus could accomplish the providence of spiritual
> salvation. Consequently, in the sphere of the resurrected Jesus, Satan's
> spiritual condition for accusation was completely liquidated, and thus,
> spiritually, this became a sphere inviolable by Satan.[25]

On casual acquaintance this passage appears to state that Jesus married
the Holy Spirit, and that the bi-polar relationship between Jesus' spirit and
the Holy Spirit constituted the Marriage of the Lamb which the Book of
Revelation predicted. This interpretation is incorrect for several reasons. It
is emphatically rejected by Unificationists,[26] and in any case the claim that
Jesus married the Holy Spirit is nonsensical. Although there are many who
believe that the statements of *Divine Principle* are indeed nonsensical, it is
a canon of good scholarship to refuse to foist a nonsensical interpretation
on someone if a more sensible one is forthcoming.

It is certainly true that *Divine Principle* teaches that Jesus and the

Holy Spirit are in the *positions* of True Father and True Mother respectively.[27] However, the *Principle* makes no reference to any such marriage; Unification teaching 'thinks of the Holy Spirit not as an individual person but rather as a sign of God's work in history and His direct influence upon our individual spiritual life'.[28] The Holy Spirit occupies the feminine *position* in the redemptive process, since it (or she) displays the 'maternal functions of comforting, nourishing and nurturing'.[29] Whether the Holy Spirit is an individual spirit is a matter on which Unificationists do not appear to agree; what is taught is that it requires and uses discarnate human spirits or angels when it needs a definite form in which to act, and, importantly, that, since *positions* typically change, the *position* of the Holy Spirit as the female counterpart to Jesus Christ the True Father will also change. The Holy Spirit is not *actually* the bride of the messiah, but occupies the *position* of the True Mother. Thus the *position* of spiritual True Mother will not be occupied by the Holy Spirit for ever, but will come to be occupied by the bride of Jesus Christ when he enters into a matrimonial relationship, which is a precondition for entry into the Kingdom of Heaven.

The identity of Jesus' bride is undisclosed. It has been speculated that God intended Jesus to restore Mary Magdalene to the *position* of True Mother, but this suggestion does not secure much acceptance in UC circles. This and other details of the restoration drama await further development as and when the Rev Moon divulges further revelations which he has received from God and the spirit world.


## UC ATONEMENT THEORY: EAST AND WEST

Viewed against the backcloth of indigenous Korean religion, I believe one can understand how Unificationism gathered momentum. The Confucian ideal of the man who marries, gives birth to children, perpetuates his lineage and lives to a ripe old age was plainly inconsistent with the biblical account of the life of Jesus. Jesus was unmarried, established no physical lineage, and had his life cut off in his prime. In the shamanistic world view, someone whose life had come to an end in such an abrupt and unnatural way would become a wandering spirit: hence the post-death apparitions which were seen by Jesus' followers. Given the Korean concept of the ideal man, it was natural to find corroborative evidence from the Bible itself that Jesus' crucifixion was not in accordance with the will of God. After all, did not the New Testament describe Jesus as the 'bridegroom',[30] and does not the Book of Revelation describe the 'marriage of the Lamb' as the culmination of humanity's spiritual aspiration?[31] Indeed, was it not the case that in Jewish society, as in Korean, it was the custom for parents to arrange the marriages of their children? Ascetics like John the Baptist and itinerant celibate teachers were very much the exception rather than the rule in Jewish society.

It is not too difficult to see how this line of theologising becomes reinforced when the problems inherent in the mainstream Christian missionary message become apparent. Did not the Bible state that Jesus prayed in Gethsemane that he should not have to undergo crucifixion?[32] Did he not weep over Jerusalem, knowing that its leaders were about to condemn him to death?[33] If the crucifixion was God's will, why is Judas Iscariot portrayed as a villain rather than a hero? Further, when viewed against the social and political background of Korea, how could it plausibly be claimed that Jesus brought full salvation when there was so much armed conflict and social unrest? Viewed thus, Unificationism could be seen as a fairly logical Korean response to the preaching of the Christian gospel.[34]

Such theological developments are understandable in Korea; but it is less obvious why Unificationism should find a following in members from different countries of origin. It must therefore be asked what reasons western members have for accepting the UC position on Jesus. I have discussed this question informally with various members of different backgrounds. I claim no scientific validity for what follows, only impressions. There is scope for further here study by those who are more able to deal sociologically and psychologically with NRMs.

Some members claim to have visions of Jesus or to feel a very close presence of him. All members I have met speak very lovingly of Jesus, although they do not pray to him, since God ('Heavenly Father') alone is the subject of prayer. Contrary to popular belief, by contrast, Sun Myung Moon is not prayed to. Since (at the time of writing) Sun Myung Moon does not inhabit the spirit world, he cannot be an object of prayer, let alone worship. The formula 'In the name of the True Parents', which members almost invariably use at the end of prayers, indicates that those who accept that the True Parents (the Rev Moon and his wife) are God's ideal now have the right to approach God in prayer and to experience a unique quality of love, which has been made possible through the True Parents' accomplishment.

Clearly those members who have come from Christian backgrounds have been dissatisfied with the more orthodox views of Jesus. One member found it difficult to see how someone's death on a cross could have salvific effects, and another said that mainstream Christian practice consisted of 'worshipping a corpse', and was 'gruesome' and 'macabre'. Another member felt that the ideal of celibacy, which Jesus represented, was unnatural. This was not simply a 'gut feeling', but was reasoned out by a process of theological summation of scripture: Adam was commanded by God to be fruitful and multiply, hence it was God's will that he should marry; Jesus, being the 'Second Adam'[35] must therefore be expected to recapitulate God's plan for Adam, but in the 'principled' manner.

It is often forgotten by mainstream Christians that the status of Jesus can actually be enhanced by accepting Sun Myung Moon as the Lord of the Second Advent. This may seem strange, but *Divine Principle* gives a solid account of achievements which Jesus is said actually to have accomplished. To some UC members, mainstream Christianity presents Schweitzer's picture of the failed apocalyptist,[36] while Unificationism presents a spiritual messiah who opened Paradise. As one member remarked, 'Jesus did more than I had ever previously thought.'

No student of religion can accept uncritically these statements of members, particularly since their interpretations of mainstream Christianity would be vigorously challenged by members of conventional churches. To say that Roman Catholicism involves worshipping a corpse would be regarded as a travesty of the Catholic faith. Comments like these may therefore tell us more about members' misapprehensions of Christianity than about real points of divergence on soteriology. One might profitably consider wherein lie the origins of such misconstructions of mainstream Christianity. One possible explanation is that members' constructions of mainstream Christianity come from Unificationism rather than from Christianity itself, and that such criticisms of religious orthodoxy are learned from within the movement. Conceivably they could be *post eventum* rationalisations for having joined the Unification Church, in an attempt to assert the doctrinal superiority of the UC account of the mission of Jesus. If it were possible to undertake a study, it would be an instructive task to examine how the role of Jesus altered in a UC member's mind after converting to Unificationism, when that member had come from a mainstream Christian background.

To accept the '*post eventum* rationalisation' thesis would place the blame for misapprehension on the Unification movement. This would be unfair, since blame must be due equally to a failure on the part of mainstream Christianity to clarify its message. Mainstream Christianity normally fails to proffer a detailed account of how atonement took place. This is partly due to a failure of mainstream Christian churches to provide anything more than a very perfunctory and amateurishly presented account of Christian theology. Sunday School impressions of Jesus rarely take a mainstream Christian's theological education beyond the simple tenet that Christ 'died to save us all', and even in the pulpit, where a congregation is addressed by a clergyman who is supposedly theologically literate, one seldom finds any attempt to explain how atonement occurred.

In fairness to mainstream Christianity, members' lack of theological sophistication on atonement theory is not entirely due to negligence. At no point in the history of Christian doctrine has any particular theory about the mechanics of the atonement been imposed on Christendom. Unlike doctrines of the person of Christ, competing theories of atonement – the 'ransom theory', the Anselmian 'satisfaction' theory, the liberal 'moral influence' theory – have been able to co-exist as legitimate competitors. No particular penchant is expressed in any of the traditional creeds, and it is sometimes suggested that mainstream Christianity has been more concerned about the *fact* of the atonement than about theological explanations. This has its merits and demerits: on the one hand, it allows healthy room for doctrinal divergence, but on the other it leaves a theological vacuum in which mainstream Christians are left without any official explanation of Christ's atoning work. It is possible that, faced with this vacuum, UC converts are grateful to have it filled with a meticulous and definitive explanation. Unlike the mainstream churches, it is impossible to join the Unification Church without undergoing fairly demanding theological instruction in the *Principle*.

The member who found difficulty with mainstream Christianity's connection between Christ's death and his atoning work appeared to overlook the fact that his own tradition makes very similar connections. It is surely just as problematic, *prima facie*, to claim that Jesus' death secured spiritual salvation as it is to claim that it fulfilled God's primary purpose of bringing full salvation to humankind. The member was also unfamiliar, no doubt, with the classical attempts in the history of Christianity to devise an acceptable soteriology. St Anselm's doctrine,[37] for example, which views the atonement as a metaphysical transaction has certain affinities with Unificationist soteriology: God's 'honour' is satisfied by humanity's payment of its debt, but God's benevolence is demonstrated by the fact that God paid the price by taking on the form of humanity in the incarnate Christ.

If Anselmian theory is criticised for entailing a rather dubious divine book-keeping approach to atonement (humanity's debt to God assumes a specific value which must then be paid off) it is difficult to see that Unification doctrine fares better. The UC presentation of the salvific work of Christ has as much a 'book-keeping' approach to atonement as that of Anselm. On both accounts of atonement God cannot simply elect to forgive humanity and cancel out original sin, even though he is omnipotent. For Anselm, God's omnipotence is qualified by an 'honour' which demands satisfaction. For Unificationism divine omnipotence is qualified by humanity's need to fulfil its responsibility in the restoration process, and particularly to establish and maintain a base on which the messiah may come. For Anselm the sacrifice of Christ, the God-man, forms part of a transaction in which men and women repay a debt which only they owe and which only God can pay. For Unificationism, the operation of spiritual laws produces a metaphysical reaction in which God enables Satan to claim Jesus' life in return for humankind's spiritual salvation which God had been preparing to form the base on which the messiah could accomplish his work.

## UNIFICATIONIST AND MAINSTREAM SOTERIOLOGY

My analysis of Unificationist soteriology has revealed similarities and contrasts between UC thought and mainstream Christianity, and indicates that these do not always lie at precisely the points which evangelical Christians typically locate. One striking contrast, generally overlooked by the UC's evangelical critics, lies in the relationship between Jesus Christ and religious doctrine. For many mainstream Christians, an acceptance of Jesus Christ is regarded as the first step in spiritual progress, and serious theologising is an optional extra which is often discouraged. For the Unificationist, however, the emphasis lies on understanding the *Principle* sequentially, rather than a simple faith in Jesus or an acceptance of the Rev Moon as the Lord of the Second Advent. Thus, acceptance of the *Principle* becomes a prerequisite for understanding Jesus' saving work and the task which remains for the Lord of the Second Advent to fulfil.

Both mainstream Christians and Unificationists might agree that there is an important sense in which humankind's salvation process awaits further completion. Whether the Christian conceives the final eschaton as an other-worldly realm which God's chosen will enter after Christ returns on the clouds, or whether the Kingdom of Heaven is to be conceived as an earth-worldly utopia in which social justice prevails, that state has not yet been reached. Indeed Unificationists will often challenge mainstream Christians to specify precisely what they do mean when they insist that Jesus Christ fully accomplished his mission. The essential theological strategies employed in the respective soteriologies are similar. The Unificationist interpretation in terms of the working out of spiritual laws has plain counterparts in mainstream Christian tradition, and not exclusively in Anselm.[38]

There are several differences between mainstream and Unificationist soteriology, however. First, if I may put it so, although the notion of soteriological book-keeping is common in both traditions, the entries in the ledger are vastly different. The interaction with Satan is absent in Anselm, although it is worth noting that other mainstream accounts of the atonement are not averse to the idea of God transacting with Satan by paying him a ransom to redeem humanity. The Anselmian and Unificationist accounts differ more fundamentally in the status accorded to Jesus: for Anselm it is crucial that he is simultaneously God and man, whereas in Unificationism the messiah, as we have seen, is not God himself.

Second, whereas in mainstream Christian thought there is a completely open choice of atonement theory, for the Unificationist there is one definitive interpretation. Because of the definitive nature of Unificationist soteriology, Unificationists will teach it as a clear part of the *Principle*, and thus members will accept official UC teaching in a fairly uniform way. Each mainstream Christian, by contrast, will devise his or her preferred view, or else, more probably, have no view at all.

Some interpretation is needed of the UC account of the respective roles of Jesus and the Lord of the Second Advent. The second messiah comes to bring physical restoration, following on from the work of Jesus Christ, the spiritual messiah, who brought spiritual salvation. It is therefore inaccurate to contend that Unificationism regards Sun Myung Moon as 'more important' than Jesus. As Unification members insist, the difference between the two does not lie in differences of greatness, but rather in differences of function: one is the 'spiritual messiah', whereas the other is the 'physical messiah', who completes the unfulfilled mission of Jesus, and continues his messianic work.

It was explained to me that the story of the woman's vision of Jesus and Sun Myung Moon does not signify that the Rev Moon is more important than Jesus, but rather that Sun Myung Moon, the Lord of the Second Advent, is the divinely appointed messiah of the new Completed Testament Era. Just as Jesus fulfilled an important part of his messianic mission in the New Testament Era, so the Lord of the Second Advent will complete the work of accomplishing physical restoration. After all, it is claimed, Jesus promised his disciples that he would be with them 'to the end of the age'.[39] Unificationists emphasise that the word 'age' is used, meaning aeon, and that this promise was not a promise that Jesus Christ would exist eternally with his disciples. The word 'age', it is contended, means the New Testament Era, which is now concluded. According to Unificationist teaching, a new era has begun, the Completed Testament Era in which the Lord of the Second Advent establishes the part of the salvific process which the New Testament age could not accomplish.

## THE MARRIAGE OF JESUS

My account so far is only a part of the Unificationist exposition of the respective roles of Jesus Christ and Sun Myung Moon. My analysis of these roles has two apparent consequences. First, if Jesus only opened up Paradise, leaving the Kingdom of Heaven unopened, there was no possibility for anyone to become a 'divine spirit' after his death. Second, the Kingdom of Heaven is held only to be attainable by married couples, not by single individuals. Adam and Eve before the Fall had reached the top of the Growth stage, at which they were almost eligible for divinely blessed marriage; reaching the Completion stage of spiritual attainment would have been accompanied by marital union. Jesus was unmarried; therefore until a bride has been found he cannot – according to Unificationist thinking – enter the Kingdom of Heaven.

But there is more: it is not the case that simply any marriage will secure the keys of the Kingdom of Heaven; the only marriages which can remove original sin are those which are solemnised by the Lord of the Second Advent at the Unificationist Blessing Ceremony. Couples who are already married when they join the Unification Church are expected to have their marriages blessed by the Rev Moon, with all the accompanying requirements which are entailed.[40] It is therefore a logical step in Unification thought to declare that, in order for Jesus Christ to gain entry into the Kingdom of Heaven, the Lord of the Second Advent must find him a bride and join them together in matrimony in a Blessing Ceremony.

It may be asked how this is possible when Jesus Christ no longer exists as a human being on earth. The fact that Jesus is no longer physically alive in fact presents no problem. The Rev Moon is empowered to marry members of the spirit world as well as those who remain on earth. One married couple informed me that at their Blessing Ceremony the Rev Moon blessed some older single members, sealing them in marriage with spirit partners. After his son Heung Jin died in 1984, a ceremony was performed in which Heung Jin's spirit was married to a Washington ballerina called Hoon Sook Pak (now known as Julia Moon).[41] The marriage of spirits need not wait until the Rev Moon's death: it is believed that he has close relationships with the spirit world and, as we have seen, he is believed to be capable of journeying into this world on occasions. Those who do not accept the

*Principle* in their physical life on earth will be able to receive appropriate teaching in the spirit world and, having accepted it, receive the Blessing and eventually gain entry into the Kingdom of Heaven.

One might have expected that the marriage of the first messiah would be a spectacular event, accompanied by great ceremony and publicity, just as the 'mass weddings' are spectacular events which are milestones in the lives of members and of the church. Not so. I understand that this event has already occurred and that Sun Myung Moon has found a bride for Jesus and performed a ceremony to solemnise the union. It has not been possible to obtain details of this event, only confirmation that it has taken place. Even UC leaders have claimed that they do not know whether or not this has happened. I am told that the details belong to the category of revelations which the Rev Moon has still to disclose to members when the time is considered to be right. No details have been given about the nature of Jesus' bride. One ex-member states that Jesus is supposedly married to an old Korean woman (it is not stated whether she is alive or dead),[42] but he provides no sources, and hence this statement must be regarded as no more than pure conjecture.

## THE HEUNG JIN PHENOMENON

The opening of the Kingdom of Heaven is not the end of the restoration process. There still remain problems in the earth world and the spirit world alike, since both still fall short of perfection. According to UC teaching, the Rev Moon's late son, Heung Jin, has done much to bring both worlds nearer their ideal state. It is appropriate therefore to look at the recent Heung Jin phenomenon. Unification members are somewhat reluctant to speak about it, possibly for two reasons. First, it is clear that the phenomenon distances the UC from mainstream Christianity, precisely at a time when the UC is anxious to be recognised as a legitimate expression of the Christian faith. Second, the phenomenon partly derives from individual experiences and visions of members, and it is difficult to give 'official' accreditation to individual revelations.

Heung Jin Moon was the Rev and Mrs Moon's second son, who was involved in a car crash on 22 December 1983. He was then 17 years old. His car collided with a large lorry which had skidded out of control; the accident left him with serious head injuries and he was in a coma for several days after undergoing brain surgery. He died on 2 January 1984. (He is usually referred to as 'Heung Jin Nim', 'Nim' being a title of respect.) Obviously this was a matter of concern within the Unification Church at the time, and an issue of *Today's World*,[43] one of the UC's in-house publications, was devoted to Heung Jin Moon's obituary and some attempt to explain why God had permitted the tragedy.

The matter remained very much an internal issue, until in December 1987 *The City Paper*, a free Washington weekly newspaper, received copies of some correspondence which had been sent to the 'Cult Awareness Network'. The correspondence consisted of three typed letters, one of which was on official UC stationery, and which purported to come from Heung Jin. One letter began:

> Dear Brothers and Sisters of the Bay Area: Hi! This is the team of Heung-Jin Nim and Jesus here. We need to establish a foothold among you and bring true sunshine here to California.[44]

Heung Jin Moon informed members that Jesus was standing by him, and he encouraged members to liberate the human race, warning them against homosexuality, asking them to pray for him, and to study *Divine Principle* and the Korean language.

Having discussed these revelations with UC members, I was informed that the informality of Heung Jin's communication was not incompatible with its being a serious revelation: Heung Jin, I was told, was a very informal, relaxed character, and, if anything, the style of writing vindicated the authenticity of the message rather than made it suspect. I was told that some members sometimes experience trance-like revelations which are transmitted by 'automatic writing' – hence the letters. The fact that one member had used official stationary did not imply that the content was 'official': most members have access to such material and are permitted to use it.

What is more significant than the correspondence itself is the explanation which is given for Heung Jin Moon's death, and the beliefs about what he is now accomplishing in the spirit world to which he has been transported. Heung Jin's death was explained as being a 'sacrificial death'. Satan, it is claimed, was attacking the Rev Moon, and the attack was made possible by a number of problems which were occurring within the Unification Church. Satan was invading the blessed couples,[45] many of whom were experiencing problems within their own marriages and many of whom did not appear to be united with the True Parents; the Rev Moon's own immediate family was apparently becoming disunited,[46] and as a consequence the Rev Moon had not succeeded in bringing the entire free world to God.

Problems in the earth world are reckoned to be intertwined with problems in the spirit world; hence it was believed that the spirit world itself had problems. Unprincipled relationships within the earth world were held to be caused by the infiltration of evil spirits who were exercising undue influence on those on earth. The spirit world itself was believed to be divided, with spirits of different levels of attainment dwelling in different areas without being able to improve those who needed spiritual guidance. Communication between good spirits and men and women on earth was hampered by impediments on travel imposed upon spirits. A spirit, it is believed, cannot necessarily travel anywhere at all, for a spirit is not a completely disembodied entity but itself possesses a spirit body as well as a spirit mind. Consequently the spirit body is more likely to be attached to one specific geographical region. A spirit who is influencing someone in Korea may have difficulty travelling, say, to the USA to influence members there.

Where humans and spirits are not acting in accordance with the *Principle*, indemnity must be paid. Satan therefore was able to demand the life of the Rev Moon. A sacrifice so great as this would have paid indemnity, but the consequences would have been too great for the Unification Church. Accordingly, it is believed that Heung Jin Moon's death was a substitutionary sacrifice for his father: he was in the *position* of Abel in the Rev Moon's family, being the second oldest of his sons.

Heung Jin Moon's entry into the spirit world is believed to have achieved very significant consequences. It is claimed that he has taught spirits in the spirit world. Previously they had received some instruction from Mr Eu, the late former President of the UC, but Heung Jin's achievement was to unify the spirit world, which had previously existed in different levels and in different factions. Spirits were elevated to new levels of attainment, as Heung Jin performed liberation ceremonies for them. Greater communication between the earth world and the spirit world is now believed to be possible as a result of Heung Jin's activities, and Heung Jin has reportedly said that we should prepare for a time when we shall have interaction not merely with the occasional individual visitor from the spirit world, but with thousands of spirits.[47] Amongst visitors from the spirit world, Heung Jin is believed to have enabled Jesus Christ and the Virgin Mary to come to earth to be experienced in a new and clearer way.[48]

Heung Jin Moon's death, however, is held not merely to be a sacrifice on behalf of his father and for Unification members and spirits. Heung Jin is believed to have died for all, to enable everyone to have a 'right to resurrection' and entry into the Kingdom of Heaven. Whereas Jesus Christ merely opened the gates of Paradise, Heung Jin has opened the Kingdom of Heaven:

Jesus opened the realm of Paradise in the spiritual world. Based on True Parents' victorious foundation, Heung Jin Nim went one step further, and opened the realm of the Kingdom of Heaven in the spirit world. After Jesus' ascension to Paradise, Pentecost came. The same thing happened after Heung Jin Nim went to the spirit world: we experienced a new Pentecost.[49]

Some comment is appropriate on the relationship between Heung Jin and Jesus. In a series of lectures to UC members, Young Whi Kim, a prominent UC leader, states clearly that: 'Father is the King of Kings, thus Heung Jin Nim, as his representative, is now called the King of Heaven.'[50] Evidently this is not merely a verdict pronounced by Unificationists, but by many saints and spirits, as well as Jesus Christ himself. As Young Whi Kim continues:

One brother has received messages from Heung Jin Nim. St. Francis, St. Paul, Jesus, Mary, and other spirits have come to him as well. They all refer to Heung Jin Nim as the new Christ. They also call him the youth-king of heaven. He is the King of Heaven in the spirit world. Jesus is working with him and always accompanies him. Jesus himself says that Heung Jin Nim is the new Christ. He is the center of the spirit world now. This means he is in a higher position than Jesus.[51]

Why Heung Jin is believed to have a higher status than Jesus is not immediately obvious. Ed Mignot, a former UC member, has suggested that Heung Jin is accorded a higher status than Jesus on account of the fact that the former is married while the latter was not,[52] but this cannot be correct – particularly since Mignot himself in the same article tells of Jesus' marriage to the Korean woman. The explanation I have been given by Unification members is that Heung Jin Moon was born into the family of True Parents. By being unable to establish a true family Jesus was unable to go to the spirit world with such a foundation.

Although it has been stated that that 'Heung Jin Nim's position is even greater than Jesus', members with whom I have discussed their relationship point out that Heung Jin has not usurped Jesus' status or demoted him in any way within the spirit world. One Unificationist offered me an analogy of achieving the four-minute mile: the first person to break this psychological barrier has accomplished a great achievement, and that achievement stands, even though others may subsequently surpass him in speed; indeed it is only through that first runner's achievement that subsequent records are made possible. Similarly, Heung Jin's achievement stands on the foundation which Jesus has made and is only made possible through that. Jesus is said to co-operate with Heung Jin, and therefore does not feel that any rivalry exists between them. It is also incorrect to suppose that Heung Jin is now regarded as more important than Sun Myung Moon. Unificationists insist that Sun Myung Moon and Mrs Moon are the only True Parents, and not Heung Jin and his wife. Although Heung Jin is described as the King of Heaven, *positions* change, and his kingship is regarded as a regency, pending the arrival of his father.

## HEUNG JIN'S 'RETURNING RESURRECTION'

Heung Jin's ascension to the throne of heaven was not the end of the matter. Just as spirits are believed to co-operate with the earth world, so Heung Jin co-operates with men and women on earth. One particular manifestation of Heung Jin in the physical world is worthy of mention. Some time after the reports of Heung Jin's 'letters from heaven', the *Washington Post* issued a report, 'Theological Uproar in Unification Church'[53] with the subtitle 'Rev Moon recognises Zimbabwean as his reincarnated son.' According to reports, a young black Zimbabwean UC member gained recognition as the special mouthpiece of Heung Jin. When the Rev Moon was informed of the phenomenon he sent the Rev Chung Hwan Kwak (one of the UC's most prominent leaders) to Zimbabwe to find out about the matter. The Rev Kwak was given a question to put to the Zimbabwean, to which only Heung Jin could have known the answer: the Zimbabwean, I am told, answered correctly. He was then brought to the USA, and when he had been introduced to the Rev Moon the latter accepted the veracity of the Zimbabwean's message and welcomed him as his own son. The Rev Chung Hwan Kwak is quoted as saying, 'Several months ago, Heung Jin Nim started working 24 hours a day through a black African brother who was specially chosen and prepared to become his embodiment. Now we can speak to Heung Jin Nim directly in a physical body!'[54]

The name of the Zimbabwean was not disclosed even to members, who refer to him straightforwardly as 'Heung Jin Nim', 'HJN', or sometimes 'Second Self Heung Jin Nim'.[55] Not being Heung Jin himself, he does not live with Julia Moon as man and wife. The Zimbabwean of course cannot strictly be a reincarnation of Heung Jin, for two reasons: *Divine Principle* explicitly rejects the doctrine of reincarnation,[56] and the Zimbabwean youth was born many years prior to Heung Jin's death. He is sometimes said to be a 'returning resurrection' of Heung Jin (a human being through whom a member of the spirit world specially co-operates), but one UC leader with whom I discussed the phenomenon believes that the concept of 'returning resurrection' does not adequately describe the occurrence. It was, he said, more like 'possession', since Heung Jin's spirit appeared to take over the Zimbabwean's body and not merely influence it in intermittent stages. However, the word 'possession' has somewhat negative connotations, and it was stressed that the Zimbabwean phenomenon was regarded by most (although not all) Unificationists as an extremely positive and important spiritual occurrence.

The Zimbabwean travelled the world, meeting members and hearing 'confessions' from them. Apparently most of these confessions related to alcohol consumption: Unificationism is opposed to drinking intoxicants, but a number of members had become lax and had engaged in occasional drinking. Other confessions may have been about illicit sexual relationships. These confessions were followed by physical beatings by the Zimbabwean, so that the penitent members could pay indemnity for their misdeeds. He preached to them, offering encouragement, and calling for spiritual renewal and repentance.

Because he is considered to have improved declining spiritual standards within the UC, most leaders regarded his presence as having a cleansing function. However, after only a few months little was heard about the Zimbabwean's activities, and members now believe that Heung Jin's spirit has left his body and returned to heaven once more. It is unclear why the phenomenon was merely temporary. Members suggest that Heung Jin performed the tasks that were needed at the time, and has returned to heaven in order to continue his work there and influence members in other ways. The UC's critics have a different explanation: by using physical violence, they allege, the Zimbabwean over-reached himself, and this state of affairs could not be allowed to continue.


CONCLUSION

Although I have devoted a significant amount of space to Heung Jin, members are now inclined to play down the phenomenon and suggest that it was a passing stage of the church's development. The Rev Moon's eldest son Hyo Jin has recently instructed members to remove Heung Jin's picture from UC prayer rooms, notwithstanding the fact that this practice is recommended in the official UC liturgical manual *The Tradition*. Nevertheless, Heung Jin Moon's death – if not the Zimbabwean phenomenon – cannot fail to have a permanent effect on Unification theology. The Kingdom of Heaven, once opened by Heung Jin, cannot readily be closed, and Heung

Jin is necessarily regarded as the first human being to have attained the status of a 'divine spirit' and progressed to individual perfection.

My task in this chapter has been to clarify the Unificationist position regarding Jesus Christ and Sun Myung Moon. Whether these teachings are acceptable to mainstream Christianity I leave readers to decide for themselves. Mainsteam Christendom will no doubt continue to insist that Jesus' status is necessarily downgraded by any claim that there was an unfulfilled part of his mission which has been accomplished by new messianic personages. Unificationists will point out that even mainstream Christendom has to acknowledge that the Kingdom of Heaven on earth has still not been established, despite the advent of Jesus Christ. What Unificationism does, it is claimed, is to specify much more precisely than mainstream Christianity the means by which the Kingdom of Heaven will be realised. To do this, members insist, is not to downgrade Jesus: Jesus fulfilled a crucial role in the restoration drama by opening Paradise and attaining individual perfection. He will, they declare, continue to co-operate with Heung Jin Moon and the Lord of the Second Advent for the accomplishment of humanity's full salvation.

# 7    The Blessing

We have seen that in Unificationist thought, God's ideal for humankind is marriage and the procreation of sinless children. Jesus was crucified before he was able to undergo matrimony, and consequently the Kingdom of Heaven was left unopened. Because the Lord of the Second Advent is believed to have taken over the unfulfilled mission of Jesus, Sun Myung Moon is accorded the achievement of inaugurating a new era of human history – the Completed Testament Era – as a result of his marriage in March 1960, when the beginning of a true family was established into which the rest of humanity could be adopted by means of the Blessing Ceremony. Only blessed couples can proceed eventually beyond Paradise into the Kingdom of Heaven, and, having had their marriages blessed by the messiah, their marriages are not merely valid 'till death us do part', but form bonds which are believed to last eternally. Unificationists have used the term 'Second Self' to describe a partner of a blessed couple. What this means is that, since humanity was created in God's image, our task is to restore the image of God which was lost in the Fall and to perfect ourselves by reaching a truly godlike state. Since God is held to have male and female aspects, it follows that the only 'Second Selves' of God can be a male and a female together who are sealed in marriage as a blessed couple. Unblessed members are not referred to as 'Second Selves' but – until recently – were called 'Chosen Ones', and it is an expectation that at some stage in the future they will undergo the Blessing.

Mainstream Christians have often expressed surprise at religious groups which believe in eternal marriage, pointing out that in Jesus' dispute with the Sadducees, he asserted that there was no marriage at the resurrection.[1] However, UC theology interprets Jesus' statement as a description of the state of the spiritual world at that time. In Jesus' time, they insist, there were no 'divine spirits' and no restored Blessing. It is only in our age, they believe, that the situation has changed, with the coming of the Lord of the Second Advent.

The mission of Jesus was to restore humanity. The second messiah must complete this task by re-enacting the events which led up to the Fall, but this time in a 'principled'[2] way, and this will enable the rest of humankind to be ingrafted into the new lineage of restored people. Since the Fall was due to sexual misconduct, this new messiah must effect the restoration of

131

humanity through 'principled' marriage and sexual activity. This is enacted through the Blessing and its related ceremonies, in which the participating couples are restored from their satanic lineage to their true divine lineage. Because of its paramount importance in restoring the Fall, the Blessing assumes outstanding significance in Unification thought.

The outline of Unificationist teaching in Chapter 2 revealed that there are three Blessings and not just one. God's command to Adam and Eve[3] was first to 'be fruitful' (attain individual perfection), to 'multiply' (marry and beget children) and to have dominion over the earth. It is the second of these three 'Blessings' which is widely called 'The Blessing' within the Unification Church, and which is popularly known in the media as the 'mass wedding'. It may seem illogical that the second Blessing should be restored before the first: after all, how can there be a perfect marriage unless the spouses are perfect individuals? The answer is two-fold. First, sinless individuals are only produced from a pure 'blood lineage' and thus a 'principled' marriage is a necessary precondition for begetting sinless children and enabling them to attain individual perfection. Second, Unificationists do not hold that members' marriages become instantly perfected and that the couples will live happily ever after, like the conclusion of a romantic novel. Marriages demand considerable effort, and the Blessing ceremonies merely act as a symbol of the purification which must take place inwardly, laying a foundation for what is still to be accomplished spiritually.

Two principal themes feature in the Unificationist account of restoration: the sexual nature of the Fall and the lost blood lineage. The practice of *p'i kareun* (bringing salvation through a sexual act between a female acolyte and the messianic leader)[4] might have been one way in which certain New Christian groups attempted to re-enact the Fall, inseminating a woman with messianic semen to bear a child from a supposedly pure lineage. Despite accusations that the Unification Church engaged in such a practice, it cannot even be established that the Rev Moon had contact with any Korean religious groups who may have practised the ritual of *p'i kareun*. As we shall see, the consummation of the Blessing ceremony involves a different set of rituals.

The theology which underlies the ceremonies and their significance synthesises several ideas from various religions which prevail in Korea. Although the sacramental wine drinking at the Holy Wine Ceremony has been compared with the Christian eucharist,[5] the theme of blood is also to be found in Korean folk shamanism.[6] We have seen how blood is associated with lineage, and the task of 'purifying blood lineage' is a central theme surrounding the Blessing. The emphasis on marriage and the family is typically Confucian, as indeed is the stress on establishing a true dynasty.

Before proceeding to discuss the Blessing, one further element of Unification thought must be noted. We have seen how everything in the universe is said to possess a *sung sang* (internal character) and a *hyung sang* (external form).[7] The physical actions which comprise the ceremonies constitute the *hyung sang*, and those few details with which the public are acquainted fall exclusively into this category. For the couples who undergo the Blessing, however, it is not the *hyung sang* which has prime importance, but its *sung sang*: what the Blessing means to them assumes much greater importance than the physical events which comprise it.

I propose to recount first the *hyung sang* aspects of Unification marriage, and second their *sung sang* nature, or internal meaning. (This is only a rough division; as will be clear, *hyung sang* and *sung sang* are inextricably intertwined.) But first we must mention the decisive event which made all these ceremonies possible, the marriage of Sun Myung Moon himself.

## THE 'MARRIAGE OF THE LAMB'

On 1 March 1960 the 'Divine Marriage of the Lamb' took place, when Sun Myung Moon married Hak Ja Han. We are told little by way of details about that ceremony, but the Rev Moon is insistent on the momentous significance of the event, even going as far as to state:

> The year of 1960 will be recorded by historians as the phenomenal and dramatic year of human history.[8]

Just as the advent of Jesus Christ marked a watershed dividing the Old Testament and the New Testament eras, establishing a new focal point for the calendar, so the Moons' marriage heralds a new era, the 'Completed Testament Era'.

This event is held to have made possible several things. First it opened the gate for 'Paradise on earth'. Jesus' crucifixion enabled the opening of the celestial Paradise which suitably developed spirits could inhabit, but now the possibility of physical as well as spiritual salvation has arrived. Second, it made possible the bearing of 'true children': the Rev and Mrs Moon have given birth to thirteen children in all, twelve of whom are still living. These children are believed to have been born without original sin, and into this family of 'true children' all humanity can become ingrafted.[9] This ingrafting is accomplished through the Blessing.

THE 'HYUNG SANG': THE FIVE CEREMONIES

Although the so-called 'mass wedding' at which the Rev Moon presides has attracted so much public attention, marriage in the Unification Church involves altogether five ceremonies, for which precise instructions are given. These are: (1) The 'Matching' or Engagement Ceremony; (2) The Holy Wine Ceremony; (3) The Blessing (the 'mass wedding'); (4) The Indemnity Ceremony; and (5) The 'Three Day Ceremony'. It is only the third of these which is ever public – that is to say, open to invited non-UC guests and occasionally given television coverage. In what follows I shall use the UC's own preferred term 'The Blessing' to describe the multiple wedding and my own term 'the Blessing ceremonies' to describe collectively the wedding and the other four associated rites.

Not all the physical details of the ceremonies are available: even the comprehensive liturgical manual *The Tradition* is singularly uninformative about many details, and for several reasons. First, some details are intimate and hence sensitive. Second, these ceremonies have been performed on relatively few occasions and the finer points of instruction can vary from one ceremony to another. Third, since all except the Three Day Ceremony currently require the presence of Sun Myung Moon and his wife[10] there is presumably no need to document every piece of fine detail.

**The Engagement Ceremony**

The process of becoming married within the Unification Church is extremely lengthy and complex, and stories which are popularly recounted about converts to Unificationism being married by Sun Myung Moon within twenty-four hours cannot possibly be true. The procedure is as follows.

Before one can be eligible to be blessed in marriage by the Rev Moon, several conditions must be satisfied. Normally one must have been in full membership for three years, one must have at least three 'spiritual children' (that is to say, won three converts for the Unification Church), and one must have made the prescribed contribution to the 'Indemnity Fund'. According to Unification theology, the doctrine of 'collective sin' entails that we all share in the sin of Judas Iscariot, who betrayed Jesus for thirty pieces of silver. For this sin, indemnity must be paid; and the indemnity in this case takes the form of paying Judas' price multiplied by four, four being – it is explained – the 'number of foundation'.[11] Normally this sum is payable over four years (although it can be paid in a single instalment), and it amounts to a total of £120 (UK), 120 US dollars or 12 000 Korean won.

In addition, a Blessing fee is payable: this is a small sum, often waived, which covers the administrative costs.

When it is announced that a Blessing Ceremony is imminent, names of candidates to take part in the Engagement Ceremony are put forward. Whether or not a member participates is a matter of mutual agreement between that member and the national leader; although a member could refuse to participate and still remain within the church, such a scenario is unlikely, since the Blessing is the culmination of everything one has been taught and has striven for.

In earlier Blessing ceremonies, attention was given to the exact number of couples to be blessed, since the total number of couples involved is given a theological meaning, worked out in terms of numerology. For example, in the first three groups of Blessing ceremonies, 36, 72 and 120 couples respectively were blessed. The number 36, being 12 multiplied by 3, signified the 12 apostles and also the 12 tribes of Israel. Three categories of participant were present: twelve couples were virgins, twelve were already married, and twelve had experienced sexual relationships outside marriage before joining the church. Apparently this was to demonstrate that salvation was available to all, whatever kinds of sexual activities they had engaged in before. The number 72 represented the 72 disciples Jesus sent out to preach[12] and 120 was the number of believers who assembled before Pentecost.[13] Although the Rev Moon aims to attain spiritually significant numbers of couples, some targets have been missed narrowly at certain ceremonies. For instance, in May 1978, the target was 120 couples, although in fact only 118 underwent the ceremony; similarly, at the 777 couples' Blessing Ceremony, the actual number was 791. Such minor discrepancies are seen as irrelevant to the programme of restoration; what is enacted is 'symbolic' and the restoration drama unfolds irrespective of the minor choreographic details. It would be tedious to rehearse all the numerological analyses of the various Blessings which have taken place; these are set out in an Appendix for readers who are interested in these finer points.

This may be an appropriate point to answer a question which is frequently asked about the Blessing ceremonies: what happens if a couple is already married before joining the Unification Church? The 36 Couple Blessing Ceremony defined a clear policy: the Rev Moon will bless an already existing marriage without any suggestion that the couple are separated so that other more suitable marriage partners can be selected. But the Unificationist Blessing Ceremony must still be conducted, for no other form of marriage, whether secular or religious, can enable a couple to gain access to the Kingdom of Heaven. Both partners must wish their marriage to be blessed: if only one partner desires the Blessing, it cannot be given. Since the Blessing is held to be supremely important, it is likely that an already existing marriage would break down if one partner wished to be blessed but the other did not. However, the Unification Church would not actively encourage a member to divorce in such circumstances: it is a member's duty to convert his or her spouse, but if this fails, divorce would be seen as, regrettably, an almost inevitable outcome of such a situation.

In earlier years, when the numbers of blessed couples were small, they were known to the Rev Moon and matched accordingly. As the Unification Church has grown, the numbers participating in these ceremonies has increased dramatically. In the Jamsil Gymnasium, Seoul, a record 5837 couples were blessed by the Rev Moon. Clearly such large numbers cannot be known personally to the Rev Moon, and there is now a Blessing Committee which considers candidates for Blessing and makes recommendations. The Blessing Committee also determines whether the various requirements relating to the Blessing, such as the separation period or the number of spiritual children, can be relaxed. Before the Blessing Committee was established, the Rev Moon himself took exclusive responsibility for selection; he himself still has the final authority to suggest a match, and it is believed that, as in the early days of the UC, he is guided by the spirit world in reaching decisions about Blessing partners.

When the Engagement Ceremony takes place, the candidates assemble in a suitably large room (not a chapel). The Rev and Mrs Moon enter, and the Rev Moon speaks to the candidates about the significance of the Blessing and how to treat one's marriage partner. The matching is then carried out: the Rev Moon points alternately to a male and a female within the congregation. The criteria for selection are not formally articulated, but particular attention is said to be paid to the nature of the respective partner's ancestors. The reason for this connects with the doctrine of 'ancestral sin'; a person inherits the sin of his or her ancestors, for which indemnity must be paid. Consequently, a couple with roughly the same ancestral sin ought to be roughly compatible in terms of spiritual development and have to pay similar amounts of indemnity for these debts.

When a pairing is made, the couple is asked to adjourn to an adjacent room and decide whether or not they accept their leader's recommendation. Normally they are happy to do so, and return and bow to the Rev and Mrs Moon, indicating their acceptance. There have been cases where the couple has declined; although less usual, this is permissible and a re-matching then takes place, perhaps at the same ceremony, or else, if this is not possible, at a later one.

Although a couple may choose to accept or reject the Rev Moon's recommendation, it is normally unacceptable for a member to make a request for a specific marriage partner. If someone were to do this, it would be construed as an attempt to base a relationship on physical attraction or earth-worldly goals,[14] rather than a recognition that marriage is predominantly spiritual and hence involves a spiritual compatibility the Rev Moon is believed to recognise more reliably than the candidates. The Rev Moon is said to have conducted an experiment prior to an Engagement Ceremony: he requested all participants to vote for their favourite potential spouse. Embarrassingly, but predictably, one third of the gathering collected nearly all the votes, indicating that the Blessing could not be enacted if it were carried out according to human standards.[15]

It is sometimes commented that the Rev Moon must sometimes make inappropriate choices, since numerous UC marriages end in divorce.[16] Although the UC boasts a very small divorce rate compared with conventional marriages, second Blessings are becoming an increasingly common phenomenon. Members will insist, however, that a divorce need not cast doubts on the Rev Moon's fitness to pair marriage partners. Although human affairs are governed by God's providence, humankind – as we have seen – is endowed with free will and has its portion of responsibility to contribute to the working out of God's plan. It follows therefore that a couple whose marriage is unsuccessful had a sufficiently sound basis on which to develop a harmonious relationship, but did not fulfil their proportion of the responsibility to make it successful.

## The Holy Wine Ceremony

Very shortly after the Engagement Ceremony, the Holy Wine Ceremony takes place, usually on the same day. When the couples are assembled, the Rev Moon addresses the gathering on the meaning of the ceremony, and then a small glass of Holy Wine is distributed to each couple. A representative couple goes up to pray with the Rev and Mrs Moon in front of all the couples. They face each other, and the bride drinks half of the cup, giving the remainder to her bridegroom to finish. The other couples then drink their wine in similar fashion. The fact that the bride drinks first is not a reflection of western respect for women: it is a reflection of the fact that Eve was the first to sin, and hence the process of restoration, being essentially a recapitulation of Eden, requires that the woman be the first to be restored.

It is worth noting here that the interpretation of the ceremony draws on the Confucian notion of changing *positions*.[17] By offering the bride the cup first, the Rev Moon stands 'in the perfected husband *position*', the bride is in the *position* of Eve, and the husband Lucifer. The restored Eve then goes to the husband who is now in the *position* of fallen Adam, who becomes 'restored'.

The Holy Wine is not only consumed by the couples. It serves a further purpose. A few drops of wine are sprinkled on a new handkerchief which each participant collects at the end of the ceremony. This handkerchief is known as the 'Holy Handkerchief' and is to be kept safely; it is needed again at the Three Day Ceremony.

## The Blessing Ceremony

The Blessing Ceremony is the culmination point of Unification membership, and a vital event in the restoration drama. The ceremony is sometimes public, but the number of guests permitted is determined by the space available; owing to the large number of participants this can be severely limited. However, it should be remembered that the Blessing is different from an ordinary marriage ceremony, for it does not mark the beginning of married life as it is conventionally regarded. It is not followed immediately by a honeymoon, setting up house together or even sexual consummation; indeed the couple may be separated for an extended period afterwards. The ceremony does not necessarily have legal validity; at the Madison Square Gardens wedding in 1982 the Rev Moon obtained a licence to solemnise the marriages, but more often a civil ceremony is needed to legalise them. Sometimes members have preferred to undergo a civil marriage even when this is not strictly necessary, so as to avoid any problems of another country's possible refusal to recognise a Unificationist ceremony. Members will normally ensure that parents and friends are invited to the civil ceremony and to any festivities thereafter.

Depending on the number of couples receiving the Blessing the liturgy will be adapted slightly. The following liturgy was followed at the International Wedding of 74 couples at the World Mission Center in New York on 21 February 1977. Although this number was small compared with other ceremonies, it was at that time the largest Blessing Ceremony to be held outside Korea.

First, twelve men and women attendants, representing couples from previous Blessing Ceremonies formed an aisle through which the True Parents, dressed in their ceremonial robes, passed. The participants then entered in procession, incorporating three symbolic sets of seven paces, interspersed with pauses. Seven is not only a sacred number in Unificationism, but the taking of seven steps is still an integral part of wedding ceremonies in the

East and reflects an ancient tradition. The requirement to enact the seven steps three times is to represent each of the three eras which precede the perfection of Eden: Old Testament, New Testament and Completed Testament. As they passed the True Parents, they were sprinkled with holy water.

The couples then positioned themselves in four columns, facing the True Parents, and the Rev Moon put the following marriage vows to them:

1.    As the restored sons and daughters of God, can you pledge that you will keep the unchanging heavenly law, becoming the ideal ancestors of goodness, the true Adams and Eves, and that you will be responsible for any errors you make from now on?

2.    As the eternal true husbands and wives, you will create not only the ideal family of God, inheriting His blessing, forever, but also you will establish the authority and dignity of Heaven and God's family. Do you pledge this?

3.    As true parents, can you promise that you will raise your children as the obedient and loyal sons of goodness to be able to inherit the will of Heaven and to establish the law of Heaven?

4.    As one of the central families of Heaven, you will become the center of the universe and through the offspring of your home, not only the family of goodness, but also the society of goodness, the nation of goodness, and finally the world of goodness will be established. Can you pledge this?[18]

To each of these questions the couples shouted 'Ye!'

The Rev Moon then prayed publicly. The text of this Blessing prayer indicates that it was probably an extempore prayer, although Blessing prayers appear to have common ingredients: recognition of God's ideal, acknowledgment of the Fall, a pledge to create a new true family, petition for the blessing of spirits who are believed to be present at the ceremony, and prayer for unification and expansion from the unified family to a unified society, nation and world.

After the prayer, wedding rings were exchanged, and two couples – one representing the West and another the East – presented bouquets to the True Parents. The ceremony ended with three cheers of victory: 'Mansei! Mansei! Mansei!' ('Mansei!' is roughly the Korean equivalent of 'Viva!') After this the True Parents and blessed couples left in procession.

After the Blessing, a reception was held for the blessed couples and guests. Despite the decisive significance of the Blessing in the restoration process, its seriousness did not prevent the reception being a festive occasion; members and guests even joined together in party games! However, the reception was not just frivolity. The fun and games were followed by the singing of Holy Songs, the giving of testimonies, the public sharing of what the ceremony meant to various couples, and expression of gratitude to the True Parents for making the Blessing possible.

## The Indemnity Ceremony

After the public spectacle of the Blessing is over, a private ceremony takes place, in which the couples ritually drive out Satan from one another. The ceremony is performed on three successive days, and the Rev Moon presides over it, to ensure that adequate indemnity is paid and that couples enter into marriage with a spouse who is suitably 'restored'. The husband takes a stick and beats the wife ceremonially, and vice versa. This is sometimes known as the 'indemnity stick ceremony' since it symbolises the paying of indemnity to lift the blessed couple from the *positions* of Adam and Eve. In Korean shamanistic folk religion, it is common for a bride and bridegroom to beat each other after a wedding in order to cast out evil spirits.

It is always tempting to ask the wrong questions about ceremonies which are unfamiliar. Questions about whether it causes pain or results in physical injury are really as appropriate as asking a member of the Baptist Church whether anyone has ever drowned or caught pneumonia when being baptised by total immersion. The baptismal candidate will insist that it is the significance of the baptism that is important, not the physical ritual, which can be made to sound strange if the physical actions alone are described without their spiritual meaning. Having talked to members about the Indemnity Ceremony, it is clear that their spiritual path which has led up to this event endows it with a meaning which, as an outsider, I cannot possibly experience. (Incidentally, I am aware of no instances where physical injury has been sustained in this ceremony.)

The period of three days symbolises the three eras through which humankind is believed now to have passed – the Old Testament, New Testament and Completed Testament Eras – and also signifies the restoration of each: God's love, which could not be experienced fully during the first two stages of humankind's history, can now be inherited from all three levels. As the Rev Moon has explained:

> . . . only by inheriting the sphere of God's love on the formation and growth stages can people enter the sphere of the Completed Testament

age. The Indemnity Ceremony has the significance of symbolically accomplishing this inheritance. The first day is to restore the Old Testament age, or fallen Adam. The second day is to complete Jesus' mission and restore the New Testament age. In the Completed Testament age, represented by the third day, the man stands as the bridegroom in the place of Jesus and recreates the bride. Then, for the first time, he can assume his proper position as a restored Adam. Restoration requires such concrete and specific indemnity conditions.[19]

The ceremony is also given a Judaeo-Christian rationale. When the patriarch Jacob met the angel at Jabbok[20] he wrestled with him; unable to overcome Jacob, the angel dislocated his thigh. According to the Unificationist interpretation, the angel was in the *position* of Satan (although not actually Satan himself), and thus the Indemnity Ceremony represents a re-enactment of Jacob's victory over Lucifer.

**The Three Day Ceremony**

Normally three years must elapse between the initial Matching Ceremony performed by the Rev Moon and the consummation of the Blessing in the Three Day Ceremony. In practice, however, such regulations are often relaxed, particularly if the partners are over thirty years of age. The reason for such relaxation is that the emphasis of Unificationism is on begetting sinless children and hence the aim of marriage is procreation. As a woman becomes older, the possibility of pregnancy and safe delivery diminishes.

Unlike the Blessing, the Three Day Ceremony is not public, and does not require the presence of the Rev Moon. Because it is private, Unification members have felt unhappy about the prospect of the details being publicly disclosed. However, rumours are rife, and one ex-member has recently stated that the ceremony involves 'a prescribed series of sexual acts. They have previously been instructed what to do and in what order by elder church members.'[21] Sex always makes for sensationalism, and it is therefore important to recognise the spiritual meaning of the Three Day Ceremony rather than make unfavourable comments on the fact that the founder-leader gives instructions to members on how to consummate their marriages. Consummation of the Blessing is certainly not the consummation of carnal desire, as sex often is in secular society; it is regarded as both the act of the restoring the Fall and of inaugurating a potential new lineage of blessed children.

The Three Day Ceremony restores the fallen relationships between Lucifer and Eve, and Eve and Adam. The couple begins the day by

praying together in private. There is no set prayer, but guidelines are
given: one should pray that the ceremony will be an acceptable offering
to God. They then shower and bathe and the Holy Handkerchief collected
at the Holy Wine Ceremony is dropped in wine, dipped in cold water and
wiped over their bodies. They then don white robes.

To symbolise the restoration of the Fall, the female superior position
is adopted on the first two nights since the wife is in the *position* of
the restored Eve and the husband in the *positions* of Satan and Adam
successively; Eve thus takes the initiative in recapitulating the two 'fallen'
sexual acts, but in a 'principled' manner, since she is having sexual
intercourse with her true spouse. On the third night the male superior
position is adopted, symbolising the restored Adam and Eve fulfilling the
Second Blessing which God had intended them to obtain at the beginning
of Creation.[22]

THE INNER MEANING OF THE BLESSING

So far I have examined mainly the external, or *hyung sang* aspects of the
Blessing ceremonies. What is more important, however, is their *sung sang*,
or inner meaning. As we have seen, the true blood lineage must be restored
and the Fall, which was due to sexual sin, must be reversed. The Holy
Wine Ceremony emphasises the former, while the Blessing and, more
particularly, the Three Day Ceremony, focus on the latter. It would be
inaccurate to state that one ceremony restored the blood and another a
true sexual relationship, for the themes of blood and sex are inextricably
linked.

The concept of 'blood lineage' envelops both these ideas, for sex and
blood are two related factors which affect one's lineage. The lineage in
which someone stands clearly depends on the sexual activity of the parents,
and the pedigree of one's parents determines one's social standing in most
societies. Allied to this, the sexual act of procreation determines the type of
blood the child inherits; medically speaking, the blood group is transmitted
genetically, and of course it is also possible to transmit certain physical
conditions via the blood.

Since the satanic lineage is not restored through *p'i kareun*, another
method is required, and herein lies the importance of the Holy Wine
Ceremony. It has been alleged that the Holy Wine contains the blood of
the Rev and Mrs Moon and that by imbibing messianic blood the 'blood
lineage' of the couples undergoing the Blessing is changed physically
as well as spiritually. This allegation has brought emphatic denials by

Unificationists. It is certainly true that the wine is prepared according to a closely defined recipe, and it takes around six months to mature. It is in fact a *shoju*, a kind of brandy, and it is composed of 21 ingredients, 21 being a sacred number (3 x 7), but whether the Rev Moon's blood is one such ingredient is unclear. In an address on the subject of the Blessing, the Rev Ken Sudo, possibly one of the most controversial Unificationist leaders, made this statement:

> In the Wine Ceremony we use a special wine which contains 21 kinds of things and also the blood of Father and Mother. When this wine was made, many came from the spirit world and asked to drink some. But Father denied it to them. People who are living on earth must be given it first. Moses and Elijah and many saints and sages are waiting for this wine ceremony, but they are not given it yet. Only we who didn't understand anything received it. Without understanding anything we experienced the changing of blood lineage and became qualified to get into the Kingdom of Heaven.[23]

However, a rather curious piece entitled 'Correction' was published almost a year later, which reads as follows:

> In the article 'Internal Meaning of the Blessing' appearing in the Summer, 1977 issue of *The Blessing Quarterly*, Mr Ken Sudo is quoted as saying on page 46: 'In the Wine Ceremony we use a special wine which contains 21 kinds of things and also the blood of Father and Mother.'
> Mr Sudo would like to correct that statement. 'I have no clear memory if I said " . . . contains 21 different kinds of things and also the blood of Father and Mother,"' writes Mr. Sudo. 'But, just in case I said that, it was my mistake. Corrected, the sentence should be: "In the Wine Ceremony, we use a special wine which contains several kinds of things, to inherit the heavenly blood lineage to separate from Satan."'[24]

To this Sudo adds two further comments. First, '"Several kinds of thing" have nothing to do with blood.' Second,'The Holy Wine Ceremony is symbolic just as the bread and wine are used to symbolize the body and blood of Jesus in Holy Communion.'[25]
The Rev Moon himself has made a statement which is equally confusing. In a speech concerning preparation for the Blessing, he says this:

So we do need the condition for a new lineage, that is the ceremony of Holy Wine and in it is represented Father's and Mother's blood, actual blood. Their blood is represented in that particular cup.[26]

This is certainly strange, and even blessed members themselves do not appear to know where the truth lies. (This is hardly surprising, of course, since they do not witness the preparation of the wine.) In June 1979, Neil Salonen, who was at that time the American UC President, is on record as stating that

It is his personal belief that several drops of Moon's blood were in the wine used in the first engagement rite in 1960; the original wine has been preserved for use in all future rite [sic], being multiplied through dilution.[27]

Although a statement from an American leader may seem definitive, it must be borne in mind that other UC leaders have emphatically denied this contention. However, Salonen's statement is not only consistent with the ambiguity of the Rev Moon's and Sudo's remarks, but is also supported, I believe, by the fact that Sudo's first statement appears to refer to a specific occasion ('when this wine was prepared') which is associated with a specific occurrence in the spirit world, when Elijah, Moses and other spirits reputedly asked to be blessed in a Holy Wine Ceremony. Salonen's conjecture is also in line with the prescription for preparing Holy Salt, where the preparation incorporates a few grains of salt which have already been sanctified, to which larger amounts of ordinary salt are added so that the Holy Salt is 'multiplied'.[28]

From a theological standpoint, the claim that the Holy Wine contains a small amount of the True Parents' blood makes sense: this could be regarded as the physical base on which a spiritual event could occur. The wine (or the blood in the wine) is the physical (*hyung sang*) aspect of what is supposedly occurring at a spiritual (*sung sang*) level. As the wine changes one's physical blood (albeit in a small way), so, it is held, one's 'spiritual blood' is changed and the participant now comes under God's dominion instead of Satan's. It is to be remembered that, according to UC teaching, the spirit body is a mirror image of the physical body, with spiritual limbs, organs and spiritual senses. Not only does the physical body contain physical blood, but the spiritual body is animated by 'spiritual blood'.[29] The function of the Wine Ceremony is to change the spiritual blood of the spiritual body.

If the Rev and Mrs Moon's blood is in the wine, does this imply that

Unificationists adopt a physicalistic account of the changed lineage? Do Unification members really hold that their physical blood is literally changed by the ceremony, and that by having some of the True Parents' blood running through their veins they are now 'restored'? Just as mainstream Christians would attach a far greater importance to what the eucharist does spiritually rather than any difference which it makes to the physical body, so in Unificationism it is not believed superstitiously that the wine has some quasi-magical causal efficacy.

The ceremony is necessary, however, because bringing about changes in the spirit world demands a physical foundation, an appropriate physical act which serves as a necessary condition for the spiritual effect. If repentance and indemnity were sufficient, the Blessing and its related ceremonies would not be accorded such momentous importance. The great achievement accredited to the Lord of the Second Advent is having made the Blessing available to the world. The Rev Moon is held to have done this as the result of the indemnity which he himself has paid in full by the sufferings endured during his lifetime. For the rest of the participants the Blessing has not been earned; the preliminary qualifications are only symbolic physical tokens which serve to lay the foundation. As the Rev Moon has said, 'You have no qualification to be blessed.'[30]

Of course, just as it is possible to partake of the eucharist and not attain spiritual benefit, it is possible to drink the wine offered by the Rev and Mrs Moon and still have 'satanic lineage'. The Rev Moon issues constant reminders to members to ensure that their participation is 'heartistic'. This is a Unificationist term: it means that it comes from one's *sung sang* (inner nature, or 'heart'); undergoing these ceremonies must not simply involve bodily compliance with a set of physical rituals. Since one's internal participation is more important than these external manifestations, UC members will no doubt feel that I have dwelt too much on the issue of the ingredients of the Holy Wine. For them the question of whether it contains a trace of physical blood is unimportant: what is more important is the spiritual accomplishment which the ceremony symbolises. The Blessing ceremonies lay the foundation for ensuring that sinless families are procreated and that sins are not passed down to one's progeny.

The Blessing Ceremony is a symbolic representation of the new lineage. It is held that the Rev Moon has pure spiritual blood, being the messiah: this is due to the nature of his ancestry, although precise details of this are not given. Despite these natural qualifications for messiahship, indemnity had to be paid for humankind's sins before the marriage of 1960 could take place, and the Rev Moon is held to have done this by his intense sufferings in prison, amongst other things. Unlike the Rev Moon, Hak Ja Han is said to have been sheltered from the satanic world, and her indemnity consisted of undergoing a period of 'heavenly preparation' by the Rev Moon.[31] The couples undergoing the Blessing do not have the qualifications of messiahship, nor have they paid sufficient indemnity to attain blood purification. The Blessing Ceremony therefore serves as a visible sign of the transference of merit which enables the blessed couples to be ingrafted into the True Family. As the Rev Moon has asserted, the Blessing itself is in a sense a payment of indemnity, being (like the Wine Ceremony) a physical base on which spiritual advancement is possible.[32]

A pure lineage requires pure parents. Of course the blessed couples do not have the purity attributed to the Lord of the Second Advent. The entire course of human history has not been preparing directly for them, but for the messiah; they do not have an ancestry which enables their spiritual blood to be pure; and they have committed many sinful acts during their lifetime for which they have not yet paid full indemnity. If the couples are impure, and only the True Parents are pure and capable of establishing a pure lineage, the only available course, logically, is for the blessed couples also to become messiahs. This is precisely what Unificationists believe is accomplished in the Blessing ceremonies: each of the blessed spouses is placed in the *position* of messiah and has the task of purifying the other spouse. Just as the Rev Moon is acting as messiah when he offers wine to the blessed couples, so the brides assume the *position* of messiah as they offer the wine to their husbands. Likewise at the Three Day Ceremony, the couples are placed in the *position* of messiah to each other, and to their children. If a sinless child can only be the offspring of a messianic lineage, the couples are (amongst other things) in the *position* of messiah to each other. The rite of *p'i kareun* thus becomes unnecessary in the Unification Church. It is unnecessary for the bride to have sexual relations with the messianic leader to inaugurate the purified blood lineage; by having sexual intercourse with one who is ingrafted into the True Family, one is performing a sexual act with one who is in the *position* of messiah.

Securing the purity of the blood lineage of one's family is of course only the beginning. Blessed couples have the task of widening the 'base' of their restoration, so that the clan, the society, the nation and the world are restored.[33] The Blessing therefore imposes on members an obligation to witness, and the Rev Moon has instructed them to beget 84 'spiritual children' in the first seven years of church life. (84 is 12 + 72, the number of the apostles plus the number of disciples whom Jesus sent out.) The establishing of the 'Home Church' programme is a further commitment recommended by the Rev Moon for blessed couples to witness. This involves each individual (ideally) taking a 'parish' of 360 families, with the aim of witnessing to them and caring for them. The 360 constitutes the 'clan' or 'tribe', the next stage to which restoration must be expanded. Further, in addition to those who are already living on earth, those who have died and moved on to the spiritual world require restoration, and this can only be accomplished through a physical base on earth. Their indemnity must be paid too.

UC marriage is therefore for a totally different purpose from matrimony as it is generally regarded in the West. The Rev Moon has pointed to a marked contrast between more conventional western-style marriages and the Blessing which he solemnises. The traditional western method of marriage is held to be self-centred; a man or a woman selects a spouse because of personal feelings of attraction. This self-centred love, the Rev Moon believes, is characteristic of humanity's fallen nature. The western system which permits mutual choice, dating and courting is firmly rejected. Special knowledge is needed to ensure that couples are suitably matched, so that undesirable ancestral tendencies are not passed on to their offspring.

The new blood lineage therefore needs to be maintained.[34] It is not a once-and-for-all miracle which is enacted by the True Parents. Particularly serious is a sexual misdeed after the Blessing, for this would be a re-enactment of Adam and Eve's sin in the Garden of Eden. It may be asked what position a blessed member is in after committing adultery. Does any salvation still remain, or is the messianic restoration offered by the Lord of the Second Advent no longer available? Sexual sin is so serious that the Rev Moon has stated that there can be no forgiveness after adultery,[35] but since Unificationism preaches universal salvation, it would appear that this is one of the Rev Moon's characteristic exaggerations to emphasise the seriousness of this sin. The Blessing symbolises the potential of the couple to pass into the 'Completion' realm: other sins may cause a member to slip backwards within the same realm or even to regress into a lower realm ('Formation' or 'Growth'), but the adulterer inevitably and unequivocally falls into the 'unprincipled realm' which Satan dominates.[36] It is of course possible to be saved from the 'unprincipled realm', since that has been the state of most of humanity until the coming of the new messiah, and the adulterer can be lifted up from his or her spiritual degradation. However, this will require the payment of indemnity not only by the offender but by the Lord of the Second Advent, who is said to suffer deeply when one of his children commits such a serious misdeed. When the final kingdom is fully restored and perfected, I have been told, the adulterer will be part of it, but the sinner will never feel completely comfortable in the presence of the Lord of the Second Advent, knowing that the latter has had to suffer so deeply through that member's own wrong-doing:

> . . . if after the Blessing you commit adultery, for seventy generations following you, your descendants will accuse you before God, and you will remain forever further away from God than you otherwise would have been.[37]

Because the Blessing is the only means of gaining entry into the Kingdom of Heaven, provision must be made for the vast majority of humankind who have died without receiving the Blessing. It is possible that the Rev Moon performs ceremonies for the bonding of spirits, just as the Mormon Church has ceremonies for the 'sealing of ancestors', but I have not received any information that this occurs. As has already been mentioned, of course, ceremonies take place in which a living member can be blessed in union with a member of the spirit world.

However important the Blessing ceremony is in Unification thought, it does not mark the completion of human attainment on earth, let alone in heaven. The couples who are blessed have not yet attained perfection, and must strive with each other's help to do so. Not only is individual perfection still to be reached, but there are many levels at which restoration and perfection must take place: individual, family, society, nation and world.

To sum up, then. The Blessing Ceremony involves a number of elements. Like western-style marriage it is a joyous occasion on which it is appropriate to celebrate. Yet this is a kind of marriage which only the second messiah can bring by paying indemnity; therefore members should feel gratitude that, by his sufferings, the Lord of the Second Advent has laid the foundation which makes the Blessing possible. The Blessing entails responsibility: responsibility to witness, and by so doing to advance the process of restoration and to widen its base; responsibility to maintain the purity of the new lineage into which the participants have become ingrafted; and responsibility to keep the four promises made at the Blessing Ceremony. Finally, the Blessing is eternal as well as temporal; it involves a very serious commitment to a bonding which extends beyond death and which serves as the prelude for those in the spirit world to enter the Kingdom of Heaven by undergoing the Blessing.

# 8 Rites and Festivals

In any serious study of a religion, attention is normally given to forms of worship, festivals and rites of passage. Public attention has focused on the Blessing, but the Unification marriage ceremonies form only a part of a complicated liturgy of devotional acts, rituals and anniversaries. It is therefore appropriate to look at some of the more important Unificationist rites. Like the Blessing, the external aspects of the ritual accomplish little in themselves: it is the member's heart which is important, and *The Tradition* states that 'restoration through Principle is not predicated upon the strict external observance of ceremony'.[1]

## THE PLEDGE

In common with mainstream Christian denominations, Sunday is the day of corporate worship. The day begins with the 'Pledge Service' which commences at 5 a.m., and which only members and their children may attend. Young children are particularly encouraged to come, even from as early an age as six months. ('Pledge' is also recited on the first day of each month and on festival days.) The Pledge takes place in a chapel or else in a room in which a shrine has been specially set up. The shrine will have a picture of True Parents in the centre, together with flowers and *shimjung* candles. (*Shimjung*, or 'heart' candles are candles which are procured by members and ritually multiplied; they are held to have the ability to weaken Satan's power.) Shrine rooms also include a wooden cross, a reminder of the spiritual salvation which Jesus Christ is deemed to have brought.

Despite the earliness of the hour, it is usual for members to assemble before the formal commencement, for meditation and silent prayer. All blessed members are recommended to wear their Holy Robes, and all members are instructed to wear their best clothes. After singing a Holy Song, the service leader announces the beginning of the Pledge. The congregation bows three times, and then recites the words entitled 'My Pledge'. The words are as follows:

1.    As the center of the cosmos, I will fulfill our father's will (purpose of creation), and the responsibility given me (for self-perfection). I will become a dutiful son (daughter) and a child of goodness to attend

149

our father forever in the ideal world of creation (by) returning joy and glory to Him. This I pledge.

2.      I will take upon myself completely the Will of God to give me the whole creation as my inheritance. He has given me His word, His personality, and His heart, and is reviving me who had died, making me one with Him and His true child. To do this, our Father has persevered for 6000 years the sacrificial way of the cross. This I pledge.

3.      As a true son (daughter), I will follow our Father's pattern and charge bravely forward into the enemy camp, until I have judged them completely with the weapons with which He has been defeating the enemy Satan for me throughout the course of history, by sowing sweat for earth, tears for man, and blood for heaven, as a servant but with a father's heart, in order to restore His children and the universe, lost to Satan. This I pledge.

4.      The individual, family, society, nation, world, and cosmos who are willing to attend our Father, the source of peace, happiness, freedom and all ideals, will fulfill the ideal world of one heart in one body by restoring their original nature. To do this, I will become a true son (daughter), returning joy and satisfaction to our Father, and as our Father's representative, I will transfer to the creation peace, happiness, freedom, and all ideals in the world of the heart. This I pledge.

5.      I am proud of the one Sovereignty, proud of the one people, proud of the one land, proud of the one language and culture centered upon God, proud of becoming the child of the One True Parent, proud of the family who is to inherit one tradition, proud of being a laborer who is working to establish the one world of the heart.

I will fight with my life.
I will be responsible for accomplishing my duty and mission.
This I pledge and swear.
This I pledge and swear.
This I pledge and swear.[2]

After recitation of the Pledge, an appointed member (or the leader) offers a representative prayer, which is sometimes followed by a speech for internal guidance. The service ends with unison prayer and a Holy Song.

Like all Unificationist ceremonies, the Pledge Service has a *hyung sang* and a *sung sang* – external appearance and inner meaning. The physical enactment of the ritual bestows no miraculous benefits on the participants:

they must concentrate their minds on God and on True Parents, they should recognise the significance of the three bows – three signifies perfection, and they may imagine that these bows are to God, True Father and True Mother respectively. The words of the Pledge should not be rushed, but spoken mindfully, and the final (fifth) paragraph enumerates seven points which comprise the ideal which members are endeavouring to create: one sovereignty, one people, one land, one language, one True Parent and one True Family tradition. In other words, humankind's ideal is to have a single heavenly citizenship under God, and hence we are a single people in a single land (the world) unbounded by national frontiers, in which the *lingua franca* will be Korean, and in which one's divine lineage will be restored with the inheritance of the True Family tradition (the Four Position Foundation, centred on God).

The reference to Korean as the universal language may seem surprising, but the Rev Moon has stated:

When you go to the Kingdom of Heaven, you will discover that its language is Korean. English is spoken only in the colonies of the Kingdom of Heaven! When the Unification Church movement becomes more advanced, the international and official language of the Unification Church shall be Korean; the official conferences will be conducted in Korean, similar to the Catholic conferences, which are conducted in Latin.[3]

Whether the Rev Moon means this literally is difficult to determine. I have noted earlier his insistence that God, Moses and the Buddha did not speak to him in Korean, or indeed in any other human language. However, I have also noted that the spirit world mirrors the physical world closely, with corresponding spiritual senses, including hearing, and it is certainly the case that members are increasingly encouraged to learn Korean. Whatever the truth of the matter, Korea is very much the 'fatherland', and members who recite the Pledge mindfully will of course recognise this as they pronounce the words. What Israel means to the Jews, Korea means to Unification members.

The UC's critics have often alleged that at the Pledge Service members worship the Rev Moon as the Lord of the Second Advent, and that the ceremony involves a declaration of readiness to commit suicide on his behalf. (It is sometimes alleged that members are given instructions about how to sever their wrists if they are physically abducted by 'deprogrammers', although I have no reason to believe that this is so.) The three-fold bowing at the beginning of the service indicates respect for their founder-leader,

but Unificationists insist that this is not worship. Certainly, the references
to 'Father' in the text of the Pledge are clearly references to God and
not the Rev Moon. By no stretch of the imagination can the Rev Moon
be believed to have 'persevered for 6000 years the sacrificial way of the
cross'. The reference to fighting with one's life is in no way tantamount
to a suicide pact: it is merely a firm commitment to strive for God's
ideal, and mainstream Christian hymns contain lines like 'Oh let my life
be given', or 'Till death Thy endless mercies seal, / And make the sacrifice
complete.' Religions have typically venerated the martyr, insisting that
death is preferable to apostasy. Whether this is what is meant by the
controversial line in My Pledge I very much doubt: the more probable
meaning is that it expresses an unrelenting commitment to working for the
ideal.

I have dwelt at length on the Pledge Service partly because of its controversial nature, and partly because of its important role in Unificationist
liturgy. It is also worth mentioning, however, that there is another Pledge
which is used additionally and exclusively by blessed members. This
Pledge is called 'The Pledge of the Families', and it is to be recited before
the more general Pledge Service begins.

The words of The Pledge of the Families run as follows:

> We families, the center of the cosmos, brothers and sisters vertically
> connected to the flesh and blood of the True Parents before the new
> heaven, pledge and swear before the True Parents to become worthy
> of possessing the glory of victors by maintaining our positions in
> responsible activities and by observing the family laws and traditions
> decreed by heaven. This I pledge. This I pledge. This I pledge.[4]

Later on a Sunday morning there is congregational worship, which
non-members may also attend. The form of the service is in the non-con-
formist 'hymn sandwich' style. There is no fixed liturgy or lectionary, but
readings are generally taken from the Old and New Testaments. I have not
personally witnessed the reading of *Divine Principle* at morning service,
but I am told this occasionally happens, and I have certainly listened to
sermons which have used *Divine Principle* in their exposition of scripture.
Mainstream Christian hymns are often used; sometimes the hymnary has
changed the words when the original wording conflicts with UC theology,
but of course the practice of adapting hymns is not by any means peculiar
to the UC: many denominations and generations have adapted and updated
hymns to suit their own ends. Prayers are normally extempore, and unison
prayer usually features in the service.

A small number of designated leaders are chosen to preside over and preach at public worship, several of whom have been given the title 'Reverend' by the Rev Moon. This is more of an honorary title than (as in mainstream Christianity) a licence to undertake special practices (such as celebrating the sacraments). Those leaders who have been accorded such titles, of course, normally have a very active role in leading the worship.

In addition to public worship, Unification Centres have a daily morning service, which consists of Holy Songs, readings, prayers and a talk. Private devotions are also considered to be supremely important, and members are strongly encouraged to develop a personal prayer life, to make 'prayer conditions' (resolutions to pray for a predetermined length of time each day over a specified period), and to study *Divine Principle* and spiritual classics.

## Birth

In any religion, festivals normally serve one of two functions. They mark events in the life of the individual follower, such as birth, marriage, and death (life-cycle rites), or they re-enact the history of the significant events within the history of the religion.[5] The Unification Church's festivals fall into both categories. We have already seen how the Unification Church treats marriage: however, the UC's commentators rarely remark on the ceremonies accompanying birth and death.

Children who are born of blessed parents are considered to have a special privilege, for never before have children been born of parents who have undergone the second Blessing. In addition, birth assumes major importance for UC members since it is taught that God imparts a human self with a spirit at the moment of the first breath; the embryo in the womb only has a 'spirit base'.[6] It is therefore important that prayers should be related to the exact time and circumstances of birth. (This is not to downgrade the importance of the embryo: since this spirit base is necessary for the spirit to grow, strict rules govern the practice of abortion, which is only permitted in extreme circumstances, notably when the mother's health is endangered, the child has a serious irreversible deformity, or where the child was conceived in 'any circumstance involving a break in the spiritual order',[7] such as rape or incest.)

The tradition of holding a ceremony to mark the birth of a child began with the birth of the Rev and Mrs Moon's eldest daughter Ye Jin in November 1960. The Birth Ceremony involves lighting 'birth candles' (candles ceremonially prepared for this event) and praying in a sanctified area. Before leaving for hospital, the parents should contact their friends who will attend, and designate one member to light the seven birth candles. These should be lit approximately five minutes before the baby is born and about five minutes after the birth. The ceremony has no fixed pattern: it basically consists of prayers, including unison prayer.[8]

The aim of the ceremony is to create a holy environment for the newly born child. This is believed still to be the period of restoration, which has not yet been fully accomplished, and the environment into which a child is born is impure and ungodly: it is therefore important that the child should be separated from Satan at the moment of birth.

## The Eight Day Dedication Ceremony

When the child is eight days old, a ceremony of dedication is performed. (The number eight signifies a new start in Unificationist numerology.)[9] Although there are fairly exact prescriptions for this ceremony it is made clear that it is the internal heart that is important rather than any external appearances: the emphasis of the ceremony is on gratitude to God.[10] Unlike mainstream Christian baptisms, it is inappropriate for parents or guests to offer gifts to the child: the ceremony is basically for God, not for the baby.

The ceremony is conducted by the parents alone, and a limited number of guests look on, participating 'internally' only – in other words, an outsider might simply construe them as observers. It would be particularly appropriate to invite what are known as one's 'trinity members': members of the UC are arranged into triads of couples, who undertake to give special support to each other and to pray regularly for each other. Parents take a bath and bathe the child before the ceremony; they don their white Holy Robes, and clothe the child in a ceremonial gown. An altar is set up in the prescribed manner, with at least one birth candle or one or two *shimjung* ('heart') candles. The parents face the altar, light the candles, pray silently and then kneel, raising the child in offering to God. The child is placed in front of the altar while the parents bow. The Pledge of the Families is recited and then (if desired) My Pledge. A representative prayer is said and the candles are extinguished. This prayer should offer the child to God, requesting that he or she should become a godly son or daughter; the parents pledge themselves to bring up the child according to God's will, and to care for the child internally and externally.

After the Dedication Ceremony, parents may decide to hold a 40–Day and 100–Day Ceremony on behalf of their child. This is optional, however. It is not a rededication, but an expression of gratitude. It is essentially a prayer service.

## Birthdays

To those outside the Unification Church it may seem surprising that birthdays form part of the Unificationist life-cycle rites, since a birthday is a purely secular celebration outside the UC. A Unification Church member has two birthdays – a physical and a spiritual. The 'spiritual birthday' marks the occasion on which the member was converted to the teachings of the church. For blessed children (those born of members) spiritual and physical birthdays coincide: the second generation of believers has been brought up within the movement and has no need of a specific point of conversion. For blessed couples, the anniversary of their Blessing supersedes their spiritual birthday, which thenceforth is no longer celebrated.

Since one's physical birth is of utmost significance it is fitting that it should be commemorated within a religious context. It is the anniversary of God's gift of life. Ceremonies for the birthdays of True Children (that is, the physical offspring of the Rev and Mrs Moon) are elaborate events, but birthday ceremonies for rank and file members are fairly simple: an altar is prepared with a picture of True Parents, a candle, and (if desired) the traditional birthday cake, and prayers are recited in the morning. A reception is held later. A traditional birthday party, to which non-members may be invited, is permitted later in the day. This is allowed because we are currently in the 'transitional era' between Fall and Restoration: but in a completely restored world such secular events would fade.

The idea of birthday celebrations is to restore a secular event into a spiritual one. Enjoyment is permitted, indeed encouraged, but it must not obscure the spiritual meaning of the day. Single members are requested to fast instead of feast on at least three of their birthdays, and the Rev Moon himself has set such an example.

## Death

Death is particularly important in one's spiritual progress since it marks the transition from the physical world to the spirit world. We have seen that for the Unificationist there is a very intimate connection between body and spirit, and hence the two must not be unnaturally separated. For this reason euthanasia is forbidden, for it is an unnatural termination of the physical body's life, and without physical bodies spiritual bodies cannot grow. (Unification ethics makes a distinction between active mercy killing and the artificial prolongation of life: switching off life support machinery, for instance, is permissible at the discretion of a dying member's family.)[11]

At death the spirit is freed from the confines of the body and is believed to have passed on to the spirit world. Therefore, far from being an occasion of sorrow, a funeral is seen as a cause for rejoicing: in fact, it is described as an event more joyful even than the Blessing itself.[12] The first part of the funeral rites for blessed members is called *Gwi Hwan*, which means 'returning to joy'.

The existing pattern of funeral rites was inaugurated in 1984, after Heung Jin Moon's death.[13] One of the many post-death achievements accredited to Heung Jin is that he has empowered members to receive the *Seung Hwa* ('ascension and harmony') ceremony.[14] The *Seung Hwa* ceremony is for members who have undergone the Blessing, and it is divided into three stages.

First there is the *Gwi Hwan* ceremony, at which members of the deceased's immediate family, close friends and trinity members pay their last respects. This is done in the home (if it is permitted to bring home the coffin), or in the hospital in which the member died. The blessed member is dressed in his or her white Holy Robes and white gloves, after these have been sanctified with Holy Salt. The Blessing ring is left on. Various items are placed in the coffin with the body, including a copy of *Divine Principle*, a book of the Rev Moon's speeches, and the member's Holy Handkerchief. A Unification Church flag is prepared, to be placed on top of the coffin.

The *Seung Hwa* ceremony may take place in the home or in a UC Centre. An altar is erected, and a new white cloth placed on it. A banner indicates the ceremony which is being performed, and the coffin, bearing the Unificationist flag, is placed in the most elevated position. Beneath it is a large picture of the member, framed and draped with a light coloured ribbon. (The conventional black for funerals is strongly discouraged.) On either side is a pair of *shimjung* candles. Brightly coloured flowers are placed on the floor beneath. It is considered inappropriate to have a picture of the True Parents in the room.

The *Seung Hwa* Ceremony itself follows the style of a conventional funeral – Holy Songs, a prayer, and a tribute to the deceased member. Members pay their last respects individually by making a full bow towards the altar and lighting an incense stick. The *Seung Hwa* Ceremony extends beyond the service, however, and lasts a total of three, five or seven days (an odd number of days is prescribed), during which a constant vigil is kept in the room, until the body is finally taken away for burial. This is performed by members of the family and trinity members, and consists of a continuous recitation of hymns, prayers and testimonies. At no time must the coffin be unattended.

After the vigil, members process to the burial ground. Unificationism holds that deceased members should be buried, not cremated, since the physical body should be allowed a natural return to the physical world. The Rev Moon has expressed an intention to create special 'Holy Grounds' for Unificationist burials, but until this is achieved, members are encouraged to select an attractive burial plot, preferably on high ground.

At the burial ground the second part of the funeral rites, the *Won Jeun* Ceremony, is performed. This is a simple service at which a hymn, prayers and a sermon are offered. A simple meal is brought to the service and placed before the coffin. After *Won Jeun* a family altar is set up in the home, bearing the deceased member's picture, flanked by a pair of *shimjung* candles. A plate of food should be offered daily at this altar, and subsequently removed for consumption by the rest of the family. (It is an ancient Confucian practice to offer food as an act of venerating the dead.)

The burial ground should be visited three days after the *Won Jeun* Ceremony, when the *Sam Oje* Ceremony – the last 'ceremony of ascension' – is performed. Flowers and incense are offered, and fruit and other simple foods are brought to the burial ground.

The *Seung Hwa* ceremony is for blessed members, and only parts of it are used for a single member's funeral. The single member, although unblessed, has nevertheless believed the *Principle* and acknowledged the Rev and Mrs Moon as the True Parents. He or she therefore has a spiritual advantage over the non-member and hence it is appropriate to celebrate the death in a distinctively Unificationist manner. At present no precise liturgy for single members' funeral rites has been formulated.

On occasions, UC members have to attend non-members' funerals. Blessed members, single members and non-members are at different spiritual levels, and it is necessary for blessed members to pay indemnity to cleanse the spirit after it has been 'connected to the unperfected spiritual level'[15] in an environment related to death. In order to return to 'God's environment' after entering 'Satan's environment', members are instructed to light a fire (preferably in an open space, but if this is impossible the back door of a Centre or one's home will suffice), walk over and then around it three times, sprinkle themselves with Holy Salt, and (if possible) take a shower.

## THE MAJOR FESTIVALS

The four most important Unificationist festivals are Parents Day, Children's Day, Day of All Things, and God's Day. True Parents' Birthday is also celebrated as an important landmark in the liturgical calendar. The UC's liturgical manual *The Tradition* states that 'Salvation actually means saving the four heavenly days also'.[16] This somewhat enigmatic remark, given the appropriate explanation, serves as the key to understanding the first four of these festivals. The celebration of these festivals signifies, amongst other things, the restoration of True Parents and Children. If Adam and Eve had not sinned, they would have perfected themselves (the first Blessing), become True Parents (the second Blessing) and given birth to sinless children. The day on which the first sinless children were born would have been the first Parents Day and Children's Day combined. On that day they would also have been the true inheritors of the earth, having accepted dominion over all things (the third Blessing) under God's 'direct dominion': such a day would therefore be simultaneously The Day of All Things. That day would indeed have been a joyful day for God – it would in fact have been 'God's Day', the day in which the first man and woman attained perfection, became husband and wife (thus establishing principled sexual relationships) and gained dominion over creation. God's Day would thus have incorporated Parents Day, Children's Day and The Day of All Things simultaneously. Of course, because of the Fall, no such day occurred, and thus these 'days' had to be restored. However, as *The Tradition* explains, in the process of restoration the four days had to be restored sequentially and not simultaneously. These four festival days encapsulate the main events of Unificationist history where these four days of restoration took place.

Parents Day commemorates the marriage of Sun Myung Moon and Hak Ja Han. This decisive event is held to have restored Eden, and marked the origin and source of new life for all humankind. Parents Day thus lies at the root of UC tradition. As the Rev Moon stated in a recent Parents Day speech:-

> Parents Day has this significance: Parents Day is the first time since God created all things and humankind that there is one balanced man, one balanced woman, balanced in love, to whom God can descend and with whom He can truly be. For the first time in human history, the original state of matrimony, the original trinity, has come into existence upon the earth.[17]

Children's Day was established on 1 October 1960 (lunar date) on the 'foundation' of Parents Day. True Parents are regarded as the spiritual life source, but their Holy Blessing was a prelude to the establishment of the Kingdom of Heaven on earth, the next stage of which is the establishment of a True Family. Children's Day signifies that all humankind can be ingrafted into the family of True Parents and become children of God.

The Day of All Things was established on 1 May 1963.[18] Humankind had to be restored before the rest of creation, since the attainment of individual perfection and principled matrimony are the first two Blessings and the dominion over creation the third. Since the restoration process involves a re-enactment of Adam and Eve's course in a principled way, The Day of All Things – signifying the unification of humankind with the rest of creation – must follow after Parents Day and Children's Day. This festival signifies the return of all things from the dominion of Satan to the rightful ownership of God.

The fourth major festival is God's Day. Although mainstream Christians have typically avoided devoting a special festival to God, holding that *all* worship and living should be so directed, Unificationists are surprised that a Being as important as the deity should be denied a festival on his own behalf. For UC members, God's Day provides an opportunity for attaining a right relationship with God (a correct 'vertical' relationship) by showing repentance and healing any broken relationships with fellow human beings (a correct 'horizontal' relationship). The festival therefore focuses on the themes of love, repentance and purity.

God's Day is New Year's Day. On New Year's Eve, members assemble to mark the beginning of God's Day with a midnight ceremony. At this ceremony, which commences on the stroke of midnight, the Rev Moon prays to Heaven that his mission for the coming year will be fulfilled. After this prayer he proclaims a motto for the year and paints it on a large white banner with a brush and black ink. In 1984, for example, the motto was 'The Creation and Building of the Fatherland'.[19]

These four Holy Days mark the stages of restoration of the Four Position Foundation. But there is also a fifth which UC members would regard as a major festival equal in importance to these four. It is January 6, which is the date of the mutual birthday of the Rev Moon and Hak Ja Han.

For all five occasions, members are instructed to prepare themselves inwardly. At least three days' internal preparation is prescribed and the three ensuing days should be devoted to gratitude for the events in the restoration process which are commemorated. Festival days begin with the Pledge Service, which commences at 7 a.m. It is customary for members to send greetings cards or gifts to the True Parents, and also to exchange cards and sometimes gifts amongst themselves. Spiritual parents would typically give a card or present to their spiritual children at these times.

The celebration of the five main festivals takes place at two levels. First, there are the True Parents' Celebrations, over which the Rev and Mrs Moon preside. These are attended by the elder couples of the movement, and a few blessed couples who represent the membership more widely. In addition, a number of blessed members are selected to represent various elements of the restoration process. Thus, one member might represent the four major 'dispensational nations' (Korea, Japan, USA, Germany), another the six continents, a third the world's major religions, a fourth the nations in which there are UC missions, a fifth the communist world and a sixth the spirit world. These categories are not fixed, and sometimes additional categories are added: for example on True Parents' Birthday, a couple might be chosen to represent True Parents' relatives.

An offering table is set out with a white cloth stretching from its surface to the ground, and with various foods and candles. A cake – rather like a conventional wedding cake in appearance – is placed at the front. Beside it is a ceremonial sword. Behind the table two places are set, and a Korean meal is prepared for the True Parents. The foods and fruits are formally set out, and the numbers of different items and the heights of the display are determined by Unificationist numerology.

The ceremony begins with the entrance of the True Parents, who check that the offering table is in order. The True Children (the Rev and Mrs Moon's family) follow their parents to the offering table and bow. The Rev Moon offers a preparatory prayer, and all of them bow – Father and Mother to the 'position of True Parents', Mother to Father, and True Children to True Parents.

The blessed couples then enter, the order of entry being determined by the length of time in which they have been blessed. Men then stand on the right, women on the left. The representative couples then bow. The Pledge is recited, after which the Rev Moon pronounces a benediction, and the ceremony closes with the cutting of the celebration cake with the sword. The service leader offers three cheers of 'Mansei', and the food on the table is shared around the congregation. The ceremony concludes with a speech by the Rev Moon: this tends to be short, since a special Holy Day sermon is usually given to the general membership immediately afterwards.

At Unification Church Centres, the festival begins with the Pledge Service at 7 a.m. Before the service members bathe, and if they cannot wear robes at this service, they should wear their best clothing. A banner is normally displayed, indicating clearly the nature of the festival, the place at which it is being celebrated and the date. Members enter the chapel according to Blessing seniority. The Pledge is recited and a leader offers a prayer, usually followed by unison prayer and a closing hymn. The leader normally gives an address at this service.

What I have described so far are the *hyung sang* aspects of the festivals, and of course members would agree that these are merely the physical manifestations of something deeper and much more important. *The Tradition* states that it is not the elaborateness of the ceremonies which is important, but cleanliness, especially one's purity of heart. Any offering which is placed on the table should be placed with much prayer, and the festivals should be approached with due preparation. If members have families, they are recommended to celebrate the festivals at a family level first (normally at 5 a.m.), and to use these occasions as opportunities to instruct their children in their faith.

The fact that these festivals are landmarks in the liturgical calendar does not mean that they are to be approached with deadly seriousness. On the contrary, parents are encouraged to train their children to look forward to these events more than to secular holidays. They are occasions when parents will present gifts to their children, and the ceremonies are followed by social events. An entertainment, an outing, games and musical events are fitting sequels to the more overtly religious parts of the festival day: but there is no sharp distinction between sacred and secular – in the midst of festivities, it is quite appropriate for members to give their testimonies to all who are present.

## MINOR FESTIVALS

In addition to the five major festivals previously mentioned, there are also five minor ones, known as 'landmark days'. These are: (1) The Day of Victory of Love (January 3); (2) The Anniversary of the founding of the HSA-UWC (May 1); (3) The Day of the Love of God (May 20); (4) Foundation Day (September 18); and (5) The Day of Victory of Heaven (October 4).

The second of these is self-explanatory. Foundation Day commemorates two rallies held on 18 September 1974 and 18 September 1976 at Madison Square Gardens and the Washington Monument respectively. These events have been given a theological significance, and are held to have achieved the 'worldwide foundation' for the restoration of humankind. The Day of Victory of Heaven commemorates the Rev Moon's release from prison, together with all the indemnity he is held to have paid for humanity's restoration. He was freed from prison in North Korea on 14 October 1950, and from prison in South Korea on 4 October 1955. The Rev Moon established this landmark day on 4 October 1976.

The Day of the Victory of Love subdivides into two dates – the Day of Unification (proclaimed on 31 December 1983), and the Day of the Victory of Love itself. The former was declared while the Rev Moon's son Heung Jin was dying in hospital and it was clear that he would not recover. The latter emanates from a 'Victory Over Communism' rally in Korea, at which the Rev Moon affirmed that Heung Jin's death had been transformed into a victory of God's love. Heung Jin is held not to have died an ordinary death, but to have conquered death. He has not died but attained *seung hwa* – ascension and harmony, opening a celestial door to save the communist and the free worlds. After he ascended to the spirit world, it was predicted by the Rev Moon that Heung Jin would travel back and forward from there as a 'returning resurrection'. The Rev Moon made the following statement on 1 January 1984 concerning the ceremony for the Day of Unification.

This morning I held a special service, called a Unification Ceremony, in the hospital chapel. On the foundation of this precious sacrifice, we called for the unity of the first, second and third Israels – Judaism, Christianity, and the Unification Church. Also we called for the unity of Adam, Eve, and the archangel nations, the unification of True Parents and their family, the members of the Unification Church, as well as all the races of the world. We called for total unification.[20]

The Day of the Love of God reaffirms the work of Heung Jin. The day marks 'the unity between True Parents on earth and Heavenly Father, Heung Jin, and Jesus in the spirit world'; as a result, 120 nations in the spirit world and 120 nations on earth now have 'the right to resurrection'.[21] (120 is reckoned to be the number of nations in the free world; since the spirit world mirrors the physical world it is therefore to be expected that spirits who have lived in 'free' countries comprise 120 different spirit nations.)

It will be obvious from the preceding account that many of these festivals are very recently established. It is therefore highly likely that the future will see further additions. As decisive events occur in the life of the church they will no doubt be commemorated liturgically. After the Rev Moon dies, it would indeed be surprising if his *seung hwa* was not accorded an important place in the UC's liturgical year.

Since the church has a very large number of festivals, some will no doubt diminish in importance, or even be passed over. This has its precedent in mainstream Christianity: how many Christians are still able to mark the date of the conversion of St Paul or the beheading of John the Baptist, even though such festivals are technically part of the liturgical calendar?

## ATTITUDES TO CHRISTIAN FESTIVALS

It is necessary to say something about the Unification Church's attitude to mainstream Christian festivals. The UC has never celebrated the sacraments of baptism and the eucharist.[22] Although the eucharist is not part of the UC's liturgy, members will normally accept the sacrament if they are attending a service in a mainstream church, provided the celebrant has no objection.

Since the UC acknowledges that Jesus' mission, although incomplete, accomplished significant results, it is appropriate that it should mark the mainstream Christian festivals which are connected with the life of Jesus Christ. Like mainstream Christians, members observe Christmas Day. However, they are more inclined to avoid the commercialism of western-style Christmases and attempt to experience its true spiritual meaning. One of the Rev Moon's Christmas Day speeches ('The Participants in Celebrating Christmas')[23] recommends that members mark the remainder of Christmas Day by continuing their street witnessing. The true spiritual meaning of Christmas for the UC member is to become one with the heart and mind of Jesus, by continuing his unfinished mission. However, it should not be assumed that on Christmas Day members do not enjoy any of the traditional festivities. On the contrary, particularly in the face of the anti-cult criticism that 'Moonies split up families', many members will visit their parents and families to celebrate Christmas in the traditional way.

Good Friday is likely to pass unmarked, since the UC's attitude to the crucifixion is ambivalent. On the one hand, the crucifixion was contrary to God's primary purpose; on the other hand, it obtained spiritual salvation for humankind. UC members are more likely to observe Easter Day, since they wish to emphasise the resurrection and continued existence of Jesus Christ in the spirit world. Easter Day worship would therefore follow the normal pattern of morning worship, with the hymns and readings directed towards the Easter theme.

## CONCLUSIONS

This elaborately complex Unificationist liturgy demonstrates that there is much more to belonging to the UC than believing the *Principle*. The *Principle* is to be lived, not just intellectually accepted, and living the *Principle* involves both ethical and religious dimensions. Corporate worship involves an unusual combination of the spontaneity and informality of American

Protestantism with the ceremonial precision associated with Confucian rites (such as the rites for the dead) and the rituals of folk shamanism. I do not know whether the elaborate ritual dimension, combined with a liturgical calendar punctuated with anniversary ceremonies, serves to explain the presence of a higher proportion of erstwhile Roman Catholics and Jews than one would normally expect within the UC.[24] It is a possible hypothesis, but much more research needs to be carried out by sociologists of religion to explain transmigrations between religious groups.

Whatever sociological conclusions can be drawn about the Unification Church, one theological conclusion is clear. If a liturgical calendar serves to highlight the significant events in a religious tradition's history, then it can be seen that the Lord of the Second Advent's work is what is given the greatest, although not exclusive, emphasis. Although recognition is given to the Old and New Testament ages, Unificationist liturgy clearly emphasises the firm belief that humanity has now passed beyond the Old and New Testament ages into the Completed Testament Era.

# 9 The Future Agenda

The most obvious immediate task of the Unification Church is the propagation of its own distinctive teachings. In the longer term, the goal of 'unifying' the world's religions must be reached, and members of different denominations and religious traditions brought together in an ecumenical context. The UC's work is targeted towards both these goals.

In addition to its traditional work of street witnessing and workshop seminars, a number of satellite organisations have been established by the Rev Moon which might be said to have the broad aim of 'unification'. These organisations are known collectively as the Unification Movement (UM), and it is appropriate to say something about the range of activities which the Rev Moon has sponsored.

The Church's initial outreach was to spread the teachings of the *Principle* to potential converts, which it did by 'witnessing' (evangelising) and fund raising. Students were particularly targeted as potential converts and accordingly the Collegiate Association for the Research of Principles (CARP) was established in Korea in 1955, and has since spread world-wide. The declared goals of CARP are 'spiritual renewal, new moral commitment and positive solutions to global injustice'.[1] As well as facilitating the study of the *Principle*, CARP has held public rallies in various parts of the world, raising public consciousness on a variety of current social issues: it has organised rallies against drugs and pornography, for example, in Great Britain and the USA.

In order to further the UC's goals it is desirable that a significant proportion of its members should have undergone a good education. The Rev Moon has a high regard for scholarship and has taken pains to ensure that the more academically able UC members obtain good academic qualifications. Far from being an eccentric community of gullible people, as is sometimes imagined, somewhere between 20 and 30 per cent of its members are university graduates. Formal training of some of the more academically gifted Unification Church members is carried out in its own seminary – the Unification Theological Seminary (UTS) – in Barrytown, New York. From time to time, promising UC members are sent to UTS for its two-year training course. It is a small seminary, staffed by some ten academics, and runs post-graduate courses for members. Of its academic staff, only two are Unification

Church members. The religious affiliations of the academic staff are reflected in the curriculum: it is not simply Unification thought which is taught, but the entire spectrum of the world's religions. Clearly, if members are to establish links with representatives of the world's major religious traditions, a breadth of religious knowledge is desirable. In 1987 the Seminary gained a provisional charter to award its own degrees – Master of Religious Education and Master of Divinity – and in 1990 the New York State Board of Regents granted it an absolute charter.

From the ranks of its graduate members, several have progressed to post-graduate study, and have attained doctorates in well accredited universities including Yale and Harvard. From time to time they have presented material at UC-sponsored conferences. By virtue of the religious viewpoint which it reflects, it is against the trend of contemporary scholarship; nevertheless, much of it is of a good standard and holds its own against mainstream contributions.

The Rev Moon's predilection for scholarship is not limited to securing high standards of academic attainment for his most promising followers. 'Unification' involves two important aspects: unifying people of diverse religious traditions, and unifying the physical world with the spiritual. For these respective purposes the Rev Moon inaugurated two large organisations: the International Religious Foundation (IRF) and the International Cultural Foundation (ICF). The IRF incorporates a body known as New ERA (New Ecumenical Research Association), which – amongst other things – has often invited academics and members of the clergy to spend several days, usually in an attractive environment, to listen to extended exposition of *Divine Principle*. At such conferences attempts are seldom, if ever, made to convert participants; the aim, rather, is to correct the stereotype of the so-called 'Moonie' presented by the media, and also – perhaps more importantly – to encourage attenders to participate in other ecumenical activities sponsored by the Rev Moon, in the name of 'unification'. In this respect the seminar is a prelude to the achievement of the UC's aim of bringing together representatives of the world's various religious traditions and denominations and to enable them to discuss issues of ecumenical importance.

The Introductory Seminars invite 'no holds barred' criticisms of Unificationist teaching, and indeed New ERA makes a practice of inviting well accredited scholars who do not belong to the UC to offer critiques of Unification theology. It is explained that the process of Unification can only be accomplished if divergent points of view are vented and discussed. At other conferences, Unificationism may not be part of the programme at all, and a theme of general ecumenical interest is debated by members from a variety of religious backgrounds.

Attendance at an Introductory Seminar is not necessarily a prerequisite for attendance at subsequent New ERA events. Although some of these other New ERA conferences are sometimes on themes relating to Unificationism (such as the ones on 'Unificationism and Socialism' and 'Eastern Interpretations of the Christian Scriptures' held in Martinique in 1985), the bulk of these conferences are on mainstream theological topics. Of particular significance is the 'God Conference' which New ERA has regularly convened since 1981, and at which eminent scholars from different religious traditions have met and discussed their respective concepts of God.

The adjective 'new' which qualifies 'ecumenism' is significant. Unlike the traditional forms of Christian ecumenism, New ERA conferences do not attempt to hammer out formulae which might enable one denomination to recognise the validity of another's ordination or to determine in what circumstances different Christian denominations might inter-communicate. Such debates would be inappropriate since attenders are not official representatives of their own denominations but come in an individual capacity. Traditional ecumenical discussions have tended to focus on differences between denominations which have formed barriers to unity; by contrast, the new-style ecumenism sponsored by the UM tends more to elicit points on which attenders are agreed. What happens after any agreement is reached is left open-ended, since there is no mechanism for implementing any decisions, even if unanimity were miraculously achieved at such gatherings.

After the first 'God Conference' in 1981, the Rev Moon proposed that the sharing of religious beliefs should not be confined to academics, but might profitably be extended to students as well. As a result, the Youth Seminar on World Religions was set up in 1982. This consisted of a pilgrimage of some 150 students from a variety of religious and national backgrounds, who traveled round the world under the leadership of non-Unificationist academics, visiting important religious sites from the various traditions of Judaism, Christianity, Islam, Confucianism, Hinduism and Buddhism. The students have traveled through Egypt, India, Turkey, Israel, Italy, Japan, Nepal, China, and the USA. In addition to the visits to the various shrines, activities have included lectures, discussions with religious leaders and scholars, and participation in the rituals of many of the religions studied. The Youth Seminar invariably ended up in Korea, and one common criticism of the venture is that it was

designed to put Korea, and specifically Unificationism, on the map of
the world's major religious traditions, thus giving a disproportionate
emphasis to the UC, which, whatever the future holds, still remains a
minor religion.

In Unification thought the unification of Christianity is a prelude
to a wider unification of religions, a prerequisite for which is inter-
religious dialogue, and the UM has financed and hosted hundreds of
inter-religious events since the IRF's inception. The scale on which
the UM operates is best indicated, I think, by a statement of a former
member of the British Council of Churches' Secretariat, who recently
remarked that

> the Unification Church (which is not an orthodox Christian Church)
> does more for the interfaith movement at an international level than
> do either the World Council of Churches dialogue unit or the Roman
> Catholic Vatican Secretariat for Non-Christians, or both of them put
> together.'[2]

The UM's most ambitious inter-religious event was undoubtedly the
Assembly of the World's Religions held at McAffee, New Jersey in
November 1985, which was attended by some 650 participants from
all of the world's major religious traditions: Jews, Christians, Muslims,
Hindus, Buddhists, Sikhs, Parsees and Jains. Three such Assemblies have
been planned, culminating in 1993, the centenary year of the 1893 World
Parliament of Religions which took place in Chicago. The Assembly's
programme was a blend of addresses, specialist seminars, and opportunities
to share in the worship and in the cultural events (such as Indian dance)
which were led by attenders from the various faiths.

Not all of the UM's work is academic. The International Relief Friendship Fund (IRFF) has been active in sending aid to underdeveloped
countries. Additionally, the Religious Youth Service (RYS) aims to pro-
mote inter-religious co-operation in relief work. Founded in 1986 as a
development of the Youth Seminar, RYS is still in its early stages, but
already a group of 120 volunteers has done work in the Philippines
in conjunction with the local communities. Projects have included re-
afforestation and the building of schools and clinics. Unlike the IRFF,
which was solely comprised of Unification Church members, volunteers for RYS are sought amongst a variety of religious denominations
and educational establishments. RYS is not exclusively funded by the
Unification Movement: contributions have been sought from previous
conference attenders.

## THE INTERNATIONAL CULTURAL FOUNDATION

Unifying the physical and the spiritual must also be accomplished, and to this end science and religion must also be 'unified'. Science cannot acceptably function in a vacuum without any regard for ethical values or without questioning the worthwhileness of its activities. Such values can only be derived from some kind of interaction between the spiritual and the physical: hence the need for the unification of science and religion. Accordingly the UM has evolved a cluster of organisations which fall under the general title 'International Cultural Foundation' (ICF).

Under the ICF's auspices many academic conferences have been convened under the title 'International Conference of the Unity of the Sciences' (ICUS). ICUS conferences incorporate all the various sciences – the physical, social and life sciences. Sometimes their themes are specific to a particular branch of science; at other times they bring together scientists from different disciplinary backgrounds to discuss scientific matters; at other times again ICUS sets as its theme some aspect of the relationship between science and values. Past ICUS conferences have attracted some important names in the field of science, including Nobel prizewinners; not all attenders are religious, and indeed some would even claim to be opposed to religion. As with the ICF organisations, ICUS is organised by a group of consultants, most of whom are independent of the Unification Church.

Very recently the Rev Moon proposed a new initiative: a World Festival of Culture in Korea in 1991. The purpose of this event was to attract major figures, not only from a variety of religions, but from the sciences, the media, economics and politics. As well as cultural exchange, athletic competition featured in the programme. Not only was this event designed to foster the spirit of unification by bringing together members of different nations to participate in events of mutual interest, but of course the Rev Moon's initiative was clearly designed to place Korea on the map in the history of the restoration process. The event was originally destined to coincide with the second Assembly of the World's Religions, but plans were changed, and it was decided that the World Festival of Culture would instead include another Unificationist international wedding. At the time of writing this event is still to occur: the precise number of couples to be blessed is as yet undetermined, but it is expected that the number of participants will break all records. Initially, the number 30 000 was mentioned, but, as the event has drawn nearer, members to whom I have spoken have told me that the Rev Moon wants the ceremony to involve as many as 50 000 couples.

UNIFICATIONISM AND WORLD PEACE

I have outlined some of the aspects of the Rev Moon's unification programme, but whatever 'unification' means, there cannot be unity while there is conflict. At the final eschaton, the Kingdom of Heaven will be a kingdom of peace: Unificationists therefore claim that their aim is to attain peace on earth, and that science and technology should be used for achieving world peace and justice, and not for destruction. The Rev Moon's belief is that international harmony should be established by forging cross-cultural links and facilitating international travel and communication. The most ambitious project conceived by the Rev Moon is an International Highway Project, which would consist of an underwater tunnel linking Japan and Korea, together with an arterial road link from Seoul through China, India and Europe. A one-kilometer neutral zone would be declared on each side of the highway so as to guarantee unobstructed passage to citizens of all countries. Already borings for the tunnel have been made, and Chinese officials are discussing plans for the Chinese section of the highway.

Physical links, of course, are insufficient to establish world peace, which involves the spiritual as well as the physical aspects of humanity. Accordingly the Professors' World Peace Academy (PWPA) was established in Korea in 1973 to bring academics together to discuss issues relating to peace. The Foundation for Peace International (another UM organisation) sponsors an independent 'Summit Council for World Peace' which has a select membership consisting of former heads of state, former heads of government, and internationally recognised figures who are renowned for their contribution to the cause of peace.

It would be wrong to suppose that the UC's goal of world peace entails that it is a pacifist movement. Far from it. Unificationists do not want peace at any price, particularly if peace means capitulation to communism. Although unification aims to unify systems of religious belief, politics and science, communism is undoubtedly and emphatically excluded from any such synthesis. Unificationists are vehemently opposed to communism and actively combat it. How far such opposition goes is a matter of speculation: critics have asserted that members have been prepared to engage in armed combat against communism, or at least to fund the arming of its opponents. In Korea, part of Sun Myung Moon's business enterprises includes the T'ongil Engineering Factory, which manufactures air rifles, and makes parts for weapons, which the South Korean government requires.

Whatever the truth of the matter, one of the UM's organisations is CAUSA, the political arm of the Unification Movement. Originally, the name 'CAUSA' was an acronym for 'Confederation of Associations for the Unity of the Societies of the Americas', but CAUSA has extended beyond Latin America and become an international movement. Unificationists prefer to explain the label as the Latin word for 'cause' – the cause being the establishment of a 'God-centred' world of freedom, brotherhood and religious unity.[3] CAUSA's membership extends beyond the Unification Church, which is why it is unfair to direct criticism exclusively at the UC when it is said to fund Nicaraguan 'contras'. Whether or not it is true that funding has been given to guerilla fighters (CAUSA denies that it has ever done so), some mainstream Christians too have presumably added momentum to CAUSA's activities. CAUSA, like the Unification Church itself, is fiercely opposed to communism, and CAUSA members describe themselves as being 'ideologically opposed' to communist regimes.

CAUSA's ideological opposition is expressed in the *CAUSA Lecture Manual* which was published in 1985. The manual, aimed not exclusively at UC members, but at mainstream clergy and others, appears to contain some of the distinctively Unificationist teachings but not others. It propagates a theology which it labels 'Godism', which it sets out as a competing and preferable ideology to replace communism: this incorporates the essentially Unificationist notions of God as male and female, the principle of 'give and take action' and O-D-U (Origin, Division and Union), the Four Position Foundation, the UC doctrine of human responsibility in the fulfilment of God's purpose, and the goal of unifying the earth world and spirit world. On the other hand, there is no material concerning the means of salvation: the Fall, indemnity, Jesus' incomplete mission, and the Lord of the Second Advent are singularly absent in the sustained account of 'Godism' which is given.[4] It is not clear why there is this selectivity. Perhaps Unificationists believe Godism will prove less controversial and thus secure wider acceptance than the entire theological position of *Divine Principle*.

Whatever form the UC's opposition to communism takes, the former's refusal to incorporate any part of communist ideology into a 'unified society' is probably to be explained by its underlying philosophy of 'give and take action'. Entities or ideas can only interact and unite when they are in subject and object *positions* to each other, each in its true *position*. In the case of Godism and communism, however, God is in the subject *position* in the ideal world and Satan in the subject *position* in communism's atheistic materialism. Two 'subjects' cannot interact: they are like similar poles of a magnet which can only repel each other. Before there can be any 'give and take' with communism, the satanic side (the 'Cain' side) has to humble itself and assume the role of object on God's side (the 'Abel' side). UC members view the recent Soviet policies of *glasnost* and *perestroika* and the collapse of communism in Eastern Europe as possible indications that this may be beginning to happen.

## THE UC'S AGENDA

The relationship between the UC and the UM is at first sight a rather puzzling one. Why does Sun Myung Moon sponsor the UM when it makes no obvious attempt to convert participants to Unificationism? The Rev Moon's insistence that he never wished to found a separate denomination may seem to fit readily with the apparently inclusivist stance adopted by the UM. Yet, paradoxically, Unificationists do not believe that each religion is equidistant from the truth: in matters of doctrine, there can only be one correct interpretation of God's word, namely theirs. It is firm Unificationist belief that it is only by recognising and accepting the Lord of the Second Advent and by undergoing the Blessing that men and women can gain entry into the Kingdom of Heaven.

The anti-cult movement's interpretation of the UM is that it is simply a means of 'gaining credibility' for a minority religious group which has attracted bad publicity. This explanation is implausible: it would be much easier to reduce the workload of mobile fund-raising teams, thus accepting a more modest income, than to continue to lavish money on academic conferences and ambitious social programmes.

If 'gaining credibility' means making one's teachings more palatable, the UM would seem to have a singular lack of success. The academics involved in UM conferences seldom even discuss the doctrines of the Unification Church, let alone act as unofficial consultants. Changes which have occurred within the UC have tended to come from within, and have actually caused outsiders to have even greater difficulties in intellectual acceptance of the *Principle*. The Zimbabwean phenomenon is one case in point, for example.

It is possible that the UC can use events within its own history as illustrations of the unfolding of God's providential plan. For example, when the Rev Moon gave tailor-made suits to all the communist participants at the Olympic Games at Seoul in 1988, members regarded this gesture as a re-enactment of the biblical story in which Jacob presented gifts to his elder brother Esau.[5] Evidently the UC saw its role as communism's 'younger brother', and offered a token of reconciliation. The UC could likewise incorporate the three Assemblies of the World's Religions into its theology. There will be three Assemblies in all, the last of which will occur on the eve of the fortieth anniversary of the founding of the Unification Church. Since the fortieth anniversary could be viewed as theologically significant (40 being a sacred number), the three preceding assemblies could be cast in the role of 'Formation', 'Growth' and 'Completion' – the three stages in UC salvation-history. The Assembly themes plausibly lend themselves to such interpretation: the 1985 focus on 'heritage' evokes the concept of 'Formation', 'Responding to Our contemporary Challenge' (the 1990 theme) the 'Growth', and 'Strengthening our Hope in the Future' (1993) might be designed to take the participants on towards the 'Completion' stage.

## THE THEOLOGY OF THE UM

Until recently the purpose of the Unification Movement has been a matter of conjecture. However, the Rev Moon has now made a definitive statement regarding its role. The UM subsidaries all form part of a 'new cultural revolution' which he is inaugurating. Establishing the Kingdom of Heaven on earth involves not only bringing about a return to religion by men and women, but an entire transformation of the physical world. The Kingdom of Heaven on earth would be a world in which there was universal peace, freedom from poverty, perfect justice and truth, and creditable cultural achievements. Given this utopian vision, we can begin to see the role of the UM's various organisations: the International Religious Foundation aims at renewing religious awareness; the International Cultural Foundation envelops the world's social and economic problems and seeks appropriate solutions; other UM organisations endeavour to relieve world famine or improve humankind's environment; the Professors' World Peace Academy and the Foundation for Peace International ostensibly aim at world peace. The Rev Moon's investments in the media (he owns the *Washington Times*, the *New York City Tribune* and *Noticias del Mundo*, amongst others) have the stated purpose of ensuring that these sectors of the media set new standards of journalism, communicating truthfully in the public interest, without distortion, propaganda or sensationalism. By owning organisations such as the Little Angels Ballet and the New York City Symphony Orchestra, the Rev Moon is endeavouring to assist human creativity in its various art forms. Industry is regarded as 'the foundation upon which God's Kingdom will be built': [6] it is a means by which humankind controls the natural world and brings it into its dominion, and of course it provides the profit which can be channelled in to the other activities which will make the utopian vision a reality.

Expressed another way, the UM's various activities are a means of attaining the three Blessings which God offered to Adam and Eve. Thus, the specifically religious projects such as IRF, New ERA, the 'God Conferences', and the Assemblies of the World's Religions have a role in perfecting individual people (the first Blessing). More secular academic research such as that of ICUS and PWPA, and also the commercial interests in the media, have the purpose of securing a properly organised society. Such a society will be one which consists of ideal family units, and thus this wing of the Unification Movement serves to restore the second Blessing. The third Blessing, dominion over creation, involves projects which impinge more directly on humanity's physical needs. For example, the International Relief Friendship Foundation (IRFF) aims at improving humankind's physical health; the Rev Moon's Ocean Church, with its emphasis on tuna fishing, demonstrates the belief that humankind's dominion over creation entails using the animal kingdom as food. The pharmaceutical and machine tool companies which the Rev Moon owns are held to serve the function of creating a prosperous society. It is not necessarily the case that any single UM organisation is targeted towards the restoration of one specific Blessing: there is overlap, but the overall endeavour is the 'new cultural revolution' in which all creation is restored.

My analysis so far shows how the various UM organisations can serve in some limited way towards attaining the UC's goals. Nevertheless, it must be remembered that, according to UC teaching, salvation is only possible by means of marriages which are solemnised by the Rev Moon at the Blessing Ceremony. The reason for apparently failing to offer UM participants the sole means of salvation is that membership itself is neither a necessary nor a sufficient means of restoration. Neither is it necessary to understand every point of theology which comprises the *Principle*. What is held to be more important is the acknowledgement of the messianic status of Sun Myung Moon and undergoing the Blessing ceremony. If UM participants agree that the Unification Movement has accomplished much, they should consider what these accomplishments indicate about the nature of its founder. Could he be the new messiah, the Lord of the Second Advent, who is commissioned to complete Jesus Christ's unfulfilled mission? Unificationists would hope that at least some of the participants would pray about these matters, even though they do not explicitly express this hope to them.

Since the Rev Moon did not set out to establish a new denomination which was separate from the rest of Christianity, the UC's ultimate hope is that Christians might acknowledge the messianic status of the Rev Moon without necessarily leaving their own denominations, and have their marriages blessed for eternity, so that they can establish a family which is ingrafted into the True Family. I am told that at least one mainstream clergyman and some academics have in fact had their marriages blessed by the Rev Moon; the clergyman has reportedly returned to his congregation, who as yet have not been informed of this event.

From the standpoint of UC theology, the possibility of making the Blessing available to those outside the formal membership of the Unification Church is made possible on account of the foundation which has been laid by Unification members who have paid appropriate indemnity and made their own blessed marriages the base on which a wider edifice can now be built. The Rev Moon has made the following highly significant statement regarding the Blessing Ceremony which will take place at the 1991 Festival of Culture:

> The model of one world family of mankind, based on true love and transcending differences of race and colour, will lead us directly to the fulfilment of world peace. Men and women subscribing to this ideal will be invited to participate in international weddings in the name of God as a demonstration of commitment to lasting family relations and eternal values. By living high ethical standards, these couples will provide a model of morality and lead the way towards the creation of ideal families, societies and nations.[7]

It will be noticed that the condition for participating is not UC membership but subscription to the broad ideal of the 'one world family'. If I understand the situation correctly, couples who are already married may receive the Blessing if they endorse this ideal, and single men and women may be matched by the Rev Moon some time before the ceremony is due to take place. Whether or not the candidates for the Blessing belong to the Unification Church, they will probably be expected to undergo the accompanying ceremonies which I have discussed earlier, and they would normally be expected to observe a period of celibacy prior to the Three Day Ceremony.

Christianity is given the first opportunity to acknowledge the Rev Moon's messiahship and his ability to inaugurate true families under God, since the UC regards Christianity as the Second Israel, to whom salvation was offered after the Jews – the first Israel – rejected Jesus Christ.[8] Being the Second Israel, Christianity is now being given the opportunity to receive the new messiah. This can be done without Christians leaving their various denominations to join the Unification Church. If Christianity does this, then it is believed that the other great religions of the world will unite behind the

Christians and, in common with them, acknowledge the messianic status of the Lord of the Second Advent.

However, just as the Jews rejected Jesus, it is possible that Christianity will fail to recognise the new messiah who is said to be now on earth. And just as the Jews lost their *position* as the first Israel, so it is possible that Christianity will lose its *position* as the new Israel which has been chosen for God's special dispensation. If Christianity fails, then the messiah will be offered to some other faith which God has elected to assume the *position* abandoned by Christianity. Already there are signs of contingency plans for such a 'failure': one version of the *Principle* has been written specifically for Muslim readers and is designed to demonstrate how the Qur'an points forward to present-day events on earth and to the dispensation which God is offering our present age.⁹

DEVELOPMENTS WITHIN THE CHURCH

In my discussion of the UC's imminent developments I have focused on the relationships between the UC and those outside its borders. Something now remains to be said about the developments which can be expected from within.

There can be no doubt about the future the Unification Church would like to see. Each Christian denomination would acknowledge Sun Myung Moon as the messiah without necessarily changing its identity. We would still continue to see Anglicans, Baptists, Methodists and Presbyterians, but they would have achieved 'unity' in their common acknowledgement of the Lord of the Second Advent. Such an event would herald similar acknowledgements by all other world faiths: the Jews would then agree that the Rev Moon was the long awaited messiah, the Buddhists would acknowledge him as Maitreya, the Confucians as Jin-In, the Hindus as Kalki (Vishnu's incarnation in the future age), the Muslims (perhaps) as the hidden Imam and the Baha'is as the messenger of the new age.

It is commonplace for religions to place humankind at the end of the age, with an eschatological expectation which remains unfulfilled. In the midst of prophecies that the present order of affairs is ending and a new age will begin, religions have either found that prophecies have not been fulfilled as expected (as with the many sects who have set dates for the world to end), or else they have been given the opportunity to claim a realised eschatology, but have deliberately and resolutely rejected the opportunity to do so. Only a small minority of Jews ever acknowledged that Jesus Christ had inaugurated the messianic age, and, despite the Christian prophecy that

Christ will return, Christianity has viewed with strong disapproval various individuals' claims to be the 'second appearance' of Christ.

Notwithstanding the ecumenical and inter-faith achievements I have described, which various prominent religious figures have been willing to support, the UC has made little headway in persuading any religious group to concede that the Rev Moon is the new messiah on earth. It might therefore be asked how successful the Rev Moon's achievement has been, from the point of view of Unificationism. Has he succeeded, or has he failed? Is it possible that the Lord of the Second Advent could fail to complete his mission and that a Fourth Adam would be needed to assume his *position*?

It has been suggested that the Rev Moon's messianic status has still to be recognised even by Unificationists. I have already noted their reticence about stating unequivocally that Sun Myung Moon is the messiah, and it has been suggested that one possible explanation for the apparent 'messianic secret' is that the messiah is indeed still to come and that the Rev Moon is only the messiah's herald.[10] This suggestion was made at a time when the 'messianic secret' was more of a secret. Now that Unificationists more openly proclaim that the Rev Moon is the messiah, this suggestion has become increasingly implausible.

I think it is unlikely that the Unification Church would ever revise its messianic teachings. It has never been stated that the new messiah will establish a perfect Kingdom of Heaven on earth in his own lifetime. Unificationists believe that what the Rev Moon has accomplished is sufficient to accord him the status of the Lord of the Second Advent: he has married, he is believed to have established a new lineage which stems from True Parents, and the Kingdom of Heaven has now been opened, making it possible for those in the spirit world to progress from Paradise to the Kingdom of Heaven. Unificationists would agree that there is still much to be accomplished and that the Kingdom of Heaven on earth is indeed a long way off; but, according to Unification thought, what remains is a matter of human effort, and no further messianic figure is needed, and no further 2000 years of indemnity will need to be paid. Since human co-operation plays such a central role in realising God's ideal on earth, Unificationism's future is unpredictable: presumably it depends on the degree to which the rest of humankind co-operates and works towards the coming Kingdom.

Yet there are some factors which are certain. The Rev Moon will die, and his position as leader of the Unification Movement will be assumed by his son Hyo Jin.[11] There will be several effects of the Rev Moon's death. It will create a gap at the top of the Unification Church. It is possible that Hyo Jin will take over his father's work in a similar way, defining doctrine and inspiring new enterprises, but much will depend on whether his leadership will be that of a figure head, or whether he will take a strong lead. He is still relatively young (born in 1962), and it is possible that the older Korean leaders, such as the Rev Chung Hwan Kwak, Dr Bo Hi Pak or Dr David Kim will dominate. The American and European academics will be a further force: whether these various parties will counterpose or complement each other is a matter of speculation.

As far as the Blessing Ceremonies are concerned, it has been determined that Mrs Moon alone will continue to preside over them.[12] The ideal, however, which has still to be attained, is the Kingdom of Heaven on earth, in which parents would be able to conduct the weddings of their own children, having aspired to the state of perfection, and thus enabled to assume the *position* of messiah on behalf of their children, having established a pure blood lineage for them.

Since there is held to be a close inter-connection between the spirit world and the physical world, I am sure that the Rev Moon will not disappear beyond recall, as far as UC members are concerned. It is more than likely that he will be believed to co-operate with members who still remain in the physical world, and members will no doubt claim to have visions of their founder-leader and messages from him. Just as Heung Jin was held to have returned in the form of the Zimbabwean member, a similar phenomenon remains a possibility with respect to the Rev Moon himself. Just as the Zimbabwean phenomenon was unpredictable, so the nature of any supposed 'returning resurrection' of Sun Myung Moon cannot be foretold. It is even possible that, just as the Zimbabwean and his pronouncements were accorded a high status, some other UC member could even be given the effective leadership of the movement on account of similar revelations.

When John Lofland wrote in the early 1960s about a small group of apparently eccentric adherents to a 'Doomsday Cult' in the Bay Area of California, he could not have predicted that the movement would develop into a world-wide organisation which would bring together such large numbers of prominent academics, clergy and religious leaders from such a diversity of backgrounds. Similarly, what the next decade or two will bring can only be guesswork, and will depend on a variety of factors: external events in the world, internal forces, missionary policies, opponents' reactions, the rise of other religious groups (which may deflect public attention away from the UC), and, above all, the revelations which members will claim to receive in the years to come.

Cynics may ask whether the UC will survive into the twenty-first century, but religious movements are singularly resilient and adaptable.

Whatever happens theologically or organisationally to the UC, its financial assets alone will secure its survival for some considerable time, and it can confidently be predicted that Unificationism will not simply vanish into oblivion in the foreseeable future. This may be depressing news for the anti-cult lobby, but there are only two factors which could bring about the eclipse of the UC: mass apostasy or gross financial mismanagement. Since neither scenario seems realistic at the moment, I believe the future will see survival amidst continuing change.

# Postscript: Some Personal Reflections

The approach adopted in this book has been phenomenological. I have attempted throughout to describe the origins, beliefs and practices of the Unification Church without imposing my own value judgements or raising external criticisms from my own religious standpoint. By doing so, however, I may be accused of having taken the easy way out and avoided some very pertinent questions about the UC. What *do* I think of the 'Moonies'? Are they really religious, or is the UM a large business operation or a political organisation masquerading as a church? Do they use dubious methods of proselytising, such as 'love bombing', 'heavenly deception', 'brainwashing' or sleep deprivation? Would I like a child of mine to 'join the Moonies'? Is the Rev Moon the messiah, or a religious charlatan who enjoys a life of luxury at the expense of his followers who sell flowers and candy bars for as long as 18 hours a day?

In this postscript I shall abandon the phenomenological approach to the Unification Church and instead give a phenomenological account of my own feelings about them. What follows is mainly a subjective reaction, based on my own personal experiences, and I fully acknowledge that others who have come into contact with the UC have gained quite different impressions, some more favourable, some less. Most of the issues I have identified above demand much fuller treatment than is possible in a postscript, and the reader will sometimes be subjected to bare assertion where fuller argument is needed.

At the end of the research which has resulted in this book I am certainly no nearer to accepting the *Principle* than I was before; indeed, many teachings turned out to be even stranger than I had expected. If the Unificationists who provided me with my material expected me to be persuaded rather than informed (which I doubt) then they have been disappointed. In the seminars I attended, the lecturers clearly believed that they were expounding the *Principle* in a logical way, but any lecture (inside or outside the UC) must make assumptions which the lecturer assumes the audience will share. It was really at this point that we had to part company: it was not at all self-evident to me that everything in the universe has a *hyung sang* and a *sung sang*, that God never uses the same person twice when fulfilling his providential plan, that a messiah must have the qualities specified in the *Principle*, or that there is any significance in the apparent parallels which Unificationists find in human history.

The methods which are used at the seminars are often the subject of criticism, so it may be useful to record my observations. The UC is sometimes accused of concealing its true identity from enquirers. Since I had deliberately set out to research the UC, there is no way in which they could have concealed their identity from me. However, in response to the criticism that its premises do not invariably bear its denominational label, I can note that, although the UK headquarters at Lancaster Gate now clearly displays the UC's name and emblem, I noticed no such identification at their seminar centres. However, these are not premises to which members of the public would wander in uninvited, and premises owned by mainstream religious organisations do not invariably indicate their identity either. For all the seminars I attended, the documentation I completed was clearly labelled with the UC's name, and no participant to whom I spoke was in any doubt that he or she was attending a Unificationist seminar or that Unificationists were 'Moonies'. Naturally UC members do not tell enquirers that they are 'Moonies', but this is because they find the nickname offensive: black people do not declare that they are 'niggers' or evangelical fundamentalists that they are 'Jesus freaks' or 'Bible thumpers'.

Seminar lecturers are often accused of 'brainwashing' their listeners, and this criticism deserves some comment. The successive seminars certainly had considerable overlap of material, but each time I undoubtedly learned something new. I would not normally use such teaching methods myself, exposing listeners to extended periods of largely one-way communication from lecturer to listener, and I think the Unification Church could profitably explore some of the newer teaching innovations which most modern educational establishments now use. I certainly do not think there is anything sinister in the UC's lecturing technique, and questions are certainly encouraged after each lecture has finished. A frequent accusation is that UC lecturers tell questioners that their query will be dealt with at a later stage, thus constantly postponing an answer which never comes. In order to confirm or deny this allegation, I made a point of noting all questions which were asked at the end of a lecture and not just my own; each one received an adequate reply. It is seldom remarked that the lecture programme is probably more exacting for the lecturer than the audience: to lecture for five or six hours a day for seven days is not a task which I would willingly undertake. What surprised me was that at my last seven-day seminar the lecturer made himself available at meals and was amenable to answering questions on the *Principle* at all times. I am still uncertain whether he was joking when he said that attenders should not talk about the weather, but about the *Principle*, and that if we talked about anything else we were wasting our time!

Conditions at seminars are basic, but tolerable. In my various stays at seminar centres, I was fortunate in securing a single room or double occupancy accommodation, unlike the majority of attenders who live in dormitories. Adequate sleep was therefore no problem, although I appreciate that I was accorded special treatment in this respect. It is fair to say that attenders are strictly advised to ensure that they go to bed at a reasonable hour in order to be mentally alert for *Principle* lectures the following day. Not every attender took this advice, however, and, especially at the last seven-day seminar I attended, most members believed that 'sleepy spirits' were at work in preventing them from staying awake at the lectures. UC leaders rejected my alternative explanation that their difficulty was due to inadequate sleep, and the remedy for their predicament was fairly stringent: adjacent attenders massaged them awake, and if that failed they stood for the remainder of the lecture at the back. One organiser confessed that his average night's sleep during that week was three hours!

Some enquirers have alleged that the UC has taken them to isolated locations and never let them out of sight, not even to go to the toilet. I understand that such techniques may well have been used in the USA, particularly in the late 1970s,[1] and leaders have stated that they then used an excess of zeal which they now regret.[2] I certainly did not experience anything of the kind, although the final seven-day seminar was very intensive: by lunch time attenders had sat through a one-hour service and three hours' lecturing, which were only interrupted by breakfast and a short break. At meal times we were asked to sit at table in pre-defined groups in order to discuss the *Principle*. After a mentally exhausting morning, I am afraid I did not particularly welcome being probed on what I thought of the lectures, and, judging by the lack of conversation at meal times, I suspect that other attenders felt that their minds had been stretched to their limits.

Critics have accused the UC of trying to gain converts by psychological means, such as the 'rest and relaxation' evening at which attenders provide entertainment for each other. It is true that 'R & R' can break down hostility, and I have seen seminar attenders approach initial lectures in a spirit of confrontation, only to find it more difficult to maintain an adversarial stance after an evening of party games and community singing. I have not found this disturbing: after all, many organisations attempt to persuade by working on the emotions as well as the intellect. I try to teach my own students by winning some degree of friendship (with varying degrees of success), rather than simply hoping that they will be persuaded by any overwhelming logic which my lectures may possess! Any sensible organisation will attempt to create the atmosphere which is most conducive to achieving its aims.

Critics are no doubt correct in suggesting that converts are often attracted by the atmosphere of the UC's community rather than the strict 'logic' of its teachings. However, being in the warm atmosphere of a community is often a reason why people join mainstream Christian denominations; conversely, its frequent absence is often a deterrent to seekers – almost every reader must be familiar with many people who feel basically religious but cannot find a religious community which will accommodate them.

Critics have sometimes use the term 'love-bombing' to describe the tactics of the UC's apparently caring community. The term 'love-bombing' requires careful examination. The expression was originally used by the Children of God, and referred to a technique whereby seekers were attracted into membership as a result of prostitution by existing COG members. This method of recruitment is known as 'flirty fishing'. The UC deplores such practices, being opposed to any form of extra-marital sexual contact. I have only once encountered the expression 'love-bombing' in UC literature,[3] and with a very different meaning, namely showing the maximum care and concern for potential converts. If concern which is greater than normal constitutes 'love-bombing', then I can recall one occasion where I sustained a very minor physical injury at a seminar: members seemed very concerned that it should be properly treated, instead of simply ignoring the mishap and leaving me to my own devices.

Some mention should be made of UC lifestyle. Much as the UC has denied various slanders, it has never denied that mobile fund-raising teams (MFTs) operate for very long hours over extended periods, and that members can work up to 18 hours a day selling flowers and candy bars on behalf of the church. Yet members do not complain: they regard it as 'indemnity' which they are paying for the sins of humanity, and even senior members are assigned from time to time to MFTs and regard it as worthwhile spiritual discipline. If we are indeed living in the last days, then it is understandable that members feel a sense of urgency which necessitates such stringent demands. After all, a doctor or a fireman would not leave an emergency on the grounds that it was bedtime! I can admire the energy and the relentlessness of Unificationists' endeavours, although perhaps they will not think it to my credit if I admit that I would not myself be prepared to offer such total commitment.

As a result of my encounters with the UC, there are several questions which I find I am frequently asked. It may be helpful to answer some of these here. First, I am sometimes asked if I have ever been tempted to join as a result of my contacts. I can only once recall being at a seminar lecture where the community spirit had built up so well that I momentarily reflected that it might be wonderful to belong to a community which seemed so enthusiastic and so idealistic. I stopped myself short fairly readily by reminding myself that I just could not *believe* what the lecturer was teaching!

On balance my reaction has been much more negative towards joining. Although the sense of community and belonging are positive features of the UC, there are times when I have wondered why Unificationism attracts a following at all. When one compares the Unification Church with the 'New Age' phenomenon, which emphasises care for the environment, disarmament, vegetarianism, feminism, animal rights, and egalitarian politics, the UC seems singularly 'untrendy'. Despite its protestations to the contrary, I still think that its teachings come over as politically right wing, as was evidenced by some members' support for Le Pen at the recent European Parliamentary elections: one UC supporter of Le Pen, Pierre Ceyrac, actually gained a seat.[4] Although members will sometimes point to the fact that *Divine Principle* in one place depicts a 'green' utopia,[5] the reference is an isolated one, and I have not detected a sustained 'green' movement within the UC. The UC makes no concessions to the vegetarian,[6] and I am told that the Rev Moon has said that members should not create divisions within the movement by unnecessarily requesting special diets. The UM subsidiary, the Ocean Church, seeks to feed the world's hungry from the sea: humanity's dominion over creation is construed as entailing the permission to kill animal and fish life, rather than to preserve it. As far as feminism is concerned, I am not convinced that Unificationist doctrines such as the 'dual nature of God' pay sufficient regard to the female gender. The men still tend to assume the dominant roles, and more often than not it is the women members who prepare meals and serve tables.

I am often asked whether I would like one of my children to join the Unification Church. The straightforward answer is no: there are many of the UC's ideals which I cannot share, and I believe that members' life-style is very demanding indeed. But I can think of worse fates for them: I would be much more concerned if they joined the National Front, or if they associated with certain other new religions which exist today.

I cannot say how I would react to a son or daughter of mine being 'matched' by the Rev Moon. I am sure that some people's negative reaction stems from racism: most parents are happy enough for their children to have European or American spouses, but find inter-racial marriages much more difficult to accept. I have no knowledge of whether inter-racial marriages work better or worse than more conventional ones. No one really knows what constitutes the recipe for a successful marriage, although the fact that both UC partners are committed to the same brand of religion is at least one very important point of common ground. The prescribed three-year 'separation period' strikes me as rather unnatural, and I do not share the view that sexual abstinence constitutes spiritual 'purification'. But this is only my personal (and here undefended) view: I am aware that many spiritual communities (the Buddhist Sangha, ISKCON, the Roman Catholic priesthood) regard sexual abstinence as a virtue. Perhaps they have a point: certainly in my own experience with the students I teach, emotional and sexual relationships cause many problems, and any religion which discourages dating, love affairs and sexual contact effectively abolishes a whole chain of human problems at a stroke – but of course at a price.

As far as the blessed couples are concerned, many appear to be very happily married, while others, I know, have experienced matrimonial problems. Sometimes these can be resolved through counselling within the church; at other times there is irretrievable breakdown. The UC boasts a very low divorce rate (only 10–15 per cent) compared with trends in Europe and the USA;[7] however, since most of its marriages have probably had a shorter lifespan than national averages, a cynic might suggest that there are many divorces still waiting to happen. I am also fairly certain that the emphasis which is placed on the family in Unification thought must exert tremendous pressure on couples to make marriages work, with the possible effect that it is particularly difficult to admit that one's marriage is simply not working.[8]

Inevitably I have been asked what I think of Sun Myung Moon himself. Although members speak lovingly and respectfully of the Rev Moon, I cannot myself understand why he appears to be such a charismatic figure.[9] Before I ever met Sun Myung Moon directly, one colleague who had done so said that I would be unimpressed. He was right: on the two occasions when I heard him speak publicly he read a script in English, and his delivery and inflexion made me wonder how well he even understood what he was saying. I had been informed that his text had been written by another (English-speaking) UC leader. Nevertheless the scale of Sun Myung Moon's Unification Movement is remarkable, although I think that some causes he has championed are more commendable than others. The academic conferences I have attended have always been worthwhile, but I cannot support UM organisations such as CAUSA. (Indeed, after reading some of CAUSA's literature, I actually decided to join the Nicaraguan Solidarity Campaign, which opposes American intervention in Nicaragua.) Needless to say, Sun Myung Moon's scale of achievement has not led me to acknowledge that he is the Lord of the Second Advent.

If my children joined, would I encourage them to leave? Having come to know many of its members, I do not think I would react as negatively or violently as some parents. I would certainly not consider hiring 'deprogrammers' (professional kidnappers who physically abduct their sons and daughters from such movements), nor would I write letters to the Prime Minister, the Home Secretary, my MP or the Archbishop of Canterbury, as one cult monitoring organisation advises. However much I can understand parental concern about their sons and daughters joining a movement which has attracted so much bad publicity, any attempt to destroy an offspring's faith is a sure recipe for a breakdown of human relationships. Where there exists the likelihood of a deprogrammer abducting someone, it is understandable that the endangered member will wish to avoid further contact with parents.

In my meetings with parents, I have found a very mixed reaction to their son's or daughter's membership. The most hostile couple have described their situation as a 'living bereavement', and their stated policy was to do something each day to hamper the progress of the 'cult phenomenon'. Some parents have proved simply indifferent, while others have sometimes perceived benefits which were not on the UC's official agenda: as one mother remarked to me, 'My son never used to cut his hair until he joined the Moonies!' I have also met parents who have even converted to the Unification Church through their son's or daughter's joining. While acknowledging that there are many genuinely distressed parents, I believe that the media have stressed the atrocity tales because they make 'good copy', and played down the more positive aspects of belonging. It is seldom noted, for example, that UC members do not smoke, drink or take drugs; they are opposed to pornography and any form of sexual promiscuity.

I am sometimes asked about the sincerity of the 'Moonies'. I believe that the Unificationists I have met are sincere about their beliefs. To claim to sense a 'spirituality' within a movement is a very subjective matter, I know. My own impression, for what it is worth, is that I have felt a spiritual atmosphere within the Unification Church which I do not always find in religious groups I visit. I have still to detect it, for example, in the Church of Scientology, if it exists there at all. Having said that, I find that I cannot relate well to the informality of their worship: I dislike the highly emotive character of its extempore prayer, and I still find unison prayer a very strange experience. I am old-fashioned enough to dislike guitar accompaniments to hymns, preferring a more dignified and traditional liturgy. But no doubt these reactions tell the reader more about me than about the Unification Church.

I believe that Unificationism is certainly a religion and not just a front for a political organisation or a conglomerate of business enterprises. Indeed, a book such as this would not have been possible if Unificationism was not a religion, and I hope I have shown the extent to which the UC's activities are founded on a highly complex theology. Whether or not one likes the UC's form of religion, the UC has few who are members in name only, and Unificationists by and large spend many more hours a day in prayer, study and worship than many of their mainstream Christian counterparts. I can see no reason why they cannot call themselves a church: the term 'church' is not a registered trade mark, and I understand that, in law, anyone can call an organisation a 'church' without seeking any kind of official approval from the state.

I have tried to avoid the question of the UC's 'orthodoxy' on the ground that what constitutes sound doctrine is determined by official ecclesiastical bodies, not by individuals, and various Councils have already made (negative) pronouncements.[10] Basically there are two unstated grounds of heresy in mainstream Christianity. One is to add to Christianity's canon of scriptures;[11] the other is to diminish the role of Jesus Christ, particularly by elevating some subsequent figure to an equal or greater messianic status. The Mormon Church has embraced the first 'heresy' by adding the Book of Mormon to the Old and New Testaments, while sects like the Muggletonians of the eighteenth and nineteenth centuries (amongst other things) ascribed too high a role to their prophetic leaders Muggleton and Reeve. In the case of Unificationism, it appears to have embraced both heresies at once. The Rev Moon is accorded the status of the new messiah, the Lord of the Second Advent, and *Divine Principle* appears to be a religious text which completes Christianity's two Testaments. (This second point is debatable: some Unificationists feel that *Divine Principle* is not part of a Unificationist canon of scripture, but more akin to a work like Calvin's *Institutes*.)[12]

Although I believe there are reasons to question the UC's claim to Christian orthodoxy, I do not believe that Unificationism is deceptive in claiming to be a Christian church. Most Unificationists sincerely believe that they are Christian, and ask how else they should be classified, since they are clearly not Hindu, Buddhist or Muslim. I do believe, however, that their urge to be regarded as a Christian denomination has caused them to highlight points of affinity with mainstream Christianity and to suppress the real points of difference, and I am sure this accounts for some of my problems in obtaining material relating to the more sensitive areas in Unification thought. Perhaps many problems in this area could be solved if Unificationists defined themselves as an independent faith, just as Baha'ism is best viewed as an independent global religion rather than a fringe Islamic sect. This would absolve the UC from at least some of the charges of deception, and might enable them to be more open about some of their more esoteric teachings.

Whatever their claims to Christian orthodoxy, my encounters with Unification members have dispelled the myth that they are only familiar with a very few selected biblical texts and that someone who is well versed in his or her Bible can readily refute their teachings. Certainly some members know their Bible better than others, just as mainstream Christians have varying levels of knowledge. (Knowledge of *Divine Principle* too varies from member to member.) Yet even when I have thought that their teachings were straightforwardly at variance with scripture, UC discussants proved more than able to defend their position. I recall clearly my first set of discussions with them about John the Baptist: I had collected together the totality of biblical evidence which did not indicate to me that John the Baptist was the feeble waverer which *Divine Principle* suggests, but invariably UC leaders were able to argue for their own distinctive interpretation. When I confronted them with John's statement about Jesus, 'He must increase, but I must decrease,'[13] and the standard mainstream interpretation that John was ascribing to Christ a higher status than himself, members insisted that an alternative reading was possible, namely that a note of jealousy on John's part should be read into the text and that it should not be assumed, as mainstream Christians do, that John was therefore expressing approval of Jesus' increasing popularity.

*Divine Principle* is certainly not constructed from careless reading of scripture and sloppy exegesis. To my mind it is a strange exegesis, and it is the result, I believe, of the fact that Sun Myung Moon familiarised himself remarkably well with Old and New Testament scriptures, but had minimal (if any) acquaintance with Christian scholarship. But I have yet to find a passage in *Divine Principle* which makes straightforward mistakes about the Bible's content. If the *Principle*'s account of, say, Moses seems at variance with the Book of Exodus, it is always possible to find some later scriptural reference, such as a speech by one of the early apostles, where the missing detail is added. There was a passage in *Divine Principle* which eluded me for a long time: it was the story where Jacob, according to the *Principle*, wrestled with an angel at Jabbok.[14] The Book of Genesis does not state that Jacob's adversary was an angel: he is described as a man, although there is a hint slightly further on that it was God himself whom Jacob encountered.[15] Why, then, did *Divine Principle* insist that it was an angel? I consulted commentaries, colleagues, even hymns which refer to the incident, as well asking Unificationists themselves. For once I was persistently defeated. It was only after many months of searching that a friend finally drew my attention to a little-known passage in the Book of Hosea, where the incident is summarised, but with the importation of the tradition of the angel. The mystery was solved: either Sun Myung Moon himself, or else the Presbyterians with whom he had contact in his early years, must have inserted this detail into the Genesis story by a process of theological addition: Genesis plus Hosea gives the account which we find in *Divine Principle*. Whether or not the Rev Moon realised it, he was in fact putting into practice a distinctively Protestant method of interpreting scripture; the *Westminster Confession of Faith* of 1647 states that not all passages of scripture are equally clear and that a passage which lacks sufficient clarity is to be interpreted in the light of other scriptural passages which speak more clearly.[16]

I have given my reflections on encounters with members, but I have often been asked whether I have given due attention to the testimony of the ex-member. I have drawn from as many sources as possible, and have certainly been careful to read the accounts given by those who have left the movement. During the time spent on workshops I inevitably encountered attenders who had come with no intention of joining, decided not to join after listening to lectures, and in one case a young woman who decided to leave half-way through a workshop. (She was permitted to telephone a boy friend, who collected her, and they departed unimpeded.) Although I have spoken to people who have belonged to the UC and subsequently left, ex-members are not very much in evidence, and at least one has declined to enter into correspondence about UC teachings to which he gained access. One young woman whom I met at a recent conference on NRMs said that she had begun to doubt the truth of *Divine Principle*, expressed these doubts to UC leaders, and then left voluntarily. A UC leader who was also present approached her afterwards and asked how she was, and relationships appeared to have remained friendly. Of course it can be argued that such scenarios have been put on for my benefit. I doubt it: in the initial stages of my workshop attendance, I discovered much to my surprise that UC members did not know who I was or why I had come!

It is perhaps not surprising that ex-members have not been particularly in evidence. This is partly due to the nature of the study of Unificationism which I have undertaken, the aim of which has not been to examine the conditions which have led ex-members to leave the movement, but rather to gain an understanding of the teachings: those who have remained in the church for a considerable time are more likely to have the detailed information which I needed. The other factor which creates problems relating to ex-members' testimonies is their reaction to past membership. On the whole, ex-members do one of two things. Either they wish to slip into oblivion, wishing that their two years (the average life-span of UC membership) had not happened, in which case they will tend to hide the fact that they have belonged. For example, if they are writing a job application they will state vaguely that they have done 'voluntary work', or that they have been an electrician or an accountant if that is what they have done within the movement. Alternatively, they will become 'heroes': they have successfully 'escaped' from the movement, or they have managed to write an insider's account of the UC in the form of a book, or they have taken up roles in the anti-cult movement: several deprogrammers have been former members of NRMs.

Obviously when we have done something which we regret, it is only human nature to seek excuses and to hope that others can be blamed for our own shortcomings. It is for this reason, Beckford believes, that ex-members (perhaps unwittingly) devise a scenario which accounts for their initial decision to join, such as their vulnerability at the time, or a 'brainwashing' theory. I believe that Beckford is right in claiming that the testimony of ex-members is problematic.[17] The 'great escape' stories do not correspond to reality, in my experience. Livingstone House at Chislehurst is five minutes' walk from the railway station along a main road and has unimpeded access to residential streets. In my sojourns there I had ample opportunities to 'escape' if escape were needed! The other centres in Wiltshire are somewhat more secluded, but it was possible for attenders to go off on their own. Although members came to look for them after some time, responsible organisers of any residential course will take steps to ensure that members do not go missing.

Two final comments are appropriate – one on the Unification Church, the other on its critics. Having completed a previous draft of this text and invited UC leaders in England to check it for accuracy, I was rather surprised to discover that they disliked a substantial amount of what I had written. I thought I had done my utmost to be fair and to correct the excesses of prevalent anti-cult prejudice; however, at least their disquiet at the substance of the book forestalls any possible suspicion that I have unwittingly acted as the amanuensis of the Unification Church. The principal objections appeared to be that I portrayed the UC as syncretistic, that I had over-emphasised the theme of sex, and that I had divulged material concerning the Three Day Ceremony.

The first comment seemed surprising in view of the fact that Chapter 1 explicitly considered whether syncretism and revelation were incompatible, and I have already argued that as an outsider I cannot possibly endorse the revelatory claims of a religion to which I do not subscribe. On the theme of sex, UC leaders did not accept my argument that the only way to rebut allegations of sexual malpractices was to consider all the evidence as thoroughly as possible; they would have preferred such discussion to be suppressed, or to have found bare assertion that no such practices existed. Members feared that their critics might be impervious to any inherent logic which my argument possessed, and tenaciously hold on to their prejudices on the ground that 'there is no smoke without fire'.

Members were concerned that details of the Three Day Ceremony might be used to discredit Unificationism: Sun Myung Moon has been accused before (misleadingly) of prescribing the manner in which blessed couples have sexual intercourse. More especially, however, it was put to me that no outsider could comprehend the significance of this ceremony without a vast amount of spiritual preparation – much more than a single book such as this could possibly provide. I think I can understand such concerns. However, no serious writer can acceptably suppress evidence or fail to consider arguments on *both* sides of a controversy. True, I have no doubt totally failed to convey the true meaning of many UC rites; but such a communication problem exists for any author who explores a religion as an outsider. It may take years of acquaintance for someone to apprehend the true meaning of the Christian eucharist, of Jewish sabbath observance, or of the Muslim's observance of Ramadan, but one would nevertheless expect to find mention of these practices in any standard textbook on religion. The reflective reader will remember that no religious practice can stand and deliver its full import at first appearance, and that most, if not all, religious practices can be made to sound silly or pointless if they are entertained in the spirit of hostility rather than enquiry.

These remarks bring me to my final comment on the attitude of the UC's critics. I have often felt very saddened in Christian bookshops as I have perused the shelves marked 'cults'. I am still surprised that some Christians can pay lip service to the Ten Commandments which forbid 'bearing false witness', but yet find it acceptable to malign other faiths, and in particular the new religions which have evolved in recent times, subjecting these faiths to ridicule, launching into criticism without giving their beliefs a fair hearing, and seldom checking their material's veracity with the relevant religious organisations. Invariably mainstream Christians focus on the shortcomings of these groups, while ignoring or downgrading whatever good they may have done. While it is reasonable for mainstream Christianity to define where its boundaries lie, and to criticise strongly ideas which it believes are unacceptable, every faith has surely a right to truthful and balanced presentation. When the UC's critics are prepared to listen with greater empathy (and empathy does not necessarily mean sympathy) then I believe Unification members might well become less defensive and secretive.

These are my reflections. Perhaps my critics will find in these pages evidence that 'the Moonies' have brainwashed me from the very start. I do not think I left my mind behind at any point, and I hope the contents of this book have demonstrated that it is possible to comprehend Unificationist teaching while remaining healthily critical. At any rate, I hope these pages have provided some understanding of Unificationist belief and practice, without which any value-judgements, whether favourable or unfavourable, lack proper foundation.

# Appendix: The Numerological Significance of the Blessings

As previously explained, the numbers of couples undergoing the Blessing are regarded as symbolic. The symbolic meanings given by the Unification Church are provided here. On occasion the actual number blessed does not exactly correspond to the symbolic number. This is deemed to be unimportant, however. When referring to a specific Blessing ceremony, Unificationists will usually cite its symbolic rather than its actual number. Thus, the 1963 ceremony is often referred to as the '120 couples', even though there were four extra couples who were allowed to participate. The analysis is culled from Unificationist literature, principally speeches of the Rev Moon and an account of his life written by a Mr Dijk.[1]

**1961: 36 Couples**

36 = 12 x 3. 12 represents the number of apostles and the tribes of Israel. 3 represents three categories of individual: (i) virgins ('Abraham type'); (ii) those who had sexual relationships within marriage ('Adam type'); (iii) those who had sexual relationships outside marriage ('Noah type'). By solemnising the marriages of 12 couples from each category, it was demonstrated that salvation was available to all.

Although the '36 Couples' Blessing' is frequently mentioned by Unificationists as if it were a single event, in reality there were three separate ceremonies: 3 couples (1960), 9 couples (1960), and a further 24 couples (1961). It is held that Jesus should have conducted the marriages of his three closest disciples: these three ideally should have included John the Baptist, who (according to Unification thought) refused to submit himself to Jesus; but through John's default the inner circle of three became Peter, James and John. This initial Blessing of an inner core of three founder-disciples (Hyo Won Eu, Young Whi Kim and Won Pil Kim) is thus a 'principled' enactment of an event which Jesus was unable to accomplish. The marriage of the further nine, of course, corresponds to the remaining number of Jesus' disciples.

**1961: 72 Couples**

Jesus sent out 72 disciples to preach (Luke 10.1): 72 = 36 x 2, representing 36 couples from the 'Cain' side and 36 from 'Abel'. Also, 72 = (12 x 2) x 3, symbolising pairs of 12 (one 'Cain', one 'Abel') from each of the three eras of history – Old Testament, New Testament and Completed Testament.

**1963: 120 Couples (actually, 124 were solemnised)**

120 apostles gathered together prior to Pentecost (Acts 1.15), and 120 represents the number of nations of the world. 120 therefore represents 'practically everybody on earth'.

**1968: 430 Couples**

1.   The 'vertical history' of Korea is 4300 years.
2.   The period of slavery in Egypt is calculated to be 430 years.[2]

These two points are linked, for both are concerned with *nations*: the Israelites became a nation after their period in Egypt. The number 430 is thus connected with the concept of 'nation'.

3.   The combination of 4 and 3 yields a spiritually significant number, because:

$4 + 3 = 7$ (a 'perfect' number)
$4 \times 3 = 12$ (a perfect number)
$4 - 3 = 1$ (signifying unity)
$4 \div 3 = 1$ remainder 1 (signifying unity twice)

This Blessing is said to have established the 'national' base from which international marriages could subsequently take place.

**1969: 43 Couples**

This Blessing has similar numerological significance to the previous one. The factor 43 provides a link between the 'victory of Korean history' and restoration on a world-wide level. The '43 Couples' Blessing' was in fact three separate Blessings: one in Korea for Japanese founder-leaders, another in America for American founder-leaders, and a third in Germany for European leaders.

## 1970: 777 Couples (actual number: 791)

777 comprises three 7s. 7 represents perfection, and three represents the three stages of spiritual progress: Formation, Growth and Completion. It marks the completion of all indemnity, enabling the Lord of the Second Advent to commence his ministry at an international level. 'This was the last conditional number to be fulfilled. After this, Father could bless any number.'[3]

## 1975: 1800 Couples

18 = 6 x 3. Three 6s form Satan's number (666).[4] This Blessing 'restores' the number 666 'in three different categories'.[5] This explanation (the exact meaning of which is not totally clear) is given by Sun Myung Moon, notwithstanding Mr Dijk's assertion that the 777 Blessing was the last ceremony at which 'restoration of numbers' was necessary.

# Notes

## 1 Examining the Evidence

1. Acts 5.1–10.
2. For an examination of the 'brainwashing' theory, see Eileen Barker, *The Making of a Moonie* (Oxford: Blackwell, 1984).
3. For a fuller discussion, see G. D. Chryssides, 'The Right to be Religious', *The Modern Churchman*, New Series, vol. XXIX, no. 3 (1987), pp. 25–33.
4. Ted Patrick and Tom Dulack, *Let Our Children Go!* (New York: Dutton, 1976), p. 127.
5. See, for example, Patrick and Dulack, op. cit., pp. 32, 240; *FAIR News* October 1982, p. 2.
6. It is important to note that 'the *Principle*' is to be distinguished from *Divine Principle*. The latter is the book which is used by the UC: this is held to be a distillation of what has been revealed to Sun Myung Moon, and it by no means contains all his revelations. The Rev Moon's revelations of these spiritual laws is known as 'the *Principle*'. There is another sense of the word 'Principle' – a technical term in Korean philosophy – which will be explained later. I have attempted to distinguish carefully between what is in the book *Divine Principle* and what is one of the Rev Moon's pieces of revelation, which (following UC practice) I have termed 'the *Principle*'.
7. Hyo Won Eu, *Divine Principle* (New York: HSA-UWC, 1973). I shall continue to use the initials 'UC' as a standard abbreviation for 'Unification Church'.
8. Peter B. Clarke, *Black Paradise* (Wellingborough: Aquarian, 1986).
9. Jan Shipps, *Mormonism: The Story of a New Religious Tradition* (Urbana and Chicago: University of Illinois Press, 1985).
10. British Council of Churches (Youth Unit), 'The Unification Church: a paper for those who wish to know more'; n.d., c. 1978. Panel on Doctrine appointed by the General Assembly of the Church of Scotland, 'The Third Adam from Korea', *Life and Work* (September 1978).
11. For an explanation of the term 'New Christian', see Chapter 5.
12. James Beckford, *Cult Controversies* (London: Tavistock, 1985).
13. John Lofland, *Doomsday Cult* (Englewood Cliffs: Prentice-Hall, 1966), ch 2, pp. 14–28. Gregory T. Tillett, 'Sources of Doctrine in the Unification Church', *Update*, vol. 8, no. 1 (March 1984), p. 3. J. Isamu Yamamoto, *The Puppet Master: An Inquiry into Sun Myung Moon and the Unification Church* (Illinois: Inter-Varsity Press, 1977).
14. The use of the title 'Reverend' juxtaposed to a surname without

forename or initials is normally unacceptable usage, and indeed is often regarded as the hallmark of ignorance. However, this is how UC members normally refer to their leader, and I have therefore followed their practice. If it is objected that the Rev Moon's title has never been conferred by any mainstream authority, I fully accept that this is so: Sun Myung Moon is reported to have said, 'I have been ordained by God: what higher ordination is needed?' The fact that Sun Myung Moon and several UC leaders assume the title 'Reverend' is part of the phenomenon of Unificationism, and I believe it to be worth reporting.

15. Yamamoto, op. cit., p. 83.
16. Young Oon Kim, *Unification Thought* (New York: Unification Thought Institute, 1973). Young Oon Kim, *Unification Theology and Christian Thought* (New York: Golden Gate Publishing Co., rev. edn., 1976).
17. Matthew 5.29–30.
18. Mark 3.31–35.
19. *Master Speaks*, 17 May 1973.
20. European Parliament, Committee on Youth, Culture, Education, Information and Sport: 'Report on the activity of certain new religious movements within the European Community'. Rapporteur: Mr Richard Cottrell, 22 March 1984. PE 82.322/fin. General Synod of the Church of England, 'New Religious Movements: A Report by the Board for Mission and Unity'; GS Misc 317, October 1989.
21. Erica Heftmann, *Dark Side of the Moonies* (Harmondsworth: Penguin, 1982), pp. 67–8.
22. FAIR (Family Action, Information and Rescue) leaflet, n.d.
23. See, for example, W. Y. Evans-Wentz (ed.), *Tibetan Yoga and Secret Doctrines*, 2nd edn. (Oxford, 1967), pp. 49ff.
24. The Holy Wine Ceremony is discussed in Chapter 7.
25. J. H. Grace, *Sex and Marriage in the Unification Movement* (New York and Toronto: The Edwin Mellen Press, 1985), pp. 139–40.
26. Chung Hwan Kwak, *Outline of The Principle Level 4* (New York: HSA-UWC, 1977).
27. See, for example, John Hick, *Philosophy of Religion*, 2nd edn. (Englewood-Cliffs: Prentice-Hall, 1973).
28. United States District Court, Southern District of New York; Colombrito v Kelly; 79 Civ 6205 (RO); 27 May 1982 (a.m.), pp. 174–5.
29. G. D. Chryssides, C. Lamb and M. Marsden , *Who Are They? New Religious Groups* (London: United Reformed Church, 1982).
30. 'My Pledge' *Update*, vol. III, Issue 1/2 (July 1979), pp. 53–4.
31. This is discussed more fully in Chapter 6.
32. See D. Z. Phillips, *Faith and Philosophical Enquiry* (London: Routledge and Kegan Paul, 1970).

## 2  Unificationist Doctrines

1. The transliteration of Korean names has presented some problems,

since different authors use different methods of rendering Korean into English script. I have adopted conventions which now appear to be securing acceptance in Great Britain, but with some exceptions. Where individuals have consciously chosen an Anglicised form of their name which runs counter to these, I have conformed to their preference. Where there are pieces of terminology which only appear in English in the non-standard form (for example, *sung sang* rather than *seung sang*), I have used the form in which the term typically appears.

2.   Kwang Wol Yoo, 'Unification Church History', *New Hope News* (7 October 1974).

3.   Stephen Annett, *The Many Ways of Being* (London: Abacus, 1976), pp. 20–1.

4.   Yoo, op. cit., p. 3.

5.   Won Pil Kim, *The Path of a Pioneer* (New York: HSA-UWC, 1986), p. 39.

6.   Yoo, op. cit., p. 7.

7.   D. S. C. Kim, 'My Early Days in the Unification Church', *Today's World*, January 1985, p. 25.

8.   James Bjornstad, *The Moon is not the Son* (Minneapolis: Bethany Fellowship Inc., 1976), p. 33.

9.   Lofland, op. cit., pp. 279–302. Michael L. Mickler, *A History of the Unification Church in the Bay Area: 1960–74* (MA thesis, Graduate Theological Union, University of California, 1980), pp. 192–255. David G. Bromley and Anson D. Shupe, Jr, *'Moonies' in America: Cult, Church and Crusade* (Beverly Hills: Sage, 1979), pp. 113–20.

10.  The title 'Level 4' is used because this work, produced in 1980, was preceded by a number of lectures which were written by graduate students of the Unification Theological Seminary in Barrytown. A 'One Hour Lecture' constitutes the 'Introduction to the Principle', while *Divine Principle, Two, Four and Six Hour Lectures* comprise the *Outline of The Principle, Levels 1, 2 and 3* respectively.

11.  Hyo Won Eu, *Divine Principle* (New York: HSA-UWC, 1973), p. 15.

12.  Ibid., p. 21.

13.  The decision regarding the use of 'inclusive language' has been a difficult one. Unificationist texts usually, although not always, use 'exclusive language'. Where their use of the masculine gender clearly includes the feminine, I have imported inclusive language, to ensure consistency within the book (for example, 'humanity' rather than 'man'). Where unspecified men, rather than women, are clearly referred to, I have used the masculine, since it would be misleading to do otherwise. Although God is said to possess 'male and female aspects', UC members invariably refer to God as 'he', and I have chosen to follow this practice. Some readers may consider Unificationism to be sexist, but my concern is for accurate portrayal. It would be misleading, for example, to imply that a 'central figure' might be of either sex when this is clearly at variance with Unificationist theology.

14. Kwak, op. cit., p. 2. (This terminology is not used in the 1973 edition of *Divine Principle*, which preserves the English translation of these terms.)
15. Eu, op. cit., p. 26.
16. For further discussion, see G. D. Chryssides, 'The Four Position Foundations', *Religion Today*, vol. 2, no. 3 (October 1975), pp. 7–8.
17. Genesis 1.28.
18. Eu, op. cit., p. 512.
19. Further discussion of 'Principle' as spiritual law will be given in Chapter 3.
20. Genesis 1.5.
21. John Andrew Sonneborn, *Questions and Answers: Christian Tradition and Unification Theology* (New York: HSA-UWC, 1985), pp. 21–4.
22. Psalm 51.5. Augustine of Hippo, *Treatise I: On the Merits and Forgiveness of Sins, and the Baptism of Infants*, Book I, ch. XX; in *The Anti-Pelagian Works of Saint Augustine, Bishop of Hippo*, trans. Peter Holmes (Edinburgh: T. & T. Clark, 1908), p. 21.
23. Exodus 20.4.
24. British Council of Churches, 'Two Months with the Moonies' (London, n.d., c. 1975), p. 9. James A. Beckford, 'Korean Christ?', *New Humanist*, vol. 91, part 5, 1975, p. 125. Jack Roundhill, 'The Unification Church' (London: The Church Literature Association, n.d.), p. 2. John Weldon, 'A Sampling of the New Religions', *International Review of Mission*, vol. LXVII, no. 268 (1978), p. 411.
25. Where the word 'position' is used with its technical meaning in Chinese philosophy I have used italics. At all other times it should be understood in its normal lay sense.
26. John Allan, *The Rising of the Moon* (Leicester: Inter-Varsity Press, 1980), p. 11.
27. Kwak, op. cit., p. 175.
28. Genesis 4.4–5. Mainstream biblical commentators have speculated about the reason for Cain's rejection. One suggestion is that God preferred Abel's offering because it was an animal sacrifice, whereas Cain offered vegetables. Another speculation is that Abel's heart was right whereas Cain's was not. Unificationism accepts neither of these speculations: of necessity, God had to reject Cain's offering, since Cain was in the *position* of Satan, and the respective acceptance and rejection of the two offerings signified God's separating the satanic from the divine.
29. Genesis 4.8.
30. Eu, op. cit., pp. 228–9.
31. If it is asked why the foundation of faith could not be allowed to stand, the answer is that it is a spiritual law that the central figure who sets up the foundation of faith must also set up the foundation of substance. There are several such laws which are stated or implied in the *Principle*.

32.    Genesis 9.20–17.
33.    Genesis 15.9–10.
34.    Genesis 22.1–18.
35.    Genesis 25.27–34.
36.    Genesis 27.1–40.
37.    Genesis 32.1–21.
38.    Genesis 32.22–32; Hosea 12.4.
39.    It may be questioned whether Israel was actually a nation at this point rather than a wandering tribe. The capture of Jericho (Joshua 6) surely marked the transition from nomadic existence to a nation with fixed territory. However, Unificationists expound the *Principle* as I have explained it here, and certainly when Moses (the next central figure) assumed his *position* Israel had become a nation. My comment does not substantially affect the *Principle*'s claim that there remained further levels to be restored than the family.
40.    Probably the allusion is to Acts 7.23: the Exodus story does not specify a 40-year time period, and *Divine Principle* provides no biblical proof-text.
41.    Exodus 2.11–14.
42.    Exodus 32.19.
43.    Numbers 20.1–13. *Divine Principle* reads additional material into the text at this point: God did not in fact command Moses to strike the rock once only: this command was given at a similar previous incident at Rephidim (Exodus 17.1–7), and it is assumed that the same command applied on this subsequent occasion.
44.    John 2.21.
45.    Exodus 32.
46.    Numbers 20.12.
47.    1 Corinthians 10.4; cf. Eu, op. cit., pp. 311, 327.
48.    Joshua 6.14.
49.    Revelation 13.18.
50.    Mark 13.26; 1 Thessalonians 4.17; Revelation 1.7.
51.    Luke 17.20; cf. Kwak, op. cit., p. 297.
52.    Hebrews 12.1. It is an interesting question how the *Principle* distinguishes between literal and symbolic passages: Adam and Eve, for example, are regarded as real people, yet the reference to eating a fruit is 'symbolic'. I am not claiming that *Divine Principle* is persuasive on such points, but merely rehearsing what it says. Presumably the means by which one distinguishes the literal from the symbolic lies in the revelation of the *Principle* which the Rev Moon is believed to have received from God.
53.    The year 1917 is precisely 400 years after Martin Luther fixed his 95 Theses to the Wittenburg Chapel. The year 1930 is also given, since 1930 years are believed to have elapsed between Abraham and Jesus.
54.    Allan, op. cit., pp. 30–1.
55.    Kwak, op. cit., p. 305.

56.  The phrase 'second Israel' is not found in the Bible, but it is popularly used by mainstream Christians as well as Unificationists to describe how God's dispensation is believed to have passed to the Gentile world.
57.  Revelation 7.2–4.
58.  Eu, op. cit., p. 16.
59.  *CAUSA Lecture Manual* (New York: CAUSA Institute, 1985), pp. 169–261.

## 3  The Korean Religious Heritage

1.   G. H. Jones, 'The Spirit Worship of the Koreans', *Transactions of the Korea Branch of the Royal Asiatic Society*, vol. II, 1902, p. 39.
2.   C. A. Clark, *Religions of Old Korea* (New York and London: Garland, 1981), pp. 137–9.
3.   Chang Ki Kun, *The Unification Principle and Oriental Thought*: in Lee Hang Nyong (ed.), *Research on the Unification Principle* (Seoul: Song Hwa Press, 1981), p. 89.
4.   Youngsook Kim Harvey: *Six Korean Women: The Socialization of Shamans*; Monograph 65 of The American Ethnological Society (St Paul / New York / Los Angeles / San Francisco: West Publishing Company, 1979), pp. 11–12.
5.   Takis E. Papayannopoulos, *Religions in Korea* (Athens, 1979), pp. 21–22. I have decided to compromise and qualify the term, using the label 'folk shamanism'.
6.   B. C. A. Walraven, 'Korean Shamanism', *Numen*, vol. XXX, Fasc 2, December 1983, p. 242.
7.   Kim Dong-ni, *The Shaman Sorceress* (London: Kegan Paul, 1989), pp. 37–41.
8.   Rainer Flasche, 'The Unification Church in the Context of East-Asian Religious Traditions'; *Acta Comparanda* II (Antwerp: Faculteit voor vergleijkende Godsdienstwetenschappen, 1987), p. 38.
9.   See Chapter 7.
10.  Kwang Yol Yoo, 'Father's Life', *New Hope News* (Washington: Unification Church Office of Communication, 7 October 1974).
11.  Michael L. Mickler, *A History of the Unification Church in the Bay Area: 1960–74*, pp. 4–5.
12.  Lao Tzu, *Tao Te Ching*, trans. D. C. Lau (Harmondsworth: Penguin, 1963), I, i.
13.  Fritjof Capra, *The Tao of Physics* (London: Fontana, 1976), p. 114.
14.  There has been disagreement amongst Confucian scholars, however, as to whether this is a linear progression with the period of unity as a final enduring goal, or whether the three stages form a cycle which is constantly repeated. Tung Chung-shu (c. 179 – c. 104 BCE) held a cyclical view; K'ang Yu-wei (1858–1927), who was deeply influenced by Chung-shu, expounded a linear view, expressed in his work *The*

*Book of Great Unity*, published posthumously in 1935.
15. *The Doctrine of the Mean*, XX.8; James Legge, (trans. and ed.) *Confucius* (New York: Dover, 1971), pp. 406–7.
16. Richard Wilhelm, *Lectures on the I Ching: Constancy and Change* (London: Routledge and Kegan Paul, 1980), pp. 71–2.
17. Ibid., p. 153.
18. Where the term 'Principle' is used in its technical philosophical sense, I have given it a capital initial letter, except where quoting. I have spelt 'principle' with a small 'p' when using it in a lay sense, and distinguished it from '*Principle*', meaning the revelation accorded to the Rev Moon by using italics.
19. Wing-tsit Chan, translator and compiler, *A Source Book in Chinese Philosophy* (Princeton: Princeton University Press, 1969), p. 635; quoted in Tu Wei-Ming, 'T'oegye's Creative Interpretation of Chu Hsi's Philosophy of Principle', *Korea Journal*, vol. 22, Part 2 (February 1982), p. 10.
20. Wanne J. Joe, *Traditional Korea: A Cultural History* (Seoul: Chung'ang University Press, 1972), p. 338.
21. Sa-Soon Youn, 'T'oegye's View of Human Nature', *Korea Journal*, vol. 25, Part 7 (July 1985), p. 9.
22. Ha Tai Kim, 'The Difference Between T'oegye and Yulgok on the Doctrine of Li and Ch'i', in Eui-Young Yu and Earl H. Phillips (eds), *Traditional Thoughts and Practices in Korea* (Los Angeles: California State University, Korean-American and Korean Studies Publication Series no. 3), p. 7.
23. Mark Setton, 'Tasan's Practical Learning', *Philosophy East and West*, vol. 39, no. 4 (October 1989).
24. *The Doctrine of the Mean*, XIII.3; Legge, op. cit., p. 394.
25. The Unificationist concept of the three stages is linear and not cyclical.
26. I have used the term 'unsatisfactoriness' rather than the more usual word 'suffering' to translate the Buddhist term *dukkha*. For an explanation, see George Chryssides, *The Path of Buddhism* (Edinburgh: St Andrew Press, 1988), p. 21.
27. As an explanation of Buddhism, this brief description is of course barely adequate. For a fuller account of the meaning of the Four Noble Truths and the Eightfold Path, see Chryssides, op. cit., pp. 20–2.
28. *Digha Nikaya*, ii.312; quoted in F. L. Woodward (ed. and trans.), *Some Sayings of the Buddha* (London and New York: Oxford University Press, 1973), p. 10.
29. *Khuddaka-Patha*; quoted in Woodward, op. cit., p. 37.
30. Peter H. Lee (trans.) *Lives of Eminent Korean Monks: The Haedon Kosung-jon* (Cambridge, Mass., 1969), pp. 78–9; quoted in Hee-Sung Keel, 'Buddhism in Korea – A Historical Introduction', *Zeitschrift fur Missionwissenschaft und Religionswissenschaft*, vol. 69, no. 2 (April 1985), p. 132.

31. Korean National Commission for UNESCO (ed.), *Main Currents of Korean Thought* (Si-Sa-Yong-o-Sa Inc / Pace International Research, 1983), p. 15.
32. A *sutra* is a scripture which records the teaching of the Buddha.
33. Hsuan Hua, *Sutra of the Past Vows of Earth Store Bodhisattva* (New York: Buddhist Text Translation Society, The Institute for Advanced Studies of World Religions, 1974), p. 20.
34. Quoted in Ko Ik-Chin, 'Wonhyo and the Foundation of Korean Buddhism', *Korea Journal*, vol. 21, no. 8 (August 1981), p. 7.
35. *Commentary on the Awakening of Faith*; quoted in Ko, op. cit., p. 11.
36. Nagarjuna, Selections from the Madhyamakakarika; trans. Paul M. Williams; *The Middle Way*, vol. 52, no. 2 (August 1977), p. 72.
37. Quoted in Choi Min Hong, 'The Unification Principle and Korean Thought'; ed. Nyong, op. cit., p. 101.
38. Ibid., p. 105.
39. *Commentary on the Avatamsaka Sutra*, ed. Nyong, op. cit., p. 104.
40. Ko, op. cit., p. 11.
41. Luke 23.43.
42. Eu, op. cit., p. 177
43. *Saddharma-Pundarika, or The Lotus of the True Law*, trans. H. Kern (New York: Dover, 1963), chap. VII, pp. 153–90.
44. Eu, op. cit., p. 529. Maitreya is called 'Miruk-Bul' in *Divine Principle*.
45. Richard Quebedeaux and Rodney Sawatsky (eds), *Evangelical-Unification Dialogue* (New York: the Rose of Sharon Press, 1979), p. 86

## 4  The Advent of Christianity

1. See, for example, Corinthians 6.11.
2. See John 16.12–15; Acts 19.1–7.
3. The Apocrypha, which consists of inter-testamental literature, officially forms part of the Roman Catholic canon of scripture, but is formally excluded by Protestantism.
4. James Gale, *Korea in Transition* (New York: Laymen's Missionary Movement, 1909), p. 138; quoted in Spencer J. Palmer, *Korea and Christianity* (Seoul: Hollym, 1967), p. 138. Gale wrote a private translation of the Bible which was brought out in 1925. This is said to be more understandable and colloquial than Ross's version.
5. Allen D. Clark, *A History of the Church in Korea* (Seoul: The Christian Literature Society of Korea, 1971), p. 322.
6. See Heber Jones, 'The Spirit Worship of the Koreans', p. 51.
7. Mose Durst, *To Bigotry No Sanction: Reverend Sun Myung Moon and the Unification Church* (Chicago: Regnery Gateway, 1984), pp. 63–4.
8. Palmer, op. cit., pp. 32–3.

9. Genesis 43.26.
10. 1 Samuel 28.14.
11. Mark 2.9.
12. See, for example, Jonah 3.6.
13. Exodus 20.4–5.
14. Donald W. Dayton, 'Protestant Christian Missions to Korea as a Source of Unification Thought', in Frank K. Flinn and Tyler Hendricks (eds), *Religion in the Pacific Era* (New York: Paragon, 1985), p. 79.
15. C. I. Scofield (ed.), *Scofield Reference Bible* (New York: Oxford University Press, 1909, rev. 1945), p. v.
16. Ibid., p. 257.
17. 1 Peter 3.20–21.
18. John 3.2.
19. Numbers 21.6–9; Eu, op. cit., p. 330.
20. Numbers 20.1–13; cf. Exodus 17.1–7; Eu, op. cit., p. 313.
21. Eu, op. cit., p. 313.
22. John 3.14; 1 Corinthians 10.4; John 2.21; John 6.49–54.
23. Eu, op. cit., p. 315.
24. Ibid., p. 314–5.
25. Ibid., pp. 311.
26. Clark, op. cit., p. 112ff.
27. H. H. Underwood, *Tragedy and Faith in Korea* (New York: Friendship Press, 1951); cited in Sylvia Norton, 'Korea's Sufferings in Christ', *Blessed Families*, no. 1, 1 April 1985, p. 67.
28. Alexandre Guillemoz, 'The Religious Spirit of the Korean People', *Korea Journal*, vol. 13, no. 5 (May 1973), p. 12.
29. Clark, op. cit., p. 131.
30. Guillemoz, op. cit., p. 13.
31. Song Kon-Ho, 'A History of the Christian Movement in Korea', *International Review of Mission*, vol. LXXIV, no. 293 (January 1985), p. 25.
32. W. N. Blair and Bruce F. Hunt, *The Korean Pentecost and the Sufferings which Followed* (Edinburgh: Banner of Truth Trust, 1977), p. 48.
33. Clark, op. cit., p. 51.
34. Testimony of Kim Myoung Hee (handwritten transcript, unpublished), p. 4.
35. Ira D. Sankey (ed.), *Sacred Songs and Solos* (Basingstoke: Marshall, Morgan and Scott, reprinted 1986), no. 145.
36. Ibid., no. 379.
37. Blair and Hunt, op. cit., p. 72.
38. Genesis 25.23; Romans 9.12.
39. *Master Speaks*: Leader's Speech, Dorney, 19 March 1972, pp. 2–8.
40. Genesis 37.22.
41. Genesis 48.12–20.
42. Genesis 38.

43.  Frederick Sontag, *Sun Myung Moon and the Unification Church* (Nashville: Abingdon, 1977), pp. 127–59.

## 5  Korea's New Christians

1.  Benjamin B. Weems, *Reform, Rebellion and the Heavenly Way* (Tucson, Arizona: The University of Arizona Press, 1964), p. 9.
2.  Ibid., p. 65f.
3.  Felix Moos, 'Some Aspects of Park Chang No Kyo – A Korean Revitalization Movement', *Anthropological Quarterly*, vol. 37, no. 3 (July 1964), p. 111.
4.  I have used the term 'messianism' to describe the belief in the imminent arrival of a supernatural figure or divine emissary. The term is not entirely satisfactory, since it is a piece of Christian terminology, and is cross-culturally applied to both Buddhism and Confucianism. It is also potentially misleading since the Unificationist understanding of the term 'messiah' differs from that of mainstream Christianity. However, I cannot devise a more accurate term, and therefore continue to employ it with these caveats.
5.  Mun Sang-hi, 'Fundamental Doctrines of the New Religions in Korea', *Korea Journal*, vol. 11, no. 12 (December 1971), pp. 18–24.
6.  Hyo Won Eu, *Divine Principle* (New York: HSA-UWC, 1973), pp. 527–8.
7.  Gernot Prunner, 'The New Religions in Korean Society', *Korea Journal*, vol. 20, no. 2 (February 1980), pp. 8–9.
8.  Won Buddhism ('*Weon pul-gyo*') is not in fact a recognised form of Buddhism, but a syncretistic new religious movement in Korea, founded in 1916.
9.  Prunner, op. cit., p. 10.
10.  Ibid., p. 11.
11.  Eu, *Divine Principle*, p. 57.
12.  Ibid., p. 11.
13.  Chung Hwan Kwak, *Outline of The Principle Level 4* (New York: HSA-UWC, 1980), p. 56n.
14  Genesis 19.1–10; cf. Eu, op. cit., pp. 78–9.
15.  *The Tradition*, p. 162.
16.  Young Oon Kim, *The Divine Principles* (San Francisco: HSA-UWC, rev. edn., 1962), p. 79.
17.  Eu, op. cit., p. 512.
18.  The term 'position' is to be understood in a technical sense here. According to UC teaching, restoration can only be accomplished through human beings and spirits occupying the 'positions' of ancestors who acted in an 'unprincipled' way in the past, and restoring the 'principled' course of divine providence. See Chapter 3.
19.  *Divine Principle* teaches that Adam and Eve were to go through three stages of spiritual development: 'Formation', 'Growth' and

'Completion'. Because they fell at the top of the 'Growth' stage into the 'unprincipled realm', the messiah must restore these spiritual stages before inaugurating the Kingdom of Heaven on earth.

20. *Master Speaks*, 27 December 1971; *History of the Unification Church*, p. 3.

21. Gil Ja Sa Eu, 'My Testimony', unpublished typescript, n.d., p. 30.

22. 'Testimony of Mr Jung' (handwritten manuscript, unpublished), c. 1978, p. 3.

23. The 'twelve and seventy' recapitulates the 12 apostles and 70 disciples whom Luke tells us Jesus sent out (Luke 9.1 and 10.1). On account of a problem of establishing the original text of Luke 10.1, some versions of the Bible give the figure of 72 instead of 70. On some occasions, the UC adopts the figure of 72 which, added to 12, yields 84: this explains, for example, why members are expected, in theory, to gain 84 converts to the UC in the course of their lifetime.

24. Cf. Won Pil Kim, *Father's Course and Our Life of Faith* and *Master Speaks*, 27 December 1971.

25. Sun Myung Moon states that this took place three times a day – no doubt a later exaggeration. See *Master Speaks*, 27 December 1971, p. 4.

26. *Master Speaks*: 'History of the Unification Church', 27 December 1971, p. 2.

27. Kyong Bae Min, *The Church History of Korea* (Seoul, 1973), chap. 9.

28. Young Bok Chun, 'The Korean Background of the Unification Church'; *Japanese Religions*, vol. 9, no. 2 (1976), p. 16.

29. Loc. cit.

30. Loc. cit. Quoted from Byun Jong Ho (ed.), *The Collected Letters of Reverend Lee Yong Do* (Seoul: Simoowon, 1934), p. 189.

31. Loc. cit. Quoted from Ho, op. cit., p. 173.

32. Loc. cit. Ho, op. cit., pp. 188–91.

33. Min, op. cit.; trans. D. Wood and H. Wood, p. 6.

34. Loc. cit.

35. Ho, loc. cit. Byun Jong Ho (ed.), *The Story of Reverend Lee Yong Do* (Seoul: Simoowon, 1958), p. 252.

36. *Master Speaks*, 27 December 1971, p. 5.

37. Loc. cit.

38. These works only exist in Korean. I have been given sight of the *Kidokkyo Keunbon Wolli*, and told the gist of its contents. It is a very long work, and it would be too onerous a task to make a complete translation.

39. Patrick and Dulack, op. cit., p. 29.

40. Yamamoto, *The Puppet Master*, p. 17.

41. 'Father's Life' (unpublished typescript 'prepared by Mr Dijk'), 27 March 1977, p. 2.

42. Loc. cit.

43. Kwang Wol Yoo, 'Unification Church History', *New Hope News* (7 October 1974). Mose Durst, *To Bigotry No Sanction: Reverend Sun*

*Myung Moon and the Unification Church* (Chicago: Regnery Gateway, 1984), p. 72f.
44. Gil Ja Sa Eu, op. cit., p. 29.
45. *T'ong-il* means 'Unification', and the UC in Korea is known as the *T'ongil-gyo*.
46. Chun, loc. cit.
47. James Bjornstad, *The Moon Is Not the Son* (Minneapolis: Bethany Fellowship Inc, 1976), p. 33.
48. William J. Petersen, *Those Curious New Cults* (New Canaan, Connecticut: Keats Publishing Inc., 1975), p. 250.
49. Sebastian A. Matczak, *Unificationism: A New Philosophy and Worldview* (New York: Learned Publications Inc, 1982), p. 10.
50. Rainer Flasche, 'The Unification Church in the Context of East-Asian Religious Traditions'; *Acta Comparanda* II (Antwerp: Faculteit voor vergleijkende Godsdienstwetenschappen, 1987).
51. Kyong Bae Min, loc. cit.
52. 'History of Blessing'; Father's Speech, 20 May 1978 (unpublished typescript), p. 2.

## 6   Jesus in Unification Thought

1. Won Pil Kim; 'Testimony of Father's Life', HSA-UWC World Mission Centre, Order Number 79–10–14: 14 October 1979, pp. 27–8.
2. Kwak, *Outline of the Principle Level 4*, p. 132; Eu, *Divine Principle* pp. 200–1.
3. Mose Durst, *To Bigotry No Sanction* (Chicago: Regnery Gateway Inc., 1984), p. 176.
4. Young Oon Kim; *Unification Theology* (New York: HSA-UWC, 1980), p. 197.
5. Sun Myung Moon, *God's Warning to the World* (New York: HSA-UWC, 1985), p. 61.
6. Moon, op. cit., 134.
7. Luke 2.7.
8. Matthew 2.12.
9. Sun Myung Moon, 'The Participants in Celebrating Christmas', Manhattan Center, 25 December 1977; Order Number 77–12–25.
10. Luke 2.46.
11. John 2.4.
12. Mark 4.31–35.
13. Malachi 4.5
14. Sun Myung Moon, *God's Warning to the World* (New York: HSA-UWC, 1985), p. 128.
15. Kwak, op. cit., p. 238.
16. Ibid., p. 238; Matthew 11.3.
17. John 3.30.
18. Kwak, op. cit., p. 238. John 1.21.

19. Ibid., p. 239.
20. Moon, op. cit., p. 122. Sang Hun Lee, *The New Cultural Revolution and Unification Thought* (Tokyo: Unification Thought Institute, 1987), p. 82.
21. Eu, op. cit., p. 148.
22. Ibid., p. 359.
23. Ibid., p. 360.
24. Luke 23.43. Ibid., pp. 176–7.
25. Eu, op. cit., p. 362.
26. Moon, op. cit., p. 136.
27. Kwak, op. cit., p. 251, Eu, op. cit., p. 362.
28. Young Oon Kim, *Unification Theology* (New York: HSA-UWC, 1980), p. 202.
29. Loc cit. Allan objects that the Holy Spirit is consistently referred to in the masculine gender in the Bible (op. cit., p. 21). This is incorrect, since *ruah* is a feminine Hebrew noun, and the Greek *pneuma* is neuter; the word *paracletos* is, however, masculine. For a discussion of this point, see Young Oon Kim, op. cit., pp. 199–202.
30. See, for example, Mark 2.19; Matthew 25.1–13.
31. Revelation 19.5–9.
32. Mark 14.36.
33. Luke 19.41–44.
34. See G. D. Chryssides, 'Syncretism, Ideology and Truth': New ERA Conference, 'Are Unificationism and Socialism Compatible?' Fort-de-France, Martinique, February 1985.
35. 1 Corinthians 15.47.
36. Albert Schweitzer, *The Quest for the Historical Jesus* (London: Adam & Charles Black, 1910).
37. Anselm, *Cur Deus Homo?*, trans. Edward S. Prout (London: Christian Classics Series, London Religious Tract Society, n.d.).
38. See, for example, M. Halverson and H. Cohen (eds), *A Handbook of Christian Theology* (London and Glasgow: Collins, Fontana, 1966), pp. 24–6.
39. Matthew 28.30.
40. David McCraw, 'Threatened by Respectability' *Dutchess*, February–March 1989, p. 34.
41. *Today's World*, January 1984.
42. Ed Mignot, 'The Cult of Heung Jin and the New Pentecost', *Areopagus*, vol. 1, nos 3 and 4 (Spring/Summer 1988), p. 52.
43. *Today's World*, January/February 1984.
44. 'Letters from Heaven', *FAIR News*, January 1988, p. 11.
45. Young Whi Kim, *Guidance for Heavenly Tradition*, vol. 2 (Frankfurt: Vereinigungskirche, 1985), p. 110.
46. Ibid., p. 149.
47. Ibid., p. 146.
48. Ibid., p. 148.

49. Ibid., p. 151.
50. Ibid., p. 166.
51. Ibid., p. 183.
52. Mignot, loc. cit.
53. 'Theological Uproar in the Unification Church', *The Washington Post* (30 March 1988).
54. *Today's World*, November 1987; quoted in *FAIR News*, Summer 1988, p. 12.
55. The term 'Second Self' was introduced into Unificationism by Heung Jin Moon, I am told. A 'Second Self' is a member, who has received the Blessing. For further explanation, see Chapter 7.
56. Eu, op. cit., pp. 187–8.

## 7 The Blessing

1. Matthew 22.30.
2. See Chapter 3.
3. Genesis 1.28.
4. See Chapter 5.
5. Sun Myung Moon, *God's Will and the World* (New York: HSA-UWC, 1985), p. 461.
6. For a fuller account see Chapter 4.
7. See Chapter 2.
8. Leader's Speech at Dorney, 19 March 1972 (typescript), p. 19.
9. Chung Hwan Kwak, *The Tradition* (New York: HSA-UWC, 1985), p. 97.
10. Both True Parents must be present at least 'symbolically'. On one occasion, in London, in 1978, the Rev and Mrs Moon's eldest daughter, Ye Jin, deputised for Mrs Moon, but Sun Myung Moon himself has always been present personally to preside over these ceremonies.
11. See Chapter 2. The allusion is to the fundamental doctrine of the 'Four Position Foundation'.
12. Luke 9.10.
13. Acts 1.15.
14. 'Earth world' is the Unificationist term for the physical world, and contrasts with 'spirit world'.
15. Chung Hwan Kwak, 'The Blessing' (unpublished typescript), October 1978, p. 19.
16. Joseph H. Fichter, *The Holy Family of Father Moon* (Kansas: Leaven Press, 1985), p. 134f. Also, J. H. Grace, *Sex and Marriage in the Unification Movement* (New York and Toronto: Edwin Mellen Press, 1985), p. 198.
17. See Chapter 3.
18. Stephanie Huber, 'International Wedding of 74 Couples', *Blessing Quarterly* (Summer 1977), pp. 31–2.
19. Moon, op. cit., p. 461.

20.   Genesis 32.22–30; Hosea 12.4.
21.   Ed Mignot, 'Marriage Rituals in Tongil'; *Areopagus*, Trinity 1989, vol. 2, no. 4, p. 37.
22.   Sun Myung Moon, 'History of Blessing'; Father's Speech (unpublished typescript), 20 May 1978, pp. 2–3.
23.   'Internal Meaning of the Blessing', *The Blessing Quarterly* (Summer 1977), p. 46. Quoted also in Grace, op. cit., p. 140.
24.   Ken Sudo, 'Correction'; *The Blessing Quarterly*, vol. II, no. 2 (Spring 1978), p. 31; see also Grace, *loc. cit.*
25.   Grace, *loc. cit.*
26.   Sun Myung Moon, *Preparation for the Blessing* (unpublished typescript, n.d.), p. 17.
27.   John Maust, 'The Moonies Cross Wits With Cult-watching Critics', *Christianity Today* (20 July 1979), pp. 38–9.
28.   Chung Hwan Kwak, *The Tradition*, pp. 49–51.
29.   Richard Quebedeaux and Rodney Sawatsky (eds), *Evangelical-Unification Dialogue* (New York: Rose of Sharon Press, 1979), p. 315.
30.   *God's Will and the World*, p. 466.
31.   'Mother's Early Life', *Today's World*, vol. 4, no. 1 (January 1983), p. 22.
32.   Chung Hwan Kwak, 'The Blessing', p. 6.
33.   Various units have to be restored in turn, and these are formally categorised by the Rev Moon: individual, family, clan, society, nation, world.
34.   Moon, op. cit., p. 459.
35.   Ibid., p. 462.
36.   This is explained more fully in Chapter 2.
37.   Quebedeaux and Sawatsky (eds), op. cit., p. 305.

## 8  Rites and Festivals

1.    Chung Hwan Kwak, *The Tradition* (New York: Rose of Sharon Press, 1985), p. x.
2.    Ibid., pp. 21–2.
3.    Ibid., p. 37.
4.    Ibid., p. 21.
5.    James C. Livingston, *The Anatomy of the Sacred: An Introduction to Religion* (New York: Macmillan, 1989), p. 97.
6.    Kwak, op. cit., p. 162.
7.    Ibid., p. 163.
8.    'Unison prayer' is explained in Chapter 3.
9.    Kwak, op. cit., p. 170. Kwak states that this is in the *Principle*, but I can find no written corroboration of this, nor any reason provided.
10.   Ibid., p. 169.
11.   Ibid., p. 204.

12. Ibid., p. 205.
13. See Chapter 6.
14. Ibid., pp. 204–9.
15. Ibid., p. 214.
16. Ibid., p. 97.
17. Ibid., p. 96.
18. This is given in *The Tradition* as a lunar date. The Korean calendar has twelve lunar months, and every two years an additional month is added. Although Korean months have their own names, the Unification Church gives them names from the western calendar. There is no merit in attempting to change these dates into solar ones: the effect of using lunar dates is that the Unificationist festivals are 'movable' in relation to our western calendar.
19. Young Whi Kim, *Guidance for Heavenly Tradition*, vol. 2, p. 322.
20. Kwak, op. cit., p. 107.
21. Ibid., p. 111.
22. See G. D. Chryssides, 'The Welsh Connection: Pentecostalism and the Unification Church', *Religion Today*, vol. 5, no. 3, May 1990.
23. Sun Myung Moon, 'The Participants in Celebrating Christmas', *Master Speaks*, 25 December 1977; Order Number 77–12–25; p. 9.
24. J. Gordon Melton, 'Modern Alternative Religions in the West'; in John R. Hinnells (ed.), *A Handbook of Living Religions* (Harmondsworth: Penguin, 1985), p. 467.

## 9  The Future Agenda

1. John Biermans *et al.* (eds.), *New Vision for World Peace: Reverend Sun Myung Moon* (New York: HSA-UWC, 1988), p. 6.
2. Kenneth Cracknell, 'Speaking Personally', *Interfaith News*, no. 10 (February 1986), p. 3.
3. *CAUSA Lecture Manual* (New York: CAUSA Institute, 1985), p. xiv.
4. Ibid., pp. 169–88.
5. 'Olympics tailor-made for a Moon mission', *The Guardian*, 22 September 1988. Genesis 33.1–11.
6. Biermans, op. cit., p. 51.
7. Sun Myung Moon, 'New Dimension In The Olympic Ideal: Proposal For A World Festival Of Culture'; Preparatory Committee of 120 Countries for the World Festival of Culture, 30 September 1988.
8. Romans 11.11–32.
9. Young Oon Kim, *Introduction to the Principle: An Islamic Perspective* (New York: HSA-UWC, 1980).
10. Joseph H. Fichter, *The Holy Family of Father Moon* (Kansas: Leaven Press, 1985), p. 106.
11. Richard Quebedeaux and Rodney Sawatsky (eds), *Evangelical-Unification Dialogue* (New York: Rose of Sharon Press, 1979), p. 188.

12.    Op. cit., p. 187.


**Postscript: Some Personal Reflections**

1.    Ken Sudo, *120 Day Training Manual*, p. 338. Contrary to popular belief, this manual is no longer used by Unificationists.
2.    William Chasseaud, *Response on Behalf of the Unification Church of Great Britain for the Inter-Church Process 'Not Strangers but Pilgrims'*, 2nd rev. edn. (London: HSA-UWC, 1987), p. 14.
3.    Although UC members are free to vote for any political party, Barker's statistics on members' political persuasion interestingly confirm my impressions: see *The Making of a Moonie*, p. 228.
4.    Sudo, op. cit., p. 338.
5.    Eu, op. cit., 443–4; cf. Kwak, op. cit., p. 270.
6.    Jacqui Williams and David Porter, *The Locust Years* (London: Hodder and Stoughton, 1987), p. 123.
7.    'The Unification Church's Quest for Perfect Families'; *Areopagus*, Trinity 1989, vol. 2, no. 4, p. 46.
8.    A full discussion of the family in Unification thought can be found in Gene G. James (ed.), *The Family and the Unification Church* (New York: The Rose of Sharon Press, 1983).
9.    For a discussion of charisma and Sun Myung Moon, see Mark Cozin, 'A Millenarian Movement in Korea and Great Britain', in M. Hill (ed.), *A Sociological Yearbook of Religion in Britain*, no. 6, 1973, pp. 100–21.
10.    For a fuller treatment of the issue, see Warren Lewis, 'Is the Reverend Sun Myung Moon a Heretic? – Locating the Unification Church on the Map of Church History', in Darrol Bryant and Herbert Richardson (ed.), *A Time for Consideration: A Scholarly Appraisal of the Unification Church* (New York and Toronto: The Edwin Mellen Press, 1978), pp. 167–219.
11.    The Book of Revelation states very pointedly: 'I warn everyone who hears the words of the prophecy of this book: If anyone adds anything to them, God will add to him the plagues described in this book.' (Revelation 22.18). The Christian churches still take this warning with due seriousness.
12.    Darrol Bryant and Durwood Foster, *Hermeneutics and Unification Theology* (New York: The Rose of Sharon Press, 1980), p. 73.
13.    John 3.30.
14.    Eu, op. cit., p. 287.
15.    Genesis 32.30.
16.    *The Westminster Confession of Faith* (1647), chap. I, paras vii and ix.
17.    James Beckford, 'Through the Looking-Glass and Out the Other Side: Withdrawal from the Reverend Moon's Unification Church'; *Les*

*Archives de Sciences Sociales des Religions*, vol. 45, Part 1, 1978, p. 112.

## Appendix: The Numerological Significance of the Blessings

1. Sun Myung Moon, 'Preparation for Blessing': Father's Speech, 19–20 May 1978.
2. Moon, op. cit., p. 8. *Divine Principle* (p. 295) states that the period of slavery in Egypt was only 400 years, but I presume that the Rev Moon holds that the Israelites spent some 30 years in Egypt under more favourable conditions, in the time of Joseph.
3. *Father's Life* 'prepared by Mr Dijk' (unpublished typescript), 27 March 1977, p. 19.
4. Moon, op. cit., p. 10.
5. Loc cit.

# Bibliography

Allan, John, *The Rising of the Moon* (Leicester: Inter-Varsity Press, 1980).

Annett, Stephen, *The Many Ways of Being* (London: Abacus, 1976).

*Assembly of the World's Religions 1985*: A Report by M. Darrol Bryant, John Maniatis and Tyler Hendricks (New York: Paragon House, 1986).

Barker, Eileen, *The Making of a Moonie* (Oxford: Blackwell, 1984).

Beckford, James A., 'Korean Christ?', *New Humanist*, vol. 91, part 5 (1975), p. 125.

Beckford, James A., *Cult Controversies* (London: Tavistock, 1985).

Beckford, James A., 'Through the Looking-Glass and Out the Other Side: Withdrawal from the Reverend Moon's Unification Church', *Les Archives de Sciences Sociales des Religions*, vol. 45, part 1 (1978), pp. 95–116.

Bjornstad, James, *The Moon Is Not the Son* (Minneapolis: Bethany Fellowship, Inc., 1976).

Blair, W. N. and Hunt, Bruce F., *The Korean Pentecost and the Sufferings which Followed* (Edinburgh: Banner of Truth Trust, 1977).

British Council of Churches, 'Two Months with the Moonies' (London, n.d., c. 1975).

British Council of Churches (Youth Unit), 'The Unification Church: a paper for those who wish to know more' (n.d., c. 1978).

Bromley, David G. and Shupe, Anson D., Jr, *'Moonies' in America: Cult, Church and Crusade* (Beverly Hills: Sage, 1979).

Bryant, Darrol M. and Richardson, Herbert W., *A Time for Consideration: A Scholarly Appraisal of the Unification Church* (New York and Toronto: The Edwin Mellen Press, 1978).

Bryant, Darrol and Foster, Durwood, *Hermeneutics and Unification Theology* (New York: Rose of Sharon Press, 1980).

*CAUSA Lecture Manual* (New York: CAUSA Institute, 1985).

Chang, Byung-Kil, *Religions in Korea* (Seoul: Korean Overseas Information Service, 1984).

Chasseaud, William, *Response on Behalf of the Unification Church of Great Britain for the Inter-Church Process 'Not Strangers but Pilgrims'* (London: HSA-UWC, 2nd rev. edn., 1987)

Ch'oi Syn-duk, 'Korea's Tong-il Movement'; *Transactions of the Korea Branch, Royal Asiatic Society*, vol. XLIII (1967), pp. 167–80.

Chryssides, G. D., *The Path of Buddhism* (Edinburgh: St Andrew Press, 1988).

Chryssides, G. D., Lamb C. and Marsden M., *Who Are They? New Religious Groups* (London: United Reformed Church, 1982).

Chryssides, G. D., 'Syncretism, Ideology and Truth'. New ERA Conference, 'Are Unificationism and Socialism Compatible?' Fort-de-France,

Martinique, February 1985.
Chryssides, G. D., *The Four Position Foundations*, 'Religion Today', vol. 2, no. 3 (October 1985), pp. 7–8.
Chryssides, G. D., 'The Right to be Religious', *The Modern Churchman*, New Series, vol. XXIX, no. 3 (1987), pp. 25–33.
Chryssides G. D., 'The Welsh Connection: Pentecostalism and the Unification Church', *Religion Today*, vol. 5, no. 3 (May 1990), pp. 6–8.
Chun Young Bok, 'The Korean Background of the Unification Church', *Japanese Religions*, vol. 9, no. 2 (1976), pp. 14–18.
Church of Scotland, Panel on Doctrine appointed by the General Assembly, 'The Third Adam from Korea', *Life and Work* (September 1978).
Clark, Allen D., *A History of the Church in Korea* (Seoul: The Christian Literature Society of Korea, 1971).
Clark, C. A., *Religions of Old Korea* (New York and London: Garland, 1981).
*Confucius: Confucian Analects, The Great Learning and The Doctrine of the Mean*, trans. and ed. James Legge, *Confucius* (New York: Dover, 1971).
Cozin Mark, 'A Millenarian Movement in Korea and Great Britain', in M. Hill (ed.), *A Sociological Yearbook of Religion in Britain*, no. 6 (1973), pp. 100–21.
Dayton, Donald W., 'Protestant Christian Missions to Korea as a Source of Unification Thought', in Frank K. Flinn and Tyler Hendricks (eds), *Religion in the Pacific Era* (New York: Paragon, 1985).
Durst, Mose, *To Bigotry No Sanction: Reverend Sun Myung Moon and the Unification Church* (Chicago: Regnery Gateway, 1984).
Eu, Hyo Won, *Divine Principle* (New York: HSA-UWC, 1973).
European Parliament, Committee on Youth, Culture, Education, Information and Sport: 'Report on the activity of certain new religious movements within the European Community'. Rapporteur: Mr Richard Cottrell, 2 March 1984. PE 82.322/fin.
Fichter, Joseph H., *The Holy Family of Father Moon* (Kansas: Leaven Press, 1985).
Flasche, Rainer, 'New Religious Foundations: Structures of their Development and the Conditions under which they come into Being, illustrated by reference to the Unification Church (T'ong'ilgyo)', *Zeitschrift fur Missions Wissenschaft und Religionswissenschaft*, vol. 68, no. 1 (January 1984), pp. 24–51.
Flasche, Rainer, 'The Unification Church in the Context of East-Asian Religious Traditions'; *Acta Comparanda* II (Antwerp: Faculteit voor vergleijkende Godsdienstwetenschappen; 1987), pp. 25–48.
General Synod of the Church of England, 'New Religious Movements: A Report by the Board for Mission and Unity'; GS Misc 317, October 1989.
Grace, James H., *Sex and Marriage in the Unification Movement* (New York and Toronto: The Edwin Mellen Press, 1985).
Guillemoz, Alexandre, 'The Religious Spirit of the Korean People'; *Korea*

216     *Bibliography*

*Journal*, vol. 13, no. 5 (May 1973), pp. 12–18.

Harvey, Youngsook Kim, *Six Korean Women: The Socialization of Shamans* (St Paul, Minnesota: West Publishing Co., 1979).

Heftman, Erica, *Dark Side of the Moonies* (Harmondsworth: Penguin, 1982).

Ho, Byun Jong (ed.), *The Collected Letters of Reverend Lee Yong Do* (Seoul: Simoowon, 1934).

Ho, Byun Jong (ed.), *The Story of Reverend Lee Yong Do* (Seoul: Simoowon, 1958).

Hua Hsuan, *Sutra of the Past Vows of Earth Store Bodhisattva* (New York: Buddhist Text Translation Society, The Institute for Advanced Studies of World Religions, 1974).

Huber, Stephanie, 'International Wedding of 74 Couples', *Blessing Quarterly* (Summer 1977), pp. 31–2.

'Internal Meaning of the Blessing', *The Blessing Quarterly* (Summer 1977), p. 46.

James, Gene G. (ed.), *The Family and the Unification Church* (Barrytown, New York: The Rose of Sharon Press, 1983).

Joe, Wanne J., *Traditional Korea: A Cultural History* (Seoul: Chung'ang University Press, 1972).

Jones, G. H., 'The Spirit Worship of the Koreans': *Transactions of the Korea Branch of the Royal Asiatic Society*, vol II (1902), pp. 37–58.

Keel Hee-Sung, 'Buddhism in Korea – A Historical Introduction', *Zeitschrift fur Missionwissenschaft und Religionswissenschaft*, vol. 69, no. 2 (April 1985), pp. 130–9.

Kim, Ha Tai, 'The Difference Between T'oegye and Yulgok on the Doctrine of Li and Ch'i', in Eui-Young Yu and Earl H. Phillips (eds), *Traditional Thoughts and Practices in Korea* (Los Angeles: California State University, Korean-American and Korean Studies Publication Series no. 3), pp. 7–22.

Kim, D. S. C., 'My Early Days in the Unification Church', *Today's World* (January 1985), pp. 22–8.

Kim, Won Pil, *Father's Course and Our Life of Faith* (London: HSA-UWC, 1982).

Kim, Won Pil, 'Testimony of Father's Life'; HSA-UWC World Mission Centre, Order Number 79–10–14: 14 October 1979.

Kim, Won Pil, *The Path of a Pioneer: The Early Days of Reverend Sun Myung Moon and the Unification Church* (New York: HSA-UWC, 1986).

Kim, Young Oon, *The Divine Principles* (San Francisco: HSA-UWC, rev. edn., 1962).

Kim, Young Oon, *Unification Thought* (New York: Unification Thought Institute, 1973).

Kim, Young Oon, *Unification Theology and Christian Thought* (New York: Golden Gate Publishing Co., rev. edn., 1976).

Kim, Young Oon, *Unification Theology* (New York: HSA-UWC, 1980).

Kim, Young Oon, *Introduction to the Principle: An Islamic Perspective* (New York: HSA-UWC, 1980).

Kim, Young Whi, *Guidance for Heavenly Tradition*, vol. 2 (Frankfurt: Vereinigungskirche, 1985).

Ko, Ik-Chin, 'Wonhyo and the Foundation of Korean Buddhism', *Korea Journal*, vol. 21, no. 8 (August 1981), pp. 4–13, 48.

Korean National Commission for UNESCO (ed.), *Main Currents of Korean Thought* (Si-Sa-Yong-o-Sa Inc / Pace International Research, 1983).

Kun, Chang Ki, *The Unification Principle and Oriental Thought*, in Lee Hang Nyong (ed.), *Research on the Unification Principle* (Seoul: Song Hwa Press, 1981).

Kwak, Chung Hwan, *Outline of the Principle Level 4* (New York: HSA-UWC, 1980).

Kwak, Chung Hwan, *The Tradition* (New York: The Rose of Sharon Press, 1985).

Kwak, Chung Hwan, 'The Blessing' (unpublished typescript), October 1978.

Lee, Peter H. (trans.) *Lives of Eminent Korean Monks: The Haedon kosung-jon* (Cambridge, Mass., 1969).

'Letters from Heaven'; *FAIR News* (January 1988), p. 11.

Lofland, John, *Doomsday Cult* (Englewood Cliffs: Prentice-Hall, 1966).

Matczak, S. A., *Unificationism* (New York: Edwin Mellen Press, 1982).

Maust, John, 'The Moonies Cross Wits With Cult-watching Critics', *Christianity Today* (20 July 1979), pp. 38–9.

McCraw, David, 'Threatened by Respectability', *Dutchess* (February–March 1989), p. 34.

Melton, J. Gordon, 'Modern Alternative Religions in the West', in John R. Hinnells (ed.), *A Handbook of Living Religions* (Harmondsworth: Penguin, 1985).

Mickler, Michael L., *A History of the Unification Church in the Bay Area: 1960–74* (MA thesis, Graduate Theological Union, University of California, 1980).

Mignot, Ed, 'The Cult of Heung Jin and the New Pentecost', *Areopagus*, vol. 1, Nos 3 and 4 (Spring/Summer 1988).

Mignot, Ed, 'Marriage Rituals in Tongil'; *Areopagus*, vol. 2, no 4, Trinity 1989, pp. 36–7.

Min, Kyong Bae, *The Church History of Korea*, Chap. 9.

Moon, Sun Myung, *God's Warning to the World* (New York: HSA-UWC, 1985).

Moon, Sun Myung, *God's Will and the World* (New York: HSA-UWC, 1985).

Moon, Sun Myung, *Master Speaks*: Leader's Speech, Dorney, 19 March 1972, pp. 2–8.

Moon, Sun Myung. 'The Participants in Celebrating Christmas', Manhattan Center, 25 December 1977; Order Number 77–12–25.

Moon, Sun Myung, 'Preparation for Blessing' (typescript, 19–20 May 1978).

Moon, Sun Myung, 'History of Blessing', Father's Speech (unpublished typescript), 20 May 1978.

Moon, Sun Myung, 'Preparation for the Blessing' (unpublished typescript, n.d.).

'My Pledge', *Update*, vol. III, issue 1/2 (July 1979), pp. 53–4.

Mun, Sang-hi, 'Fundamental Doctrines of the New Religions in Korea', *Korea Journal*, vol. 11, no. 12 (1981), pp. 18–24.

Palmer, Spencer J., *Korea and Christianity* (Seoul: Hollym, 1967).

Papayannopoulos, Takis E., *Religions in Korea* (Athens, 1979).

Patrick, Ted and Dulack, Tom, *Let Our Children Go!* (New York: Dutton, 1976).

Petersen, William J., *Those Curious New Cults* (New Canaan, Connecticut: Keats Publishing Inc., 1975).

Prunner, Gernot, 'The New Religions in Korean Society', *Korea Journal*, vol. 20, no. 2 (February 1980), pp. 4–15.

Quebedeaux, Richard and Sawatsky, Rodney (ed.), *Evangelical-Unification Dialogue* (New York: The Rose of Sharon Press, 1979).

Quebedeaux, Richard (ed.), *Lifestyle: Conversations with Members of the Unification Church* (Barrytown, New York: Rose of Sharon Press, 1982).

Roundhill, Jack, 'The Unification Church' (London: The Church Literature Association, n.d.).

Setton, Mark, 'Tasan's Practical Learning', *Philosophy East and West*, vol. 39, no. 4 (October 1989).

Shimmyo, Tadaaki, 'The Unification Interpretation of Cain and Abel In the Bible'; New ERA Conference: 'Eastern Interpretations of the Christian Scriptures': Fort-de-France, Martinique, February 6–10, 1985.

Song, Kon-Ho, 'A History of the Christian Movement in Korea'; *International Review of Mission*, vol. LXXIV, no. 293 (January 1985), pp. 19–36.

Sonneborn, John Andrew, *Questions and Answers: Christian Tradition and Unification Theology* (New York: HSA-UWC, 1985).

Sontag, Frederick, *Sun Myung Moon and the Unification Church* (Nashville: Abingdon, 1977).

'Secret Sayings of "Master" Moon, The', *Time Magazine*, 14 June 1976.

Sudo, Ken, '120–Day Training Manual' (unpublished typescript, New York: HSA-UWC, 1975).

Sudo, Ken, 'Correction', *The Blessing Quarterly*, vol. II, no. 2 (Spring 1978), p. 31.

'Theological Uproar in the Unification Church', *The Washington Post*, 30 March 1988.

Tillet, Gregory T., 'Sources of Doctrine in the Unification Church', *Update*, vol. 8, no. 1 (March 1984), pp. 3–8.

Tu, Wei-Ming, 'T'oegye's Creative Interpretation of Chu Hsi's Philosophy of Principle', *Korea Journal*, vol. 22, Part 2 (February 1982), pp. 4–15.

Underwood, H. H., *Tragedy and Faith in Korea* (New York: Friendship Press, 1951).

United States District Court, Southern District of New York; Colombrito *v* Kelly; 79 Civ 6205 (RO); 27 May 1982.

Weldon, John, 'A Sampling of the New Religions', *International Review of Mission*, vol. LXVII, no. 268 (1978), pp. 407–26.

Wilhelm, Richard, *Lectures on the I Ching: Constancy and Change* (London: Routledge and Kegan Paul, 1980).

Williams, Jacqui and Porter, David, *The Locust Years* (London: Hodder and Stoughton, 1987).

Woodward, F. L. (ed. and trans.), *Some Sayings of the Buddha* (London and New York: Oxford University Press, 1973).

Yamamoto, J. Isamu, *The Puppet Master: An Inquiry into Sun Myung Moon and the Unification Church* (Illinois: Inter-Varsity Press, 1977).

Yoo, Kwang Wol, 'Unification Church History' (*New Hope News*, 7 October 1974).

Yoo, Kwang Yol, 'Father's Life', *New Hope News* (Washington: Unification Church Office of Communication, 7 October 1974.)

Youn, Sa-Soon, 'T'oegye's View of Human Nature', *Korea Journal*, vol. 25, Part 7 (July 1985), pp. 4–15.

# Glossary

The following are terms which are not necessarily defined at the places where they are used, and which are potential sources of confusion. Their presence here does not indicate that they are necessarily the most important concepts within Unificationism. Where a term belongs to a religion other than Unificationism, I have indicated this.

| | |
|---|---|
| *Archangel* | Lucifer, also referred to as Satan. |
| *bodhisattva* (Buddhism) | A celestial being who foregoes entry into final nirvana in order to secure the enlightenment of all living beings. |
| *central figure* | A person particularly chosen by God to fulfil God's providential plan. |
| *ch'i* (Confucianism) | Material Force. |
| *Completed Testament Era* | The age which began in 1960, superseding the Old Testament and New Testament Eras. |
| *direct dominion* | Humankind's ideal state in which men and women can communicate directly with God, without the intervention of prophets, religions or religious leaders. |
| *dispensational history* | The course of history, which is ordained and ordered by God. |
| *divine spirit* | A spirit who has reached the 'Completion' stage of spiritual progress. |
| *form spirit* | A spirit who is at the 'Formation' stage of spiritual progress. |
| *Formation* | The first stage of spiritual progress. |
| *foundation of faith* | The state of affairs, brought about by a central figure, which re-establishes correct relationships between God and humankind. |
| *foundation of substance* | The state of affairs, brought about by a central figure, which re-establishes correct inter-human relationships. |
| *Four Position Foundation* | The base of all activity within the world. Ideally this comprises: Origin (God), Division (male and |

|  | female), Union (sinless children). |
| --- | --- |
| *give and take* | Reciprocal interaction between subject and object. |
| *Godism* | The part of the *Principle* which encompasses the doctrines of Creation and Fall (not Restoration). |
| *Hak Ja Han* | Wife of the Rev. Moon. |
| *Hananim* (Shamanism) | The Korean name for the high God. |
| *hell* | State of being (not a place) where the individual is below the three stages of 'principled' spiritual growth. |
| *heavenly deception* | The doctrine attributed to the Unification Church that perpetrating a falsehood is justifiable for a higher religious purpose. (Unificationists deny holding such a doctrine.) |
| *horizontal relationship* | Inter-human relationship. |
| *hyung sang* | External character; what can be perceived by the senses. |
| *indemnity* | The settlement of a debt (which may not necessarily be a full repayment); acts performed to atone for sin. |
| *invisible substantial world* | The spirit world. |
| *jen* (Confucianism) | Virtue. |
| *li* (Confucianism) | Principle. |
| *life spirit* | A spirit who has reached the second ('Growth') stage of spiritual development. |
| *Maitreya* (Buddhism) | The Buddha of the coming aeon. |
| *mudang* (shaminism) | Female shaman. |
| *NRM* | New religious movement. |
| *O-D-U (Origin-Division-Union)* | (See 'Four Position Foundation'). |
| *Paradise* | The spiritual state of spirits who have progressed to the 'Growth' stage in the spirit world. |
| *Physical Fall* | Eve's act of seducing Adam; more generally, broken interpersonal relationships which resulted from this event. |
| *p'i kareun* | A religious ritual involving sexual inititiation with a religious leader to purify one's blood lineage. (It is unclear which religious groups may have practised it.) |
| *position* (Confucianism) | A situation which changes with the time. |

| | |
|---|---|
| *Principle* | The revelation believed to have been given to Sun Myung Moon. |
| Principle (Confucianism) | Metaphysical substratum underlying the physical world. |
| *principled* | Done according to the *Principle*, or in accordance with God's will. |
| *providential time-identity* | The theory that history can be divided into sections which parallel each other in the various eras (especially Old Testament and New Testament eras). |
| *representative prayer* | A prayer said by one member of a congregation on behalf of all attenders. |
| *returning resurrection* | The manifestation of a spirit in the physical world after he or she has died. |
| *samsara* (Buddhism) | The cycle of birth and rebirth. |
| *Second Self* | A partner of a blessed couple. |
| *Seung Hwa* | 'Ascension and harmony': the accession upon death of an individual to the spirit world; also refers to the Unificationist funeral ceremony. |
| *shaman* (shamanism) | A person recognised for his or her power to establish links between the physical world and the spirit world. |
| *shimjung* | 'Heart'. |
| *shu* (Confucianism) | The Way. |
| *Spiritual Fall* | Lucifer's seduction of Eve; more generally, the 'fallen' state in which humanity's relationship with God has been broken as a result of this event. |
| *stages (Formation, Growth, Completion)* | The path through which every living being in the universe must progress. |
| *sung sang* | Internal character. |
| *sunyata* (Buddhism) | 'Emptiness'; the unconditioned ultimate reality which defies verbal description. |
| *symbolic offering* | A physical token required from central figures to establish the foundation of faith. |
| *T'ongil* | Unity. |
| *T'ongil-gyo* | Unification Church. |
| *t'ang gam* | 'Indemnity'. |
| *Tabernacle* (Judaeo-Christianity) | God's portable residence before the building of the Jerusalem Temple. |

| | |
|---|---|
| *T'aeguk* | Korean term for the impersonal force which is believed to sustain the universe. |
| *trinity member* | A member of a group of three Unificationist couples, who are so grouped to offer mutual support. |
| *True Parents* | The Rev and Mrs Moon. |
| *typology* | A method of analysing the Bible which presupposes that details within earlier events prefigure later ones. |
| *UM* | Unification Movement (abbreviation). |
| *Unification Movement* | The multiplicity of organisations sponsored by Sun Myung Moon. |
| *unison prayer* | Congregational prayer in which all attenders pray their personal prayers aloud, simultaneously. |
| *unprincipled* | Not conforming to God's will. |
| *unprincipled realm* | The state of being below the 'Formation' stage of spiritual development (also known as 'hell'). |
| *vertical relationship* | The relationship between humanity and God. |

# Index

Aaron 38, 82
Abel 35, 36, 37, 39, 45, 82, 126, 171, 194
Abraham 32, 36–7, 75, 193
Adam 27–30, 34–6, 38–9, 42–3, 100, 102–3, 107, 123, 132, 138–43, 158–9, 162, 174, 193
Aladura 83
Amitabha 65–6, 92
ancestor veneration 78, 157, 164
angels 38, 91, 117, 141, 188
Anselm, St 120–2
anti-cult movement 4, 5, 9, 10–13, 105, 114, 163, 172, 179, 186, 190
Appenzeller, W. G. 75
Archangel 28, 30, 38, 91, 99
Aristotle 55
atonement 75, 117, 119, 120, 122
atrocity tales 2, 4, 186
Assemblies of the World's Religions 168, 172, 174
Aum, Mr 21

Baha'ism 176, 188
baptism 75, 77, 113, 140, 154, 163
Baptist Church 140, 176
Barker, E. 196, 212
Beckford, J. 8, 190
Bible 19, 20, 22, 24, 28, 32, 36, 69, 70–9, 82, 89, 91, 153, 187–8
Bible translation 70–3
birth 153–5
Bjornstad, J. 105
Blair, W. H. 77, 80–1
Blessing, The 10, 11, 17, 23, 44, 49, 50, 106, 123–4, 131–48, 149, 153, 155–6, 169, 172, 174–5, 178, 193–5
see also Moon, S. M.
blood 53–4, 79, 80, 98, 115, 142, 144
blood lineage see lineage

blood purification 54, 99, 100–1, 146
see also p'i kareun
bodhisattva 61–2
see also Kshitigarbha, Maitreya
Book of Changes, The see I Ching
Book of Rites, The 55
brainwashing 2, 5, 6, 12, 16, 180, 190, 192
British Council of Churches 168
Buddha, the 14, 46, 49, 60, 66, 67, 151
see also Amitabha, Maitreya
Buddhism 3, 10, 13, 20, 46, 60–8, 84–8, 113, 167, 176, 185, 187

Cain 35–7, 39, 45, 82, 171, 194
Calvinism 62, 187
cargo cults 83
CARP 165
CAUSA 170, 171, 185
central figure 34–40, 54, 114
ceremonies see under individual names and Holy Days
Ceyrac, P. 184
Ch'amwisol 86
Ch'oe Che-u 85–7
Ch'ondogyo 85–7
Children of God 183
Chou Pong-jun 86–7
Christmas 163
Chu Hsi 52, 54
Chun, Young Bok 103–5
Chung Gam Nok 88–9
Church of England 69, 176
Collegiate Association for the Research of Principles (CARP) 165
communism 43, 45, 160, 162, 170–1
Completed Testament Era 92, 122, 131, 133, 140, 164, 194
confession 33, 81, 129
Confucianism 46, 50–2, 54, 58–62, 65, 77, 84–6, 88, 93,